Changing Journalism

Journalism is in transition. Irrevocable decisions are being made, often based on flimsy evidence, which could change not only the future of journalism, but also the future of democracy. This book, based on extensive research, provides the opportunity to reflect upon these decisions and considers how journalism could change for the better and for the good of democracy. It covers:

- the business landscape
- work and employment
- the regulatory framework
- audiences and interaction
- the impact of technology on practices and content
- ethics in a converged world.

The book analyses research in both national and local journalism, broadsheet and tabloid papers, and broadcast, newspaper and online journalism, drawing comparisons between these different outlets in the field of news journalism, thus making this essential reading for scholars and students of journalism and media studies.

Peter Lee-Wright is Senior Lecturer in the Department of Media and Communications at Goldsmiths, University of London. His career as a journalist/producer ranges from the BBC World Service, the BBC Caribbean Service, the Overseas Regional Service, BBC Continuing Education, the Open University and BBC Documentaries. As an independent and freelance producer, his work ranged from award-winning documentaries to a critically acclaimed feature drama for Working Title.

Angela Phillips is Senior Lecturer in the Department of Media and Communications at Goldsmiths, University of London, where she teaches feature writing and journalism studies. She has been a journalist for over thirty years and has worked for national newspapers, magazines, television, radio and online. She is also a committee member of the Association for Journalism Education.

Tamara Witschge is a lecturer at the Cardiff School of Journalism, Media and Cultural Studies. Tamara is the General Secretary of the European Communication Research and Education Association and is a member of the editorial board of the international journals *New Media and Society*, *PLATFORM: Journal of Media and Communication* and the *Global Media Journal: German Edition*.

Communication and Society

Series Editor: James Curran

This series encompasses the broad field of media and cultural studies. Its main concerns are the media and the public sphere: on whether the media empower or fail to empower popular forces in society; media organisations and public policy; the political and social consequences of media campaigns; and the role of media entertainment, ranging from potboilers and the human-interest story to rock music and TV sport.

Changing Journalism

Peter Lee-Wright, Angela Phillips and Tamara Witschge

Routledge
Taylor & Francis Group

LONDON AND NEW YORK

First published 2012
by Routledge
2 Park Square, Milton Park, Abingdon, Oxon OX14 4RN

Simultaneously published in the USA and Canada
by Routledge
711 Third Avenue, New York, NY 10017

Routledge is an imprint of the Taylor & Francis Group, an informa business

British Library Cataloguing in Publication Data
A catalogue record for this book is available from the British Library

Library of Congress Cataloging in Publication Data
A catalog record for this book has been requested

ISBN: 978-0-415-57954-4 (hbk)
ISBN: 978-0-415-57955-1 (pbk)
ISBN: 978-0-203-80903-7 (ebk)

Typeset in Baskerville by Taylor & Francis Books

Contents

Part III
Changing journalism   115

Acknowledgements

This book is based on the Goldsmiths Leverhulme Media Research Centre project 'Spaces of News', which ran from 2007 to 2010. In addition to the authors of this book, the following people participated in the research on which this book is based: Nick Couldry, James Curran, Aeron Davis, Natalie Fenton, Des Freedman and Joanna Redden. We would like to thank them for sharing their research material, reading drafts of our chapters and most of all for the very enjoyable and inspiring meetings and collaborations throughout the duration of this project. We would also like to thank others who have provided input by commenting on draft chapters: Laura Juntunen and Andy Williams. We would like to extend our thanks to the three research students who coded the interview material: Veronica Barassi, Mireya Marquez Ramirez and Su-Anne Yeo. Lastly, this book would not have been possible if our interviewees had not given time to reflect on the current changes in the field of journalism and adjacent fields. In addition, the access to the newsroom granted by the BBC, the *Guardian* and *Manchester Evening News* has provided us with invaluable insight into the changing journalistic practices. We acknowledge that these are trying times for news organisations and are therefore all the more appreciative of the time and access offered for ethnography and interviews. We hope that by sharing our analyses in this book we will help preserve if not change journalism for the better.

Introduction

It has been a tumultuous time for news journalism. The speed and intensity of change has engendered a feeling of crisis and many a debate has been held to discuss the future, indeed the survival, of journalism. As far-reaching managerial decisions are made, journalists are made redundant, and newsrooms closed, it is important to capture, reflect on and analyse the underlying trends and the consequences of all this, not only for the field of journalism itself, but also for society and democracy.

This book is a response to this need. It is based on a large-scale study into the field of news journalism carried out between 2007 and 2010. While sketching broader current trends (with a historical grounding of the changes), it provides ample detail of the practice of journalism. Based on ethnographies and interviews – supplemented with discussions of comparable international research – we interrogate the way in which journalism is changing, and the consequences of these changes for the role that journalism plays in democratic societies.

In times of transition, it is important to take stock and decide whether all of the changes taking place are desirable, or even necessary, and if there is action that ought to be taken to counter some of these new trends. The aim of this book therefore is not only to describe and analyse what is happening now, but also to discuss how journalism might change for the better in the future.

Many of those debating the future have focused on the impact of technology on changing news practices. For better or for worse, they suggest, the nature of news and the way in which it is produced could be turned on its head as 'new technologies re-engineer the relationship between how views and information are exchanged, judged and assigned significance, and how public opinion is formed' (Lloyd and Seaton, 2006: 1). Moreover, the three major constituencies in the world of news – journalists, newsmakers and the audience – are expected, in this analysis, to blur into each other, with audiences becoming part of the process of journalism (Gillmor, 2004: xxiv–xxv) and the professional culture of journalism becoming more diverse, open and dynamic (Deuze, 2007).

However, though the focus in the recent debates around the future of news has been on the technological changes that affect news journalism, there is a range of other factors – social, economic and cultural – that have contributed to the current state of the news industry. In this book we discuss the changing context, the changing practices and the changing outputs of news journalism. We also present different ways in which actors in the news industry (whether these are established organisations or new entries in the field) can respond. We hope to do justice to the complexity of the situation that news journalism is faced with by attending to: business models, employment, regulation, convergence, work cultures and practices, audiences and ethics.

Some argue that the shifts in practice currently underway are for the better, others that they will mean the demise of news journalism. Throughout the book, we aim to explore the implications in the broadest sense, placing them in a comparative context where possible (both in historical and national comparative context).

By focusing on the changes in the field, we do not wish to imply that there used to be a stable, uniform mode of journalism that has made way for a new, uniform mode of journalism. Journalism has always been a field in flux, and we do not envisage it will become a homogenous field in the future. The changes at hand, however, raise some fundamental questions in relation to journalism, such as: who is a journalist (and who is the audience); what is the role of journalism in contemporary societies; and whether, and if so in what form, journalism will survive?

The trends in the changing landscape of news media

The challenges that are discussed in the literature include (but are not limited to) the following: increased speed of reporting; decreased autonomy of journalists and changing employment modes; a general decline in the quality of journalism and quantity of investigative journalism; de-professionalisation of the journalism field and increased output by non-professional actors; a further blurring of the categories of news and entertainment; a challenge to the authoritative position of professional journalists in the field; and a challenge to the current dominant forms of funding and ownership of news production.

New media technologies are credited with introducing a number of changes to the news production process. Some are positive: in particular the reduction in the cost of dissemination and the range of new possibilities for researching, capturing and presenting material; but many are also considered negative. The speeding up of news cycles as connected to online news – characterised by immediacy and brevity (Singer, 2009: 375) – are seen to affect the quality of the journalistic output (Weaver, 2009: 396). The merging of genres and professional groups is seen further to diminish the quality.

Managerial changes in newsrooms, changing practices and altered views on journalistic work are all argued to have a detrimental effect on professional autonomy, crucial to well-functioning news media in democratic societies (Weaver, 2009: 396; Deuze, 2009b: 316). These different trends are together seen to be responsible for a general decline in the quality of journalism and quantity of investigative journalism. Furthermore, they indicate a de-professionalisation of the field of journalism at a time where there is increased output by non-professional actors. Nossek remarks: 'it seems that the threat facing journalism is de-professionalization, which means that everyone can be a journalist and nobody actually is one' (Nossek, 2009: 358).

We agree with Schudson that these current developments and the entry of new voices in the field of news (even though valuable) do not 'make the professional journalist obsolete. The matters of professional training, experience, and judgment are as, or more, important than ever' (Schudson, 2009b: 370). Moreover, we share his worry 'that the organizations at the institutional heart of providing that training and honing that judgment – metropolitan daily newspapers and the wire services – are in serious economic trouble with no general solutions in sight' (ibid). This book then aims, not only to take stock of the changes in journalism, but also to discuss the way forward, to ensure we will have quality journalism in the future.

By arguing that we need to find ways in which we can ensure quality journalism, we do not mean to suggest that we need to protect the current commercial business models to keep shareholders happy. Nor do we mean to imply that we should not look critically at current practices of news journalism, or that the only actors contributing to the public domain are journalists. However, we do suggest that we need to consider what the value of journalism is, and how we can protect this. With the safeguarding of journalism there is more at stake than the economic interests or individual jobs of journalists. As we will discuss further in this book, there is an important role for journalism in democratic societies – when practised well, journalism is of public value: 'A free and diverse media are an indispensable part of the democratic process ... If one voice becomes too powerful, this process is placed in jeopardy and democracy is damaged' (House of Lords, 2008: 6).

A note on the research methodology

This book is based on the Goldsmiths Leverhulme Media Research Centre project 'Spaces of News', which ran from 2007 to 2010. The research involved interviews, newsroom ethnographies and content analysis. To capture the trends in the field of journalism and the adjacent fields (of politics, public relations, and new spaces of news, such as citizen journalists and bloggers), a multi-methodological approach was used.

The main body of data consists of 170 semi-structured interviews, conducted with a wide range of actors active in the field of news and adjacent fields. The sample was stratified by type of media, geographic reach, professional roles (generalists, specialist correspondents, dedicated new media staff, production and editorial staff, managerial and business personnel), and included both local and national (UK based) broadcasting (commercial and public sector), as well as local and national (UK based) print newspapers and local, national and global online-only initiatives. We also interviewed representatives of news agencies, non-governmental organisations, freelance journalists, MPs, new sources of news (bloggers and 'citizen journalists') and online, alternative news producers. This diversity of sources ensured a multiplicity of views – not just those held by 'traditional' news producers – on the current and future situation in news journalism.

The second strand of research included mini-ethnographies in three newsrooms at the forefront of the technological developments: the BBC, *Manchester Evening News* (MEN) and the *Guardian*. At the time of the observations, the BBC and the *Guardian* were preparing to move to a converged newsroom (and follow-up visits have captured the change in work environment), whereas the MEN was already functioning in a fully converged newsroom with print, broadcast and online journalists working side-by-side in a multi-platform environment. These news-room ethnographies have allowed us to observe the newsroom practices in action, and they have provided invaluable insights, complementing those gained through the in-depth interviews.

Based on this empirical material this book reports on research in both national and local journalism, and broadcast, newspaper and online journalism. As such, it is able to draw comparisons between the different outlets in the field of news journalism. While informed by a range of theoretical perspectives, it in particular draws on Bourdieu's field theory to reflect on the changes in the field of journal-ism (even though more as a general framework than a specific guide for analysis). Based in practice (two of the authors have a background in journalism), but with a solid theoretical understanding, this book bridges the gap between theory and practice.

This book forms an in-depth follow-up from work earlier published by the Leverhulme Spaces of News research team: Natalie Fenton (ed.), *New Media, Old News: Journalism and Democracy in the Digital Age* (Sage 2010). Whereas *New Media, Old News* discusses the broad themes of news journalism and democracy from a historical, political-economic, social and production perspective, this book delves into more detail on the practice of journalism. We address the changes in jour-nalism from a variety of perspectives, and provide a rich description and nuanced understanding of the current practices in the field.

As argued above, the current changes need to be explored in context: the historical, political, economic, social, cultural and technological context. Or as Steensen puts it:

> Contemporary changes in the role of journalists must be understood in line with two axes: a vertical axis where the societal factors that shape the role of journalists throughout history are traced, and a horizontal axis where the influence of contemporary trends in work culture and new perceptions of labour is taken into consideration.
>
> (Steensen, 2009: 703)

Structure of the book

The first section of the book considers the changing political and economic structures of journalism. Chapter 1 discusses the economic context exploring existing business models and new models for funding news production. It examines the disruptive effect that new entrants into the media field have had on the traditional link that existed between advertising and news production – a connection that is under threat, thus challenging the economic underpinning of the news businesses. Chapter 2 views the changes in journalistic work from a historical perspective, considering issues of employment, the status of the 'profession' of journalism, and newsroom cultures. Chapter 3 discusses the changing nature of regulatory frameworks, introducing a political economy perspective to the analysis of current developments.

The second section focuses on the way in which practices of news production are changing and what the consequences of these changes are for the quality of journalism. It starts with a critical examination of the ideas behind and implications of multi-platform journalism and the multi-skilled journalist (Chapter 4). Chapter 5 then discusses the ongoing trends of more speed in news production and homogenisation of news content. While both Chapters 4 and 5 consider the role of technology in these changing journalistic practices, Chapter 6 focuses specifically on the impact of new media technology. Or more precisely, it considers the way in which the discourse on technology has been used to implement non-technology-related change in the newsroom.

The last section considers the future position of journalism in the changing mediascape. It first asks whether the role of the journalist is changing in light of the changing role of the audience. Chapter 7 critically examines the attitudes of news workers to audience participation. Chapter 8 moves to a more normative exploration of future news practices: what are the ethical responsibilities of journalists and do high-speed, interactive technologies make different ethical demands? Last, in the Conclusion we critically reflect on how these current changes in journalism impact on the future of news.

Part I

Changing political and economic structures of journalism

1 The changing business of news

Sustainability of news journalism

Angela Phillips and Tamara Witschge

Information is to democracy what oxygen is to fire. Without one the other cannot survive: an un-informed voter cannot use her vote intelligently, nor hold power to account. That is why democracy and the independent news media have developed hand in hand, and why any threat to the survival of organised news in the public interest (however flawed it may be) is also a threat to democracy. Today we face a crisis in the business model of news. It is not a crisis of demand – audiences ebb and flow, and may be deeply sceptical at times – but the thirst for news and information has not disappeared; it comes down to a crisis of funding.

Quality news production feeding relevant information to societies on a structural basis is not cheap. It requires large numbers of highly trained personnel, organised to respond to every change and wrinkle in domestic and world events. This chapter examines the way in which the current changes in the production and organisation of news has shaken to its foundation the business model on which news delivery has long depended. As media companies struggle 'to adjust to wide-ranging changes that are increasing competition and eroding their audience and advertising bases' (Picard, 2005: 344), we ask how it is possible to maintain the vital functions of news journalism.

No one has paid the full cost of news since the advent of advertising in the middle of the nineteenth century (Curran, 2002). On commercial television and radio, news has always been cross-subsidised by the lucrative sale of advertising around popular programming. On subscription channels also, it is the popular entertainment programming that attracts the audience. Newspapers, depending on scoops and story telling to keep circulation high, have had some means of recouping at least part of their own costs via sales, but the advertising subsidy has kept the cost of news at a price that is far below what it takes to produce. Today, audiences have many other sources of entertainment, a major one being the internet. As audiences move on to the net, so too do advertisers (K. Allen, 2007; Holton, 2008) but those advertisers are finding new ways to get directly to their audiences which do not require them to pay for space in news media as they have done in the past. Popular and local newspapers and TV have always attracted the lion's share of advertising and shareholders expect high revenues as a result, so when the level of advertising started to drop, it created anxiety in boardrooms and a large number of closures, particularly in the USA and UK.

In this chapter we trace the problems that current news businesses face and the consequences of them. Commercial news on the web appears to have limited options for recouping production costs through sales. Moreover, it finds itself sharing a space and a funding method, not only with radio and TV, but also with the new entrants into the news business: the aggregators. Aggregation sites such as Google News, together with the fast distribution potential of the internet, are undermining the unique selling point of news organisations – the scarcity value of being first with the news. They could also be fatally damaging to brand identification for all but the very largest and best known news organisations, and thus strike a further blow to the business models of news media and to the requirement of democracy for a diversity of news media.

There seems little reason to suppose that advertisers are going to take up the cost of news production across all these platforms, when they now have a plethora of different, and more direct, ways of getting to their audiences. Currently the favoured method for most news organisations is to reduce the cost of news-gathering (House of Lords, 2008: 9), exploring, for example, the use of amateurs (citizen journalists) to provide what journalists used to be paid for. Other ideas include: bundled subscriptions providing access to news and other services, iPad and iPod applications, pay-walls and micro-payments. However, these explorations have not yet produced a final answer to providing sustainable business models. This chapter maps the different responses and discusses the success (or failure) of different business models, drawing on examples from within and outside the field of news journalism. We also ask whether the market model is sustainable into the future or whether different models have to be worked out. What possibilities for alternative funding and delivery are already available, and to what extent are they capable of delivering a service that is relatively free of interference from the state?

The dual role of news businesses

News media are businesses that at the same time fulfil a public service: they provide valuable information to citizens. These two roles, as Picard points out, 'create tensions within media companies and among media policy-makers that require careful balancing if society is to gain the benefits of a free and independent media system' (2005: 337). With the current challenges facing news businesses, these tensions are intensified as both the business side of media and their capability (and inclination) to cater to the public interest of citizens are put to the test. These two roles of news have been analytically separated into the 'market model' and 'public sphere model' of media, each of those models evaluating media on a different basis (Croteau and Hoynes, 2006: 16). We maintain that, to assess the functioning of news media properly, you need to look at both roles at the same time.

News media play an important 'role as facilitators of social and political expression' (Picard, 2004: 109). They are expected to serve the public interest, but when exactly public interests are being served, is difficult to gauge. Brian

McNair (1995: 21) suggests that news media in an idealised society should: inform, educate, give publicity to governmental and political institutions; scrutinise these institutions and provide a platform for public political discourse. To allow for a consideration of changing views on public interest, Croteau and Hoynes maintain that media 'serve the public interest to the extent that they portray the diversity of experiences and ideas in a given society' (2006: 34).

The idea of public service is often seen to be diametrically opposed to the economic or business interests that guide media behaviour: commercial media will seek to fulfil economic motives before public service motives (Picard, 2005: 338). Moreover, 'most of the activities that support public interest and democratic processes ... do not attract large audiences, are often costly, and are typically less profitable than producing other content' (ibid). In many countries media regulation and/or incentives have been put in place, focussing mainly on news, as an attempt by policy makers to ensure that news is not squeezed out by more popular programming, and also to ensure diversity in the public sphere (the issues relating to regulation will be discussed in more detail in Chapter 3).

In some countries, the public service nature of news media has resulted in direct subsidies, providing the economic basis that is needed to continue delivering this service. In Nordic countries, for instance, in response to earlier economic crises, there has been support for the newspaper industry, to reflect the social, cultural and political role they play in society (Picard, 2007: 236–37; see also de Bens, 2007: 373–75). In most of Europe, public service radio and television are subsidised either directly or indirectly by government.

However, even though the 'broad public purpose of media' is widely accepted (Croteau and Hoynes, 2006: 33), news has always been primarily a business (Cranberg, Bezanson and Soloski, 2001: 1), albeit involving a wide variety of actors (see below). Viewing media as a business, allows us to consider managerial and economic conditions that result from different forms of ownership and different business models (Picard and van Weezel, 2008), an angle particularly important for current analyses of the news field.

Ownership models

Understanding different funding models is of great importance to understanding the functioning of news media in general. As Picard notes: '[b]usiness models need to account for the vital resources of production and distribution technologies, content creation or acquisition, and recovery costs for creating, assembling and presenting the content' (Picard, 2002: 26). Hence, content is inextricably linked to ways of funding news. Leaving aside state owned, or subsidised, media there are different types of ownership and, in different national and regional contexts, different models dominate: private ownership, publicly traded media, foundation-funded or not-for-profit ownership and employee owned media. Each of these forms of news media ownership 'produces different operational and performance contexts' (Picard and van Weezel, 2008: 23).

Worldwide, the majority of newspapers are privately owned (60 per cent), most of the rest are owned by governments, and only a small minority are publicly traded (3 per cent) or employee owned (4 per cent) (ibid: 24). In the USA, most news businesses were in private hands until the last quarter of the twentieth century, when many were subsumed into public companies. Now, 40 per cent of news organisations are owned by public corporations, and many of the privately owned organisations are not single local papers, but chains with diverse media interests (ibid). There are a number of reasons for this (including the effect of inheritance tax on family-owned businesses which forced families to sell), but key amongst them has been the extraordinary profits that could be drawn from newspapers enjoying local monopolies in many American cities. Between the 1991 recession and 2000 (the peak of the dot-com boom), newspaper advertising revenues rose by 60 per cent and profit margins nearly doubled to 27 per cent (State of the Media Report, 2004).

In the UK, the local and regional press has seen a particularly marked consolidation of ownership in recent times. Currently, four publishers dominate the market, with a 70 per cent market share across the UK (House of Lords, 2008: 46). In the national broadcasting market, we see a comparable situation in news production: there are three dominant players producing national television news (BBC, ITN and BSkyB) and three producing national radio news (BBC, Independent Radio News and Sky News Radio). In commercial radio, four companies have an almost 80 per cent share of the market (House of Lords, 2008: 49–52).

The increased profitability of commercial news organisations has inspired an ongoing debate about what can be considered ' "[a]ppropriate" profit levels for media companies' (Picard, 2005: 341). In many cases, the panic in the boardrooms after 2000 was a reaction, not to a collapse, but to a drop in the expected level of profit. In other cases, over-leveraged companies – bought with big loans during the boom times – simply collapsed under the weight of their debt repayments, when the crash of 2008 hit advertising across the board (Picard and van Weezel, 2008: 5).

Commercialisation

Given the dominance of players in the field, whose responsibilities are to themselves or their shareholders, rather than to their role in a functioning democracy, there are concerns that news media are now too focussed on the 'business' side of things. As Picard and Van Weezel (2008: 8) point out: 'Public ownership ... is accompanied by significant financial pressures, separation of ownership from management, and increased organizational size and complexity'. Because commercial news is first and foremost a commodity enterprise which is run by managers who put the economic motives above the public interest function, there will always be 'less flexibility ... in making judgments about coverage', and this means 'potentially important stories whose yield is uncertain' are not followed through (Cranberg et al., 2001: 12).

The focus on the bottom line can lead, as Cranberg *et al.* (2001: 2) suggest, to a position in which 'news has become secondary, even incidental, to markets and revenues and margins and advertisers and consumer preferences'. One of many examples is the *US Tribune*, bought by Sam Zell in December 2007. He saddled the company with levels of debt that could only possibly have been paid for in a boom and filed for bankruptcy the next year. The Tribune group (like many other news companies) entered a period of restructuring and cuts. Zell, in a meeting with *Tribune* staff, betrayed his attitude towards news-gathering when he described the *Tribune* Washington Bureau (which reports on government) as a non-revenue generating 'overhead' (Folkenflik, 2008).

The pressure to increase profits to shareholders has the additional effect, documented by a succession of writers (e.g. Cottle, 2003; Bourdieu, 2005), of moving all the big players towards the centre ground where, it is assumed, the biggest audiences and therefore the biggest profits lie. This 'homogenising effect' operates against the assumption that a market model will ensure a market place of ideas (thus increasing diversity): 'One of the paradoxes is that competition has the effect ... in fields of cultural production under commercial control, of producing uniformity, censorship and even conservatism' (Bourdieu, 2005: 44).

So, commercialisation of media – where economic motives drive content – seems to be detrimental for the public service function that news media play. At the same time, as Picard (2005) argues, a sound and healthy financial situation needs to be the basis of any news company, and financial strength is required in order to ensure the independence needed to operate as a watchdog with regard to government and other organisations. When 'conditions are stable and companies are financially secure, they tend to exhibit more willingness to attend to public functions than when conditions are turbulent and their financial performance is poor' (Picard, 2008: 212).

Currently, there are very pressing threats to both the economic sustainability of news media and their public service provision. As Currah (2009: 12) fears, 'the financial lifeblood of professional journalism is being constrained by the societal and technological dimensions of the digital revolution'.

Challenges to traditional business models of news

The past decade can be seen as an extremely 'tumultuous period for media firms', where they have had to 'seek ways to maintain viability in a rapidly changing business and social environment' (Owers, Carveth and Alexander, 2004: 3–4). These changes have impacted on news journalism in a variety of ways (including employment, its practice and its relationship to the audiences, which we will address in subsequent chapters), but most significantly in light of this chapter, and perhaps also for news media in general, it has impacted on the viability and sustainability of existing business models.

The very core of journalism, the value of news – whether monetary, cultural or social – has been put into question in the changing societal context and by the changing consumption patterns of news. As Tim Gardam states, in the foreword to a report examining the shifting economic foundations of news journalism:

> What is the future business model for commercial news gathering, and, more fundamentally, what is the future for professional journalism when the price of information has in many places dropped to zero? News today is ambient and access to news is free. ... What is beyond dispute is that the basis of journalism as a transaction, where in the past the many have paid to gain access to the writings of the few, has changed fundamentally. In an age of real time information, and limitless distraction, journalists can no longer assume that their 'professionalism' has a secure value.
>
> (Gardam, 2009: 3)

Even though we do not wish to downplay the importance of technological changes, we do wish to stress that these technological changes have gone hand in hand with economic, social, cultural and political changes in the context in which news media operate (see also Rice, 2008: 3). Technology, thus, is only one of the factors 'threatening professional journalism'; phenomena such as '[e]conomic globalization and changes in media outlet ownership and media audiences' are equally important (Nossek, 2009: 358). However, even though technology is not the sole reason for the current woes of the news industry, the ways in which the technology has been adopted has certainly exacerbated the difficulties it faces.

New media technologies and the abundance of 'news'

When viewing the sustainability of business models, and the value of the product 'news', we need to consider what now constitutes the journalism field. With the rise of the internet we have seen a dramatic increase in the types and number of news suppliers. In economic terms, this 'growth of media supply is far exceeding the growth of consumption in terms of both time and money' (Picard, 2008: 213). These new types of market players are eroding the 'customer and financial bases of existing media' (Picard, 2005: 344). It is clear that such fundamental change is detrimental to the existing suppliers of news, and it as yet uncertain whether (or when) alternative news suppliers with viable business models will rise to take their place.

Even though most new players online are not of equal standing (in size or reputation) to the legacy news outlets, they have created significant changes to the supply of information in general, as well as news and commentary in particular. The most important change has been the huge increase in competition, from other platforms (newspapers, radio and TV now share the same space, see Chapter 4), rival organisations and an increasing number of new entrants attracted by low start-up costs. These developments have resulted in an abundance of easily accessible information. Moreover, where they had been in control of their own content, existing news organisations have had to accept that their information is distributed freely and widely, by other organisations:

The social and institutional dynamic of the web is anathema to the pricing strategies of news publishers: their content is effectively commoditised into a stream of bits, which is freely available through sharing and linking. As a result, media businesses have had to retreat from subscription-only walled gardens and instead embrace an open access model, supported by advertising.

(Currah, 2009: 14)

This change has had considerable implications for their business models. Free access to news is not in itself a new trend. Both radio and television have been, in the main, free to viewers and listeners at the point of delivery and, in the 1990s, the rise of 'free-sheets' provided readers with free news (P. Bakker, 2010). With the exception of some publicly subsidised and subscription-based media, all were paid for by advertising. The business model depended on a buoyant advertising market, few direct competitors and (in the case of free newspapers) much-reduced editorial input compared to 'paid for' publications. We will come back to the issue of advertising below, but will first explore the issue of news dissemination in more detail.

New ways of dissemination

In the twentieth century, news by and large was channelled, 'via the scarcity of print and the broadcast spectrum' (Currah, 2009: 11). Now, of the top ten news websites through which the UK audience accesses the news, four are online-only news organisations or aggregators: Google News, Yahoo! News, AOL News and MSN News (Ofcom, 2007). The content of aggregating sites comes largely from other news organisations or news agencies, for which these aggregating organisations do not pay, as they consider that displaying snippets of the articles falls under 'fair use' (Pérez-Peña, 2009; *The Economist*, 2009).[1] Moreover, they argue, the effect of this service is to drive more people to the websites of the major news organisations, which they suggest is a service provided rather than content stolen. According to Currah, 'over 70 per cent of the traffic to a news website tends to enter from the "side door" of search results and "really simple syndication" (RSS) feeds, rather than the home page of the website' (Currah, 2009: 14).

This gave rise to the idea of a 'link economy', in which canny news organisations should: 'Do what you do best and link to the rest' (Jarvis, 2009: 26). New entrants to the news market did precisely that. Examples such as the *Huffington Post* and *The Daily Beast* employ a small core staff who trawl other websites for interesting snippets and video which they link to and contextualise, using their own commentators. The sites are popular but they pay little towards the production of the news stories that they offer to their audiences. They do, however, take all the income from the advertising on their own sites.

Apart from a major cultural effect, this change in accessing news has had a major economic and institutional impact: 'the consumer is increasingly unwilling to pay for news, and prefers instead to read selected parts of the news agenda' (Currah, 2009: 5). News online is 'commoditised' and 'atomised' (ibid). More importantly, in particular for the sustainability of news production, the 'economics of the web favour skills such as aggregation, indexing and search, as opposed to the original gathering and reporting of the news' (Currah, 2009: 15).

Search and linking in fact benefit the brand and advertising opportunities of news aggregators, rather than the news producers, and raises questions. How will news production be paid for in the future? Who will pay the salaries of the people who routinely gather, analyse and produce information for consumption by the general public and in the public interest? The suggestion that this service will simply emerge from a form of 'crowd-sourcing' (Beckett, 2008: 53; Jarvis, 2008) – in which a small number of professionals effectively 'harvest' the work of unpaid contributors – is examined in more detail below.

Changing audiences and audience fragmentation

News journalism has always been relatively resilient. Changes in technology may have changed the way news is delivered, but have never before threatened professional journalism itself. From the 1960s, newspaper circulations shifted, as television became the primary news source in the developed world (Franklin, 2008b). But the change has not all been in one direction. In the UK, for example, the numbers reading the 'quality newspapers' increased by 27.5 per cent between 1965 and 2007 (Franklin, 2009) whereas circulation of Sunday newspapers and mid-market tabloids sharply declined. Internationally, newspaper sales are rising because of huge surges in literacy (and interest) in India, China and Africa (Franklin, 2008b: 631). News is now accessed via a myriad of sources including free papers, 24-hour TV news and the internet. It is this very abundance that has 'contributed to a far more volatile and unstable environment for news organisations' (Witschge, Fenton and Freedman, 2010: 12).

Where media organisations were deemed to be in control of the media space and market, now 'consumers are gaining control of what has become a demand market' (Picard, 2008: 215; see also Currah, 2009: 11). The abundance of choice available to consumers outlined in the above section has split audiences into fragments (Currah, 2009: 15). Those accessing news stories via search engines rarely stay and browse and, even though their numbers may be very high, they do not constitute the loyal and focussed audiences that advertisers prefer (Fletcher and Peters, 1997: 537).

Advertising is 'Googled': Changes in advertising models

News media (unless subsidised) have always been highly dependent on advertising revenues even when they can, like newspapers, be sold. De Bens points out that to 'survive well, a newspaper has to realise at least 50 per cent of its income this way' (de Bens, 2007: 262–63). Even though they 'receive income from advertisers and readers', newspapers became 'increasingly dependent on advertising throughout the twentieth century' (Picard, 2005: 341). Up to 80 per cent of paid newspaper revenues (100 per cent of free sheets' income) now come through advertisements (Franklin, 2008b: 636; see also Picard, 2004: 113).

Economic recessions have always impacted on advertising income (Picard, 2005: 342), but this time around there are fears that the advertising revenue will not return to the traditional news media. Newspapers in particular are 'struggling to maintain historic levels of revenue from advertising' (House of Lords, 2008; see also de Bens, 2007).

The reasons for this struggle are not entirely related to declining circulation. The greatest threat is not declining readership per se, but the threat of a competitor who grabs a bigger share of the available readers. American newspapers, for instance, did very well out of advertising (in particular classified advertising) in spite of declining circulation, until a rival came along in the shape of the internet, and in particular Craigslist, a website specialising in local classifieds (Auletta, 2009: 12).

Classified advertising had accounted for about one third of all newspaper advertising revenue in the USA until Craig Newmark launched a website where people could post ads for free (ibid). What none of the newspapers had anticipated was the way in which this altruistic endeavour would eat up one of the main pillars of local news. Soon people were posting job ads and advertising their apartments and spare rooms on Craigslist, instead of paying the few dollars it cost to put them in the newspaper. Craigslist had the added advantage of being searchable – a real boon for those who knew exactly what they needed and wanted only to get to it quickly. Craigslist not only united the public with their purchases, it did so without exposing them to display ads along the way, as was the case in the traditional media spaces for classifieds. If you could find it online, why bother browsing through the paper and possibly noticing a news story and an ad for something you didn't know you wanted?

For small local news organisations, the existence of free listings took away one of the most reliable sources of income; and moving online did nothing to restore advertising, because local shops and venues who may pay for advertising in a publication now expect any such advertising online to be free. At the same time, in the UK, local councils started producing their own newspapers, in competition with local papers, and using them to post adverts and notices – once a good source of income for local papers. In 2010 the government announced that it was going to ban such local authority free sheets (Lambourne, 2010), a move which could restore at least one income stream to the local press.

The loss of classified and local authority advertising was just the start. The next interloper into the field was Google. The Google search engine, it has been argued, is a positive force in the news ecology, because it allows people to find stories that, in the old days, they would never have seen (see for instance Jarvis, 2009: 124). 'Links get audience', the argument goes, and news organisations need to make those links, increase traffic and exploit this by selling audiences to advertisers. An interesting model in theory, but practice learns that search and aggregation organisations, which distribute news but do not produce it, have quickly and quietly taken the lion's share of advertising revenue (Currah, 2009: 5).

Ken Auletta, in his book *Googled* (2009), spells out the ways in which Google has gobbled up the online advertising market. In 2008, the company was taking

40 per cent of online advertising revenue across the globe and, at the same time, systematically destroying advertising as a source of steady revenue for any organisation which is not as big as Google. It wasn't its intention to do so; it was merely a by-product of its methods. By allowing advertisers to enter an automated online auction for advertising space, Google has made it possible to force down the price of advertising. Given that, in comparison to print, there is also less space for advertising on a typical webpage, and the typical visitor is only popping in for information, rather than staying around to browse, it is not surprising that, even with online audiences that are far bigger than newspaper audiences (the *Guardian* for example has 300,000 print and 30 million online readers), the websites are still bringing in only a fraction of their revenue. In 2009, the adver-tising income of newspapers in the USA was a little under $37.8 billion; the advertising spent online was a mere $3.1 billion (Chittum, 2009; see also Franklin, 2008b). Globally, the ratio is even less: '5.7 per cent share of the $425 billion global advertising market, while newspapers secured 29.4 per cent of revenues' (Franklin, 2008b: 634).

Legacy news organisations are trapped. If they give up their expensive printing and distribution and move online, they also give up more than 90 per cent of their income. Yet, at the same time, circulations are declining – a trend observed by advertisers who are actively searching for cheaper and more direct methods for getting their products to people. We are currently at the point where soon print audiences will be 'too small to sustain the centuries-old business model of selling mass audiences to advertisers' (Singer, 2009: 377). At the same time, news organisations have not yet found reliable ways to 'return to a subscription based strategy since charging for site access reduces reader traffic and with it the vital advertising revenues' (Franklin, 2008b: 636).

With the migration of advertising revenues to the web (de Bens, 2007: 264), and the changing relation between news media and advertisers, new media technology has been put at the centre of the debate.

Increased commercialisation and the democratic deficit

The challenges outlined above have resulted in an ever-increasing commercialisation of news media, where the focus is on consumers rather than citizens. As argued above, news has always been a business, but we can see an increase in the role that economic motives play in news production – at the cost of public interest content – in the current media environment:

> Because market-based media face levels of competition never before experienced and their markets are more unstable than in the past century, and because they operate in a system in which the primary driver is self-interest and heavy commercialization of content, the movement away from serving public func-tions is clearly evident and is breeding discontent among social observers and citizens.
>
> (Picard, 2008: 212)

Media firms aim for larger audiences, particularly in the context of declining audiences and audience fragmentation (and the resulting decline in advertising), and 'commercial pressures dominate content decisions' (Picard, 2005: 343). News organisations, in a bid to cut costs, are reducing staff yet increasing output. The number of specialist reporters and foreign correspondents in the UK news industry has been cut considerably (House of Lords, 2008). Moreover, the remaining newsroom staff are increasingly expected to supply more and more material (see Chapters 4 and 5), taking material from other news sites in order to fill gaps more quickly (see for instance Davies, 2008; Phillips, 2010). The result of these measures is an increasingly homogenous news environment (Redden and Witschge, 2010), as will be further discussed in Chapter 5. We are thus faced with the contradiction that increasing commercial pressures imperil the public service function of media, yet a stable financial base is necessary for media to function well, let alone fulfil any societal needs in terms of information provision for citizens.

New models of news-gathering and dissemination

Citizen journalism

The hope of those seeking a new and more democratic journalism via the internet has been that the old media, with their narrow and populist agenda, would simply fall away, to be replaced by a new and far more plural media form. The low costs of entry online would ensure that everyone would have the opportunity to speak and be heard. In the words of Raymond Williams, the media would be 'genuinely multiple,' where 'all the sources have access to the common channels' and all those involved would be able to communicate and achieve '[a]ctive reception and living response' (Williams, 1983: 304).

Many similar hopes were raised at the start of the digital age, when (in the 1970s and 1980s) direct entry computer setting and digital printing lowered the costs of entry to newspapers. In reality, the big news organisations used the new technology to cut costs and entered into a period of consolidation and commercialisation in which the number of newspapers decreased (Herman and McChesney, 1997).

The changes ushered in by the internet have led to similar optimism, not only about the lower costs of entry and chance of a more plural media, but also of a more democratic form of 'networked' journalism. For 'new media' evangelists such as Charlie Beckett (2008), Clay Shirky (2008a) and Jeff Jarvis (2009), the move online opens up never-before realised opportunities for better and more collaborative journalism. Certainly their vision seems compelling:

> By joining and creating networks of journalistic effort – helping with curation, editing, vetting, education, and yes, revenue – these news organisations can, indeed, grow. Newspapers can get hyper-local or international. TV stations can have cameras everywhere. Investigators can have many more hands helping them to dig.
>
> (Beckett, 2008: viii)

The idea is simple: anyone with a computer and a connection to the internet can now contribute to the democratic conversation and the job of journalists in the future will be to collect and collate all these contributions (see also Chapter 7).

The web has proven successful at collecting together diverse audiences around particular, niche interests (Anderson, 2006). Social networks such as MySpace and Last.fm offer new opportunities for listening to, and talking about music (alongside opportunities for buying related products). Politics also attracts a big audience online, comprising 17 per cent of the top stories on US blogs. Eight per cent of the US blogs are technology-related compared to a mere 1 per cent of top news stories in the mainstream press (Pew Project for Excellence in Journalism, 2010c). Networked journalism and Clay Shirky's dictum of 'filter after the fact' (Shirky, 2008b) work well with this kind of very active, engaged and dedicated audience, where there is a genuine exchange between readers and collators, and 'facts' are rapidly corrected where they are found to be inaccurate.

Amateur photography and video are other examples of successful new entrants into the field. Images sent in by members of the public who have witnessed breaking news are now widely used. Indeed, such was the deluge of material that the BBC, for example, set up a special team of 15 journalists just to wade through it (Beckett, 2008: 81). This hub, specialising in user-generated content (UGC), comes into its own when there is a big event such as a terrorist attack. However, even though sometimes new stories are originated through this method, the cost/ benefit ratio of keeping 15 trained people tied up all day combing through amateur material is questionable, particularly for less well-funded news media.

But, where opportunities present themselves, businesses are never far behind. There are now agencies moving in, dedicated to the job of sifting amateur footage and linking it with professional news sites. Demotix, for example, was set up precisely to offer a route for citizens to access mainstream media, splitting the fees raised 50:50 with contributors (Witschge, 2009). In 2010, Demotix joined up with Publish2 (Oliver, 2010b) to provide a dedicated network for mainstream news organisations to access amateur footage. News organisations can also find a wide range of amateur photographic material free online on sites such as Flickr.

While these new routes and voices have certainly widened contributions to the public domain, they have also raised very important questions for the sustainability of dominant news production models. Amateur photography has forced down the rates paid for images and, despite many endeavours to safeguard copyright, control over material has been undermined. Most importantly, these trends make it increasingly difficult for anyone to work professionally in the field. As Turi Munthe, the CEO of Demotix acknowledges in an interview, contributors to the site would not be able to make a living from it: 'What I hope we'll be able to do is to supplement the income of professional journalists, and what I really hope we'll do is reward political participation, essentially' (in Witschge, 2009). There is no space here to discuss the possible long-term effects of this de-professionalisation on careers in the creative and media industries (uncertainties and developments in employment and work conditions are discussed in Chapter 2), but they need to be borne in mind as one of the costs of the changing news ecology.

The limits of citizen journalism

While niche sites have prospered, and news organisations now benefit from access to cheap amateur video footage and images, more general news sites have not done so well. The model for a general news site in which the vast majority of material is produced by amateurs is the South Korean OhmyNews, which employs a staff of 70 journalists to edit a vast quantity of incoming material. OhmyNews entered the scene at a critical junction in South Korea, at the very start of the liberalisation of the news media, and before commercial organisations had managed to create strong brands online. At the start, it attracted a great deal of advertising and was able to pay its contributors. In 2009, however, the model of payments was replaced by one of prizes and, in the spring of 2010, it sent out a fund-raising message asking readers to help keep it going (Oliver, 2010a, 2010d).

Outside niche subject fields, the difficulty lies in monitoring and gathering relevant information, and in building up sustainable audiences. On a general news site, there is little reason to assume that active and engaged citizens will be available, or indeed willing, over a very wide range of subject matters to supply, as well as quickly correct, erroneous material. The cost of verifying sources and information is high and has to be done by trained staff, in order to guard against legal action and ensure that information is reliable. In 2010, Ohmy News International closed because, according to a post on the site, 'it was impossible for our editors to accurately check each story. Fact-checking is one of our core principles' (Oliver, 2010c).

In spite of the trend of amateur contributions to the news, citizens who want to know what is happening to their hospitals and schools are still dependent on the every-day routine work of the beat and specialist journalists who write on these subjects. It is this sustained work of public scrutiny which does not lend itself to the operation of ad-hoc groups or enthusiasts. Indeed, as the Pew Center Project for Excellence in Journalism found:

> blogs still heavily rely on the traditional press – and primarily just a few outlets within that – for their information. More than 99% of the stories linked to in blogs came from legacy outlets such as newspapers and broadcast networks. And just four – the BBC, CNN, the *New York Times* and the *Washington Post* – accounted for fully 80% of all links.
>
> (Pew Project for Excellence in Journalism, 2010c)

Thus one of the big hopes for new, networked journalism – that at the local level a stripped down journalism staff and a lot of user-generated content would promote greater diversity and accountability – has proved disappointing so far (Fenton *et al.*, 2010). There are certainly now a number of such sites in the UK run by single reporters or enthusiasts and even more have been established in the USA, but they have not turned out to be as successful as many had hoped. As the recent study by the Project for Excellence in Journalism (2010a) confirms, 'all of these sites tend to operate with small staffs, even among volunteers, and thus can produce only a limited amount of content.' Thus, online news media offer 'substantially less reportorial content than legacy media' (ibid).

Even the key value that Beckett (2008) refers to, of a 'networked journalism', opening a conversation between citizens and journalists, is much harder to realise than the initial enthusiasts imagined. Our interviews found that journalists now have so much information pouring into their 'inboxes' that they are more likely than before to screen out messages from people or organisations they do not know (Phillips, 2010). People working for NGOs also complain that they find it harder than ever before to attract attention and time from over-stretched journalists (Fenton, 2010).

Thus, even though different voices can speak online, it is still difficult to intervene in a public debate. The idea of 'web neutrality' (equal access to all without favour) is at the heart of the way in which the web works. Search engines pre-structure access to information using mathematical formulae rather than giving the top spot to the highest payer (Koopmans, 2004; Hindman, 2009) but, as internet users do not often go beyond the first results on the search engines (Jansen and Spink, 2006, 2005; iProspect, 2008), it proves difficult for alternative voices to get heard. As Hindman (2009) shows, the very infrastructure of web search militates against all but the very biggest and the very smallest (niche) organisations. Thus the operation of 'web neutrality' actually augments the 'homogenising tendencies' mentioned earlier and effectively decreases the number of voices being heard.

Commercial light on the horizon?

Small 'citizen' media organisations, which should now be springing up to fill the 'democratic deficit' left by the ailing 'legacy media', find themselves with the same problem as the organisations they hope to replace: finding sustainable models of funding. The Pew Center reports:

> The major impediment to citizen journalism success is that the sites that do not have the financial backing of foundations, the work of professional journalists, or some supportive links with legacy media are usually fuelled only by personal motivation and when that disappears, so will the site.
>
> (Pew Project for Excellence in Journalism, 2010a)

The 2009 Conservative Party policy statement on the future of local news in the UK also connects 'legacy media' to citizen journalism (Parry, 2009). Here, however, it wouldn't be the big organisation helping smaller ones; the advice is to suck volunteers into struggling commercial news organisations to provide free labour: 'Collaboration between professional staff and unpaid community volunteers is central to making economics work' (ibid: 6). As we have set out above however, with these models of unpaid journalism it is difficult to sustain a diverse news agenda and supply a constant flow of quality content.

How then, given the economic realities of the news industry, can we make sure there is diverse, independent and quality news, that covers issues of public interest at the local, national and global level? In the music industry, we can observe similar problems with finding a new business model in light of its changing cultural, social and technological environment. The big beast was brought low by file sharing and a growing belief amongst young people that music should be free (see for instance Lessig, 2008). Money started to trickle back when new models of purchasing music were introduced. It seems that people didn't so much mind paying as they minded the difficulty of registering and entering credit card numbers; iTunes made spending simple.

Even though the issues in the music industry are by no means settled yet, they do offer some possible models to ensure the sustainability of news. Solutions based on strong brands providing quality content, such as simple micro-payment service (for example iTunes), subscription services or paid-for applications on the iPad or iPhone have, against all expectations provided a new income stream for music and may still hold opportunities for news (*The Economist*, 2010). Commercial media may also find a way back towards profitability – through changes in the way advertising is organised, or a better response to the market logic of Google. Alternatively, we may see media organisations such as Google and AOL move into news origination, elbowing out the legacy organisations. AOL has already started hiring journalists from leading quality news outlets, and now focuses on 'original reporting, analysis and commentary'.[2]

However, it is unclear how any of these models could break the trend towards ever-greater homogenisation and ensure a continued investment in a diversity of high-quality news. As the House of Lords Select Committee on the state of news in Britain reports: '[w]hile there has been a proliferation of ways to access the news, there has not been a corresponding expansion in professional journalism' (2008: 9). It is not coincidental then that the Pew Center, in a case study on news media in Baltimore City, found that 95 per cent of new information introduced in the public domain is provided by traditional media (mostly newspapers), rather than new media (Pew Project for Excellence in Journalism, 2010b).

The same study also found, however, that eight out of ten stories did not contain any new information, and that the main suppliers of new information, the press, are 'also offering less than they once did' (ibid: 2). This suggests that news media today are less able to provide a public service than before, and the question remains: how to fund (as well as regulate and disseminate) news that is in the public interest? As Bird argues, 'some stories ultimately matter more than others, and we need journalists to report them' (Bird, 2009: 295).

Public subsidy of news

More and more, there are calls to find alternatives that are not based on the commercial business model. To quote the Digital Britain report of 2009:

> To sustain the vital civic function of journalism, citizens, Government and business will need collaboratively to devise new ways of funding the news. The commercial model will continue to play an important role, especially as publishers explore the potential of new platforms and technologies. But it will

> also need to be supplemented with a range of alternative models – for
> example, local ownership, community media and non-profit organizations.
>
> (Digital Britain, 2009: 149)

By proposing public funding in the news industry, we do not suggest propping
up existing news media to satisfy shareholders. We propose introducing more
public funding to ensure quality content in the public interest. While we
acknowledge public funding of the media brings a new set of issues, we argue that
professionally produced news is an important condition for democratic societies to
function well.

In Witschge *et al.* (2010), a number of measures are discussed that can be taken
to support public interest practices in the news industry, including: charging news
aggregators that exploit news content; industry levies; tax concessions; and direct
taxation. Support of this kind can be distributed in a number of ways to ensure
neutrality and media independence. In the Nordic model, newspapers are subsidised in light of their societal function via a number of neutral instruments to
ensure that government cannot operate the subsidy system in its own interests. In
Scandinavia, for example, with the highest newspaper circulations in Europe (de
Bens, 2007), such support has been available for decades, paid via a number of
instruments such as subsidising the cost of newsprint. In the Netherlands, specific
subsidies exist for both press and broadcast that aim to increase diversity,[3] as
many state subsidies aim to do (McQuail, 2001).

As explained above, online news aggregators disseminate news and take a
considerable share of the advertising revenues, but do not produce original content. This broken link between content producers and advertisers is a serious
threat to the continuation of news production, as we have noted. One way of
dealing with this would be to ensure, through public regulation, that aggregators
pay their share for the material that they present to audiences – a measure that
has been asked for by British newspapers (Pérez-Peña, 2009).

An alternative way of charging aggregators and other profit-making organisations
in the field is to ensure there is funding for the public interest function of the
media through industry levies. These have proved popular in many European
countries, and involve a surcharge or a tax on the revenues or profits of certain
sections of the media industry. The British Institute for Public Policy Research
has shown how this could function in the British context, and has conducted a thorough investigation into the potential of industry levies as a means of funding
public service media (Institute for Public Policy Research, 2009).

Possible tax measures include direct taxation to provide subsidies for public
service media and tax concessions for media companies that provide this public
service (for a discussion of the possibilities of the latter in the British media
environment, see Currah, 2009). A variety of tax measures is already employed in
different European countries. In the UK, the relief from Value Added Tax (VAT)
is also an indirect subsidy and the BBC is paid for through a licence fee. In most
of Europe, public service TV and radio are to some extent subsidised by direct or
indirect taxation.

These types of measures, which subsidise professional journalism in the public interest, allow for a more stable income flow for the news media, and could work in a media environment that includes many different forms of funding and different ownership models. There are other models possible beyond the commercial model of media ownership. In the USA, for instance, we see that more and more initiatives are springing up where journalism is funded by charitable giving (Christoffersen, 2009). Another model that has proved to be successful is that of trust funds; they are seen as a good alternative to the commercial business model, particularly in the local press, where the issues have been starkest. The income could come from a mix of funding, including local advertising, local public funding and a return to paid local government advertising in local media (Fenton *et al.*, 2010: 48), as well as the support of larger news organisations. To ensure quality content, the trusts would have an obligation to provide 'good reporting, fair rules and open access, and you could have independent local news across web, print, radio and television offering a genuine community service' (Toynbee, 2009).

Alternatively, we can consider broad networks or partnerships between public and commercial media, to ensure sustainable news flows on matters of public concern. Sharing cost, infrastructure, expertise and, some advocate, content may prove a viable way, particularly for smaller news organisations, to benefit from established partners. However, the danger is that cooperation diminishes diversity rather than enhancing it. Thus regulation and governance of these partnerships and consortia need to be considered. (For more on the different ownership models, as well as the pitfalls, see Witschge *et al.*, 2010.)

The main point is that there is a variety of models to sustain news availability beyond the commercial model. Professional news is of such importance to democratic societies that we need to be resourceful in finding sustainable models. Some type of public intervention may be needed to get there.

Conclusion

In this chapter, we have outlined the current issues that the news industry, not unlike other cultural industries, is faced with. A range of technological, social and cultural changes has impacted on the viability of existing business models. The traditional link between advertising and news audiences, as mediated by news providers, has been broken and thus the production of news content – that never has been fully paid for by its audiences – is under threat.

We have discussed a number of trends that we consider to have had an impact on the business models and the functioning of news media. New ways of dissemination have distorted the control news producers traditionally have had (to a certain extent) over their material. The change of advertising models – where aggregating organisations such as Google offer, but not produce, material – and a change in the way in which advertisers use media, has in addition meant a decline in advertising revenues for the professional news producers. Last, all these trends suggest an increased commercialisation and homogenisation of news content, at the cost of content that is in the public interest.

To be sure, the dual nature of news, being both a business product and a public service, has always led to tensions. However, if we acknowledge the public service nature of news production, its sustainability ceases to be a mere economic enigma that media businesses need to crack themselves. To protect the flow of professional content in the public interest, we need to consider ways in which we can support content production.

New media have certainly lowered the barriers for new entrants to come into the field of news. However, thus far, most of these organisations are not bringing new information to the public domain. They aggregate news, disseminate news and comment on news. These are all valuable acts that can provide a public service. But we need to ensure that there continues to be news to aggregate, disseminate and comment upon. News, like democracy, is too important to leave to the vicissitudes of the economic cycle or the whims of technological fashion.

Notes

1 More and more news producers take legal actions against these aggregators. (On the Associated Press actions against news organisations that do not obtain permission to publish their material, or newspapers' actions against Google, see Pérez-Peña, 2009.)

2 As is reported on its website, www.aolnews.com/about/ (accessed February 2011). Subsequent to this, AOL bought the *Huffington Post* to drive its news content business http://www.huffingtonpost.com/2011/02/07/aol-huffington-post_n_819375.html (accessed March 2011).

3 See also www.ejc.net/media_landscape/article/the_netherlands/ (accessed February 2011).

2 The return of Hephaestus

Journalists' work recrafted

Peter Lee-Wright

In protestant cultures in particular, work defines who we are and the value society puts upon us, but the way we view work changes with time and economic circumstance. Until well into the nineteenth century, work was what people who had no property, little education and no vote did. When politicians spoke of 'the people', workers were excluded. The emergence of the working class as a political entity – with a voice that superseded the age-old cry of the mob – was paralleled in and promoted through the rise of the press. The press blossomed, from the weekly pamphlets, such as the *London Gazette* of the seventeenth century, to the dailies – the first of which was the *Daily Courant* in London in 1702 – and by the end of the eighteenth century there were 278 newspapers, journals and periodicals produced in London, mostly in Fleet Street and its immediate surroundings.

Writers from abroad commented on how these absorbed not just the middle classes, but workers who patronised the coffee houses. One writes: 'Workmen habitually begin the day by going to coffee-rooms in order to read the latest news' (Ferdinand de Saussure quoted in Ackroyd, 2000: 402). The UK press discovered early the ability to appeal to the crowd, the taste for sensation and scandal, the demotic voice. The process of news-gathering also came from the streets, was one of enterprise and individual effort, often 'one-man bands' (Schudson, 1978: 65), with news purveyors involved in all stages of collecting, writing and distributing information. Because of the increased mechanisation and productivity of late nineteenth-century printing presses, the divisions of labour along familiar capitalist lines were established, with the controllers of distribution in charge – the proprietors and their editors being the lords of the fourth estate – while the toilers in the field, the journalists, harvested the grains of truth. Örnebring charts this evolution of 'Journalism as labour': 'What quickly emerged was a division where the labourer responsible for the basic gathering of information, the reporter or newspaperman, had a distinctly low status' (Örnebring, 2010: 62).

From those humble beginnings journalism emerged as a craft, with its own culture, standards and traditions essentially learned on the job, through working apprenticeships as in other crafts. In 1907, the National Union of Journalists (NUJ) was formed to codify those standards and represent members in negotiations, effectively becoming a closed shop, so that membership was an essential prerequisite to employment in journalism. Two world wars and the establishment of a welfare state bred successive generations of collectivised aspiration and assumption of work as a right.

That era came to an end in the 1980s with the Thatcher government's all-industry war on trade unionism and outlawing of the closed shop, liberating some journalists to join the editors as high-profile, high-earning stars of the journalistic firmament. Journalists were now mostly graduates, attracted by both the potential pay and the public prominence. The late twentieth century can be seen as the apogee of this period of autonomy, with journalists exercising their 'cultural capital' in influencing every aspect of the public sphere, from popular culture to political morality. But the fragmentation of markets and the contraction of income promoted new technologies and ways of work which have progressively revoked that freedom, proving Bourdieu (2005) correct in calling journalism a 'weakly autonomous field'. Now, highly trained individuals find themselves virtually chained to their desks, not free to go out and source original stories because of the growing demands of productivity, and fearful if they did there would be no desk or job to return to. This precarity of employment has been given physical substance by some organisations' deployment of 'hot-desking', where you have no permanent station but take whichever desk is free – an unhappy adult version of Musical Chairs.

Acquiescence to this loss of liberty is directly related to the loss of jobs that has hit the industry in recent years. Over 160 titles ceased printing in the UK and the USA between 2007 and 2010. The Business Insider website estimate of total industry job losses in the UK and Ireland between December 2008 and April 2010 was 8,800 (Pompeo and Jedrzejczak, 2010). By March 2009, the NUJ had recorded over 2,000 job losses in regional newsrooms alone (National Union of Journalists, 2009). In the USA, between September 2008 and September 2009, it is reported that the print sector lost more than 24,500 jobs, while the broadcast sector eliminated over 8,300 posts (Pompeo and Jedrzejczak, 2010). A further 1,892 US newspaper layoffs were reported in the first half of 2010.[1] The European Centre for Journalism (Romero, 2009) reports similar losses across Europe, from *c.* 1,000 in Germany to 1,500 in Spain in the first six months of 2008, leading to the setting up of the Facebook group *Por la dignidad de los periodistas y los trabajadores de los medios* (For the dignity of journalists and media workers). This chapter aims to chart not just the practical changes in journalists' work but, through the experiences of those we have interviewed, the impact on their dignity, sense of value and purpose.

The loss of the collective

Richard Sennett's disquisition on *The Craftsman* ends with the line: 'The clubfooted Hephaestus, proud of his work if not of himself, is the most dignified person we can become' (2008: 296). Hephaestus, blacksmith to the gods and craftsman of all their miraculous things, was the only Greek god expelled from Olympus subsequently to be readmitted, the apotheosis of craft over connivance. Not only have many journalists been metaphorically expelled from Olympus, but journalism itself has fallen from whatever grace it may once have had, noted in terms of loss of trust (Seldon, 2010) as well as 'churnalism' (Davies, 2008). It remains to be seen whether the craft will regain its former ascendancy in new forms more suited to the remodelled communications landscape. As we shall see, this is as likely to be driven by individual human agency as by corporate fiat. Sennett (2008: 287) writes of the synchronicity between work skills and life skills – 'the capacities our bodies have to shape physical things are the same capacities we draw on in social relationships' – and the importance of others' experience in transmitting and embedding those skills.

The mentoring relationship is not only vital to the development of the individual journalist, but crucial to the retention of journalistic experience and values. The wise old bird took the new recruit under their wing and imbued in them the traditions and sensibilities of the particular paper or organisation. Former *Press Gazette* Deputy Editor turned blogger Jon Slattery feels that the loss of this process is one of the less well remarked declines in the intellectual capital of journalism. 'As everyone over 40 seems to have been removed from newsrooms, and the few left are spread too thin to continue that tradition, so nothing is passed on', he says.[2] Jenny Lennox, the NUJ assistant organiser for the North of England and Midlands, reports:

> Newspapers have traditionally been staffed by keen young people and older experienced staff. That relationship is key to a good newspaper. There will be a lot of graduates competing for jobs with experienced journalists who have been made redundant.
>
> (Lennox quoted in Slattery, 2009)

Each newsroom used to have a distinctive timbre which informed the voice of the journalism that emanated from it. In reflection of the ordered society it served, it required a degree of compliance, which in turn granted the individual welcome to the 'club' with all the perks of membership, including a growing degree of autonomy. But that had to be earned. So woe betide any newsroom trainee who dared to question editorial priorities and decisions, as this luckless writer once did. Older colleagues' outrage at my presumption was accompanied by a sneering contempt for the lack of 'professionalism', which disguised embarrassment at their tacit acceptance of the shared beliefs – what Bourdieu terms 'doxa' (Bourdieu, 1977) – normally dictated by the unmentioned, unmet, but omnipresent, pay-master. The reward for quiescence was understood to be a job for life. That promise – for historical, economic and technical reasons explored in the previous chapter – has now been largely withdrawn, leaving employees to reconsider the value of corporate conformity and unswerving loyalty. They are deprived of the certainties that make work familiar, reassuring and predetermined, replacing those shared values with what the Becks identify, in their charting of society's *Individualisation*, as the 'encumbrance, exertion and stress imposed by the destruction of routine' (Beck and Beck-Gernsheim, 2002).

Journalists are experiencing what others have before them, the withdrawal of the collective umbra which protects workers from the constant stress of responsibility for every decision in their working life. As one former *Telegraph* journalist said of the new conditions of work:

> I just had daily fights with them. I'd stand at the newsdesk and go: 'But why do you want me to run it? It's not true'. ... it's just a fundamentally different approach ... What's the worse they can do? Give me a cheque to go away?
>
> (Specialist reporter, *Telegraph*, interview conducted in 2008)

Which, in this reporter's case, duly happened. One thing worse than an imposed set of beliefs is the absence of any, causing many of the formerly combative to look back with unanticipated regret for the innocence of former times and clearly drawn lines.

> With the Great System of which they were all more or less the victims they were quite content, being persuaded that it was the only one possible and the best that human wisdom could devise. The reason why they all believed this was because not one of them had ever troubled to inquire whether it would not be possible to order things differently.
>
> (Tressell, 1914: 202)

In 2009, a book that was first published in 1914 – and subsequently credited with helping deliver Labour's earliest UK electoral victories – re-entered the Amazon best-seller lists, to the surprised delight of the several publishing houses with out-of-copyright editions to sell. Robert Tressell's *Ragged Trousered Philanthropists* is a semi-autobiographical, political novel, attacking the bosses who exploit a team of house painters and demean their craft, by forcing up productivity through making them 'slobber over' jobs, which previously demanded more care and attention. Set in the fictional town of Mugsborough, Tressell's socialist tract does not spare his fellow workers who, as the opening quote says, unquestioningly buy into the system that is ultimately their own downfall. The suspicion that we are all mugs who fail to question our condition is clearly behind the newfound popularity of this century-old book.

A similar phenomenon occurred in Japan in 2008, when Takiji Koybayashi's 1929 book, *Kanikōsen/Crab Cannery Ship*, sold over 600,000 copies to the growing numbers of urban Japanese working in poorly paid, insecure jobs. Its tale of fishermen's fight against wretched conditions, protesting for trade union rights, mirrors Tressell's English narrative, as did its posthumous publication – although Tressell died of tuberculosis, while Koybayashi was tortured to death by the Japanese secret police.[3] While we would not suggest that life is anything like as hard as it was in the early twentieth century, the casualisation of employment within consumer culture has created a different dynamic.

The common response to casualisation is to knuckle down and take whatever they must to keep working. The growing number of people in the freelance market tend to accept whatever work is going. Those metaphorically hanging on by their finger-nails to staff jobs recognise the need to adapt and acquiesce. Typically the attitude we encountered was: 'Obviously people deep down hold this different view but anybody who is going to kind of succeed and have a career here knows that's the future and gets on with it.'[4] Underlying that fatalism is the recognition that, employment contraction notwithstanding, corporate news careers will still exist, albeit demanding greater degrees of flexibility and accommodation.

The casualisation of labour can produce contrary reactions, for which the corporations largely responsible seem unprepared.

> We may have reorganised the workforce more efficiently, but we have yet to recognise that there is a cost in the different attitudes people bring to work. ... I had one young man, halfway through a year's contract others would kill for, come in and say he had to pack it in because it was interfering too much with his social life.
>
> (BBC News executive, interview conducted in 2009)

In *New Capitalism? The Transformation of Work*, Kevin Doogan 2009 questions the conventional, apocalyptic vision of an industrial world in meltdown, supporting this with data suggesting 'job stability has not declined' (Doogan, 2009: 4). While contesting the prevailing view – such as Castells' (1996) conclusion 'that we are witnessing the end of salarisation of employment' – Doogan argues that workers underestimate the value that employers still place on labour retention and disempower themselves by imagining the worst.

> To understand new capitalism, at the end of the day, is to understand an ideological offensive, a mode of domination, as Bourdieu suggests, that seeks to create uncertainty and anxiety and fear on the side of labour to guarantee its compliance. Accordingly, sympathetic commentators should recognise the risk of self-inflicted weaknesses created by the overstatement of capital mobility, job instability and powerlessness.
>
> (Doogan, 2009: 214)

No-one can deny the seismic impact of contraction on the newspaper industry and, in a Pew Research Center Project for Excellence in Journalism survey of news editors in April 2010, fewer than half (46 per cent) were confident that their organisations would still be in business in ten years' time (Pew Project for Excellence in Journalism, 2010d).

Middle-aged employees with large mortgages and families rightly fear the axe of redundancy and the difficulties of re-employment. Their craft is calibrated to the conformity and consistency required by corporate employers, and their compromises are traditionally repaid in a monthly paycheque. Once the paycheque disappears, those compromises seem pointless, and the habits of the self-employed freelance are not easily acquired overnight. But industry entrants who have no expectation of a permanent, pensionable job are developing the survival instincts and approaches that temporary work patterns require. One feature under-remarked is that freelances are not covered by the indemnity insurance corporate employment affords, making them more likely to be risk averse. They are on their own, they know they face an uncertain future, but the upside of a portfolio career is that they owe little to any individual employer, and are clearer what works for them. To appropriate – and invert – the J. F. Kennedy maxim, the paradigm shift seems to be: 'Ask not what I can do for the company; ask what it can do for me.'[5]

From hot press to cold calculations

The emergence of a 'self-culture' in which people have moved from 'living for others' to 'a life of one's own' (Beck and Beck-Gernsheim, 2002: 22) has been defined as the key social transformation of the last few decades by the Becks (2002), Bauman (2007) and others. Within journalism in the UK, the origin of this elevation of individualist values can be traced back a generation to the Thatcher era assault on collective bargaining, not least in the newspaper business. Elected in 1979 after a period in which trade union resistance had, in her belli-cose phrase, 'held the country to ransom', Margaret Thatcher's government set about dismantling union power. Unions were then closed shops in UK news-papers and ITV – you could not work without belonging to one: NUJ for reporters, National Graphical Association (NGA) for skilled printers, Society of Graphical and Allied Trades (SOGAT) for the lower grade technicians and Asso-ciation of Cinematograph and Television Technicians (ACTT) for all commercial television technicians and production staff.

The seminal newspaper dispute featured a maverick proprietor, Eddie Shah, who not only refused to recognise the unions' closed shop but also did not join the employers' organisation, the Newspaper Society, thereby freeing him from any pressure to observe existing agreements. Shah ran a free-sheet business in the north of England, and disagreement over work terms and conditions in the introduction of new printing presses at the *Stockport Messenger* led to a strike and illegal picket, which enabled Shah to be the first to invoke new Tory employment legislation to seques-trate the assets of the print union, the NGA. The progress and union-busting out-come of this dispute in 1983–84 was watched and covered with great enthusiasm by Rupert Murdoch's newspaper empire, particularly by *The Sunday Times* and its then editor, Andrew Neil, who saw its potential lessons for the national press.

The new technologies being developed as a result of computers, still relatively new at the time, promised the revolution of cutting out the costly and time-consuming process of type-setting, enabling journalists to type their stories directly into an electronic system which would emerge as the finished article. This would, by definition, cut out most of the printers, who were not only vital to the existing 'hot press' production, but had manipulated this power to achieve very lucrative pay deals and work conditions. News International built a new printing plant in Wapping, notionally to produce a new freesheet, *The London Post*, but actually with the intention of moving production of all its titles there. While this development went ahead, protracted negotiations were held with the unions, ostensibly to secure agreements to operate the new system. With the new plant ready to go, a final meeting with the print unions was held on 23 January 1986, which hindsight suggests was calculated to provoke the inevitable NGA/SOGAT strike that was called the following day, losing that day's *Sun*.

The company invited its journalists and other staff to turn up for work the next day at Wapping, or face the sack. Most reckoned the work preferable to the dole, and no further newspaper editions were lost, despite an acrimonious printers' strike which went on for over a year, leading to clashes with police, 1,262 arrests and the claim of 410 police injured. Andrew Neil called it 'a necessary watershed' but, as the investigative journalist Linda Melvern wrote, 'two hundred years of Fleet Street history were over' (Melvern, 1986: 153). The attack on unions did not meet with universal resistance, not least because many journalists resented the printers. Roy Stockdill was working on the *News of the World* at the time, when David Montgomery was its editor.

> I can recall little of the anguished debate that followed, save to say that in the end a large majority voted to go to Wapping for a one-off payment of £2,000 plus an extra £2,000 a year on their salaries. What I do recall is a strong sense that at long last the print unions, whose huge wages were much resented, were getting their come-uppance and that finally journalists would become the most important people in the business – well that was what David Montgomery told us, anyway.[6]

For many, the Wapping dispute remains a crushing defeat for the principles of communal solidarity at work, the creative industries' equivalent of the 1984 miners' strike, the other great tragic ending of an era. But for many others, it represented the dawning of a new age of opportunity, the freeing of the entrepreneur to exploit the new technology with newspaper products more suited to the age. On 4 March 1986, Eddie Shah launched a new mid-market national newspaper, *Today*, the first to use full colour offset printing. It had one Alastair Campbell as its political editor and his partner, Fiona Millar, as news editor. Undercapitalised and underequipped, *Today* was soon sold to Lonhro, who closed the Sunday edition and sold out in 1987 to News International, who kept the ailing title going until 1995. But it had led the new technological way for other newspapers to follow – all did within two years – and other titles to launch. On 7 October 1986, the *Independent* was born, as a centrist rival to *The Guardian*. Despite that political stance, its launch editor Andreas Whittam Smith said: 'Until 1986 nothing had changed in newspaper publishing. The industry was in a time warp. What Rupert Murdoch did was break the logjam and bring us into the 20th Century' (quoted in Aaronovitch, 2006).

Disempowering the collective

The Wapping revolution did not just break the technical logjam and release profits; it also heralded social and cultural change. The heroic reporter had notionally sat at the top of a production hierarchy involving copy takers, sub-editors, printers and copytasters. As each of these roles was made redundant by modern technology, the supporting pyramid disappeared from beneath the reporters, making them more self-reliant. Mobile phones and internet made communications more direct, the latter enabling direct filing from the field. As the doyenne of British foreign correspondents, Ann Leslie, says, 'I love my mobile phone. It's changed my life. In Moscow, for example, you used to have to wait for hours to get a line to London. It was quicker to fly to Helsinki to file.'[7] But Ann Leslie was an early harbinger of change in more ways than merely technological.

Ann Leslie was a bright Oxford English graduate parachuted into a 1963 Manchester *Daily Express* newsroom composed of hard-bitten reporters of the old school, who had usually not been to university and had unreconstructed views about the role of women. 'You needn't come up here with your fancy ways and tell us what to do. Go and make the tea', was the sort of routine misogyny that she records in her memoirs (Leslie, 2008). With her gender, education and, above all, class, she defied the prevailing archetype which then staffed the newsroom. Making news was a craft and its practitioners overwhelmingly drawn from the communities they reported, learning through apprenticeships on the job. It meant that they knew their beats well and understood implicitly what their readership wanted, but it was not a culture that welcomed change, or the 'officer class' coming in above their heads. In all this, it mirrors the police force, also a plebeian body with a canteen culture resistant to evolution, and to fast-tracked graduate imports. Like medieval guilds, police and press proudly and jealously preserved their traditions and knowledge as a kind of sacred trust; and, like Tressell's ragged trousered philanthropists, they felt threatened by the imposition of new management and purposes. The unions in the press were strong precisely because of that shared sense of craft – what Richard Sennett in *The Craftsman* calls 'a closed knowledge system' – and demoralised by the imposition of change (Sennett, 2008: 26).

There are instructive parallels to be drawn with broadcast news, which evolved at a later stage and in a different form. BBC Radio News was, in its early pre-war days, very much an establishment mouthpiece, with the unseen newsreaders wearing formal dinner suits to enunciate announcements in the received tones of the King's English. Any socialist concerns that this was not as broad a cast as it might have been were suppressed as the country hung on those words during the Second World War. The post-war relaunch of the BBC's fledgling television service did not immediately lead to TV news as we now know it. The then Director-General of the BBC, Sir William Haley, a former editor of *The Times*, did not think news appropriate on television.

A proper television news service was not established until November 1954, and there Ann Leslie, had she not still been at school, would have been very much at home, for the tone remained 'posh', even if the newsroom had to be staffed largely with 'ruffians' from Fleet Street. Even Independent Television News (ITN), which launched the following year, 1955, was initially presented by the champion athlete and future Tory MP, Chris Chataway. In fact, precisely because the recruitment from Fleet Street imported pre-war ways of work, news remained a rather more reactionary arena than the rest of television. But the driving motor of broadcast journalism, in both radio and television, came from the separate arena called Current Affairs, where the news is analysed and the issues discussed at greater length.

Broadcast current affairs production, unlike the newsroom, was largely staffed with bright young graduates, many from Oxford and Cambridge, who saw the chance to make the new medium their own. Recruitment to BBC 'general traineeships' was straight from university, becoming one of the dream career tickets of the 1960s. This generation had avowedly dispensed with conservatism and deference and brought a more questioning approach to both the subjects they covered and the ways programmes were edited. Their view, that no subject should be excluded and no opinion exempt from criticism, led to growing battles within the BBC and with political forces outside. Variously accused of 'newsmongering' (*The Times*),[8] 'journalistic irresponsibility' (*Telegraph*)[9] and 'bias' (newspapers and parties of all hues), the 1970s and 1980s were a combative and crisis-ridden time for BBC journalism, admirably covered by David Hendy in his history of Radio 4, *Life on Air* (2007), as well as in the magisterial *History of Broadcasting in the United Kingdom* by Briggs (1995). But this merely reflected the wider picture of a society in which political and social consensus was breaking down, traditional industries collapsing, causing a recriminative class war, and major stories – such as Vietnam and Northern Ireland – rendered traditions of objectivity and balance ineffective.

Chained to the bottom line

Consistent with the social levelling of the time, those elite corps exist no more. Though the vast majority of journalists are now graduates, this elevation of all to an equal footing does not complete a process of professionalisation. Witschge and Nygren (Witschge and Nygren, 2009: 39) say: 'Media scholars have thus considered journalism as a semi-profession, mostly because of this reason of not being able to exclude non-professionals from the field of journalism.' The explosion in the number of journalism graduates does not necessarily challenge that assessment, as the trade's professional profile and economic values have diminished. In broadcasting, successive reorganisations and 'efficiency savings' have cut current affairs departments down in size, virtually obliterating the genre from ITV, significantly reducing its power and position in BBC TV (though not on BBC Radio 4), and only maintaining its former airtime share on Channel 4.

The former arrogance may have been ameliorated, but with it the confidence and a lot of the ambition. The former BBC TV flagship, *Panorama*, is reduced to a lightweight ghost of its former self, a *Marie Celeste*, progressively more risk averse and neutered (Lindley, 2003). In January 2008, it featured a film about the Colombian cocaine trade fronted by Blur bassist Alex James, appointed because he had claimed to have 'consumed a million pounds worth of cocaine and champagne', not because he had any journalistic pretensions, nor managed to ask any penetrating questions.[10]

Meanwhile News has grown, to encompass a 24-hour rolling presence and its multimedia operations, while staff are spread more thinly over that output-hungry machine. The emphasis with rolling news is to be the first to get a story up, undermining the usual professional caution of dual sourcing before publication, albeit that such stories are often flagged by a cautionary caveat such as 'unconfirmed reports'. Where once a clear editorial ethic would determine the agenda and attitude of each distinct newsroom, this convergence means that rival TV news bulletins can frequently share the same stories and running order, often using the same pooled footage (see Chapter 5).

The paring of processes to the bone, the growing reliance on common sources and the increased mobility of labour have all contributed to this uniformity. As one editor said, 'Increasingly news, home news has been commodified.'[11] Once the unique quality of a story lovingly crafted by a reporter, who had lavished time and shoe-leather chasing original lines of inquiry, was the distinctive marker of value within each newspaper. The stranglehold of the bean-counters can now put a cost value on every column inch, meaning stories 'scraped' from other newspapers' websites or recycled from press releases are infinitely more cost-effective than sending reporters out of the office. For the same reason, expensive specialist correspondents have been replaced by much cheaper general reporters, who cannot bring the same investigative depth to bear on subjects outside their knowledge.

Our research found that journalists on both national and regional newspapers could list specialist portfolios that had gone, with their beats re-assigned to general reporters. A health specialist reporter, now working freelance, recalled how, some years before, she had been given three months off to master her brief and make contacts, from whom she would then get stories over long lunches.[12] A similar observation was made by a specialist reporter on the *Telegraph* (interviewed 2008). Many journalists confirm the essential feature that sources only trusted reporters with the specialist knowledge to convey their information responsibly. Conversely, one specialist reporter mentioned a former colleague at *The Times*, who allegedly wouldn't credit a story that he had not received face-to-face over lunch, where confidences were routinely shared. Now, she says, even those few specialist correspondents who do remain are expected to cover every story that every other paper is running in their field, leaving the editor to decide which to use, but leaving the journalist too little time to get out and originate stories. NUJ General Secretary Jeremy Dear anatomises this erosion of the knowledge that was the cultural capital of the press:

> In big regional newspapers, it's the specialisms that have gone. So the politics correspondents based at Westminster, they're no more; they get it from PA [Press Association]. The crime and education correspondents have gone, and now there's general reporters who cover all these things. In the nationals, it's been international that has suffered the most, and what we describe as resource-intensive journalism that has suffered the most, investigative journalism.
>
> (Jeremy Dear, interview conducted in 2008)

Many journalists we spoke to complained of being unable to escape their desks, having to beg permission to spend ten minutes with a source, not having the freedom to get out of the office and acquire the local colour that makes a piece distinctive. Most recognised the enormous advantages the internet has brought journalism, particularly in the speed and convenience of accessing and processing information, but regret the distance the screen has interposed between them and their subjects. 'I think some of the richness of investigation, all those things you found by serendipity, have gone by the wayside, very sad', said one *Times* section editor at Wapping. 'I always encourage my team to go out and meet people but, the problem is, it's cheaper to have newspapers in places like this and people don't really want to go out – because the traffic's bad.'[13] Newspapers' physical relocation to the outskirts of town mirrors the technical and logistical distancing from their human material.

Machill's and Beiler's survey of 'The Importance of the Internet for Journalistic Research' reminds us that 'the most important computer-aided research tool is e-mail', but still second in importance to the telephone (Machill and Beiler, 2009: 185). Ninety-four per cent of the journalists they surveyed said that 'journalistic work without the internet would no longer be conceivable'. But they admit that 61 per cent say that the selection of information is more important than the acquisition of new information and 55 per cent that 'journalistic quality suffers as a result of everyone being able to disseminate information via the Internet' (ibid: 196). They conclude with the finding that 'a cross-check on [internet] research hardly occurs and that, essentially the validation of sources does not take place at all' (ibid: 201). As Phillips found, internet sourcing can allow richer and more diverse sourcing, but only where journalists have managed to 'fight for the right to work autonomously, against news editors who seem determined to chain them ever more tightly to their computers' (Phillip, 2010: 100). As the specialist journalists, with their unique contact books, are replaced by younger, cheaper generalists, the critical bar inevitably falls. As one section editor explains:

> The people who spend their whole day sitting at their desks researching on the internet don't get the stories. They've broken the link between the unique relationship part of journalism, which is number one of what journalism is about, and the greater efficiency that the net can bring. It's only a tool and people forget that sometimes, they think it's the whole thing. And unless you have relationships, you can't do it.
>
> (Section editor, national newspaper, interview conducted in 2008)

The modern metropolis

The essential element of a craft is the individual pride taken in work, with the personal credit acquired for good work traditionally given a byline in newspapers, a name-check or screen credit in broadcast. The Wapping revolution initially gave newspaper journalists a sense of enhanced control of their craft, with responsibility for design and layout reverting to the newsroom. 'Getting rid of the old printers ... empowered the journalist' one regional editor says, but he admits it was a short-lived luxury, before the twin impacts of managerial cost-saving and digital media changed the landscape forever. Now the carefully crafted exclusive has largely been replaced by the hastily posted breaking news, with the diminished distinction of being the first site to break it (as will be explored further in Chapter 8). And that machine can have the effect of demolishing the sense of ownership that journalists like to feel.

Emma Hemmingway, writing of her experience at BBC regional news in Nottingham, describes servicing a digital hub that consumed her material, losing control to a technician who digitised that material and distributed it to a news machine for universal use (Hemmingway, 2008). It is efficient and cost-effective, but can tend to the soulless. Where once the news cycle had the natural human, parenting satisfaction of 'putting the edition to bed', now the child has grown into a hungry monster who never sleeps and requires constant feeding. 'You cannot be precious in news', as a regional news editor says; but, if the process deprives the craftsperson of the satisfaction of seeing their material through, then the reduction of role from engineer to stoker sets in train an inevitable disengagement, just as it did with the painters in *The Ragged Trousered Philanthropists*.

One particular role former *Press Gazette* editor Jon Slattery identifies as declining is that of the sub-editor, whose mature eye and measured judgement was always the heart and soul of every news organisation. In recent years, news organisations like Northcliffe, Trinity Mirror and the Johnston Press have centralised subbing, cutting many jobs in the process. Others have outsourced it, as far abroad as India, and some commentators, like former *Daily Mirror* editor Professor Roy Greenslade, have argued that the role is now largely redundant, a view we will discuss further in Chapter 4: 'Most subbing, most design, can be done in another country, another place, or collectively by groups of people working on different titles.'[14]

As traditional news organisations squeeze their operations to extract maximum profit from diminishing returns, there is a growing critique that the production models themselves are fatally flawed, ill-suited to the new digital world. The absence of older staff, subs and would-be mentors from newsrooms may be fine, some argue, since their knowledge is anachronistic and only the young are equipped to evolve new models of production suited to the age. In this discourse, the internet is not just a new platform which has yet to find the appropriate mechanism for monetising content and thus re-establishing the classic media market. It is a totally different ecosystem, requiring new paradigms for evaluation.

Conservative blogger Paul Staines, aka Guido Fawkes, addressed a London NUJ conference on 'New Ways to Make Journalism Pay' with the challenging observation that he had no need of the NUJ. 'I have achieved the Marxist ideal. I own the means of production and distribution. I have job security, I can't be fired and do much better than many journalists.'[15] The day before, at the *news rewired* conference at City University, the Telegraph Media Group's director of digital development, Greg Hadfield, struck a similar note, while announcing his resignation and telling delegates to 'learn the skills of journalism but do it in an entrepreneurial way. The future is individual journalists, not big media.'[16]

Entrepreneurialism is a very current buzz-word, with the view that it is fast becoming an essential skill that journalists need to be taught if they are to survive. It is more in tune with the analysis of American academics like Clay Shirky (2008a) and Andrea Press and Bruce Williams (2010), who are less concerned with new technologies than the uses they are put to. Magazine start-ups used to cost hundreds of thousands of pounds, making access to production an exclusive filter. Now access to a computer and the net makes the process open to most people, giving rise to the contentious claims of so-called 'citizen journalism'. Dan Gillmor thinks we should be worrying less about who is a journalist and more about what journalism now is (Gillmor, 2004).

Anyone can do it: de-professionalisation and the bottom line

While it is not appropriate to discuss the merits of non-professional journalism here (which we do in Chapter 7), it is worth considering the impact this presumption – that anybody can do it – has on the professional corps. Nick Couldry's survey (2010) of what he prefers to call 'writer-gatherers' finds little evidence for their muscling in on professional space, but considers their value as 'source-actors', a potentially beneficial counterpoint to journalists' over-reliance on official sources. However, scepticism abounds in the industry, with comments like this common: 'It irritates the hell out of me. It's not news. It's people wanting their five minutes of fame and it's not accurate because they haven't spoken to anybody.'[17] And:

> It has increased because they all think they can be journalists, you know, and they can't – it's dire. Now I wouldn't put it in the newspaper. So why, just because I can, should I pour all this crap into the website?
>
> (Editor, regional newspaper, interview conducted in 2008)

Others, particularly editors, take a more nuanced view:

> There's the fact that journalists feel threatened ... And you see internet participation portrayed as the great unwashed and just a load of punch-ups and all this sort of stuff in the press a lot, and it really isn't that accurate in my view. ... I mean I wade through the rubbish every day, but then I think that some of the most exciting stuff I read is online and through blogs and all of that. So I would, I just want journalists to get excited about it rather than being defensive about it.
>
> (Section editor, national newspaper, interview conducted in 2008)

As mentioned in the previous chapter, the BBC, keen to establish a more sympathetic, interactive relationship with its audience, introduced a UGC (user-generated content) unit in its newsroom and makes impassioned pleas to its various audiences to share visual material, stories and opinions with programme makers. BBC News sees it as central to the mission of arresting audience decline and refreshing public engagement. Anna Mainwaring is a producer in the BBC News UGC hub, and describes it as a revolution in news-gathering. 'Instead of teams going out to get stories, stories are coming to us', she says, instancing the story of a spate of young men being stabbed in London the year before:

> In the old days, we would have sent a team of hacks to doorstep, knock on doors to try and interview the relatives, the teachers, the girlfriends. Now we sit in the newsroom and the girlfriend has already contacted the BBC message board. We've got her e-mail. A journalist phones and interviews her and she's on air in minutes ... The speed is phenomenal.
>
> (Anna Mainwaring, interview conducted in 2009)

Some professional journalists contest the value of such passive journalism, believing that populist passion replaces perspective, encouraging the creation of instant urban myths, also mentioning the stabbing story above as being exaggerated by this unchecked word of mouth.

Risto Kunelius recognises in this trend a systemic shift towards manufacturing the news event, which 'adds value' for the audience and reinforces the institutional brand of the particular news outlet, albeit at the cost of declining autonomy for the individual journalist:

> Instead of cultivating individual 'professional reporters' who provide reliable snapshots of the current 'social map', newsrooms now look for flexible teams that will adapt to the multimedia, constant-deadline corporate newsroom which packages information.
>
> (Kunelius, 2009: 344)

Managing the news

In a climate where a diminishing news audience is seen as a dangerous hostage to fortune with a BBC encircled by hostile forces, any initiative that forges a constructive relationship with the audience is seen as 'a good thing'. But, as news producer Anna Mainwaring – who is also Mother of Chapel for the NUJ (i.e. the union rep) at BBC News – admits, it does change the nature of the broadcast journalist's job. There is less call for the reporter in the field, more for the specialist in the newsroom, whose expertise in a given field can be called upon to help winnow the grain from the chaff among the virtual truckloads of unsolicited material they receive.

> Some information you just know is genuine, because you have the wires coming in. You have cross-referenced it and you know that what they are saying correlates with everything else, especially in a breaking news context. Other stories are much more intricate and need to be put on the back burner

and researched properly by our teams. ... The big shift is, the public are actually doing the journalist's job, so our job is getting more narrowly defined as processing this stuff.

(Anna Mainwaring, interview conducted in 2009)

Print journalists express concern that this processing is becoming the dominant culture, with online sites echoing the output process of broadcast news, rather than the generative process of news-gathering. 'They have no real relationship with ... the tools of news-gathering and. ... the thought processes of getting a story together. ... you've got to protect this.'[18] Irrespective of the value of material so generated, its attractions – of being both free and abundant, as well as generating a closer relationship with audiences – make it attractive to executives, concerned about the bottom line. This has created a recalibration that Mark Deuze (2009b: 316) identifies as 'a sapping of economic and cultural power away from professional journalists to what I like to call "The People Formerly known as the Employers"':

> For all the brilliance of those advocating a more democrative media system (and in all fairness I have been among such voices), there is generally not much investigation in their analysis that challenges this erosion of power, this wholesale redistribution of agency away from those who tend to crave only one thing: creative and editorial autonomy.
>
> (Deuze, 2009b: 317)

Mainwaring paints a disturbing picture of a once great journalist culture at the BBC cut to the bone, spread impossibly thin, demotivated and reduced to the 'churnalism' that Davies (2008) found throughout both press and broadcast. Despite still being majoratively unionised, BBC News has been subjected to 5 per cent 'efficiency savings' each year over the five years 2007–12, and the results are most clearly noticed in the diminished teams of which Mainwaring is part. The *One O'Clock News*, she says, is now produced by just five people, 'scrambled' on air without rehearsal and with insufficient time and resources. The overnight staffing – when the News Channel becomes BBC World – used, she says, to be twelve or thirteen people, now it's just four 'producing output for 200 million people around the world. If a breaking story goes off, they have four people in charge in that newsroom.'

Worse still, Mainwaring complains of a poor management culture that has stopped the career breaks that were the best chance of escaping the quotidian grind, and fails to reward or even credit initiative when it occurs. She was on the night shift the night that the kidnapped BBC Gaza correspondent, Alan Johnson, was released. She recalls that it was she who thought to phone Hamas to verify his release. She was put through to him and put him straight on air. Then she made way for the managers who flocked to the building to take over and take credit. She says this is a common experience for fellow journalists and, along with there being no prospects of promotion, leads to a disincentivised culture in which no one feels inclined to 'go the extra mile. We just rewrite copy. That's what we do.'[19]

While admitting that economies have stretched resources and forced tough choices, not everyone sees it as quite so discouraging. One BBC News executive says that anybody who is 'shit hot' will make it. That begs the question of what standards apply, whose judgement it is, which 'shit' is currently 'hot'. The executive admits that one of the inevitable outcomes of reorganisation and budget cuts has been to make the whole news operation a much tougher environment for journalists:

> [The BBC]'s in transition. It is much more state of nature than it used to be. It's quite brutish in its way and people are judged much more harshly than they would have been. The bit that I know – News and newsgathering – it is nothing like as paternalistic as it once was. I don't think it's got to the *Telegraph* level of brutishness, but it is much more hard-nosed than it was. ... It's a competitive environment. People are actively competing with each other to get their ideas on air.
>
> (BBC News executive, interview conducted in 2009)

Coming together again

As the traditional news media struggle to adapt, there is a natural resistance to the notion that revolutionary change is under way, requiring a jettisoning of the support structures and shibboleths of the past. Quite the opposite is a more natural human response, as with the risk-averse BBC managers Anna Mainwaring identifies, hanging on to their desks, full-time posts and final-salary pension schemes, while those options are no longer available to the incoming generation.

Mark Deuze describes how 'what Richard Sennett calls the "culture of the new capitalism" draws our attention to the current reorganisation of the workplace and the field of work towards an almost exclusive emphasis on individualised responsibilities' (Deuze, 2009a: 84), with managers demanding enterprise of individuals rather than of the corporate system. He writes of the 'functional flexibility' demanded both of staff media workers in covering more bases within organisations, and of the growing number of contract workers having to duck and dive on the periphery. As we shall see in the next chapter, industry entrants are expected to have an ever-expanding portfolio of expertise, while at the same time quiescently plugging into and serving the machine, as and when it demands. However, there are signs that journalists are beginning to organise in some ways to confront the erosion of their cultural capital.

> Informal networks of media workers have emerged online that contribute to a renewed sense of self among especially younger professionals in such industries. This new kind of self-identification among cultural labourers can be seen as a trans-local social movement of precarious workers, emerging beyond the traditional institutional contexts of governments, employers, as well as outside of unions or guilds.
>
> (Deuze, 2009a: 89)

In April 2010, the UK saw the unusual event of a strike by 200 largely un-unionised freelance writers and photographers. They had been regularly employed by three music magazines (*Kerrang!*, *Q* and *Mojo*) owned by the German Bauer group, which had bought these – along with a swathe of popular magazine titles – from EMAP in December 2007. The freelances had been presented with a non-negotiable contract to sign, forcing them to forgo all financial and moral rights in re-use of their material in any platform, existing or yet to be invented, while demanding they accept legal liability for any action occurring as a result of any such use. Threatened that they would not work for these titles again unless they did, and advised that Bauer intended extending these draconian conditions to all their magazines, they refused on principle.

As an agreed freelance statement said in May 2010: 'Attempted rights grabs like Bauer's are far more than an assault on a specific group of music writers and photographers – they undermine the viability of freelance journalism as a whole.'[20] At the same time, a Hamburg court was declaring each and every feature of the same Bauer freelance contract illegal in Germany, confirming the freelances' rights in their material and its re-use, and striking out the open indemnity clause. Ulrike Maercks-Franzen, of the journalists' section of the German union ver.di, expressed the hope that the ruling would convince German publishers – who impose conditions which weaken the legal rights of journalists and burden them with financial risk – that such oppression is now *verboten*.[21] At the time of writing, the UK situation is unresolved. But, as Vincent Mosco has written, 'Specifically, the future health of journalism depends on the ability of journalists to come together nationally and internationally to defend their interests' (Mosco, 2009: 351).

Elsewhere, journalist networks have been established not just to represent and lobby for freelances, but also to distribute their work. The Berlin-based Network for Reporting on Eastern Europe (N-Ost) has a subscription network of 250 journalists and media initiatives from all over Europe, and a client base of European media organisations, mostly German. If articles they distribute are not paid the going rate, the organisation responsible is banned. GlobalPost is an American operation distributing writing on international affairs by part-time correspondents all over the world. Each journalist and employee has a share in the business, making it, in the estimation of the Carnegie Trust report *Protecting the News*, 'an interesting model that could also function as a trust model' (Witschge *et al.*, 2010: 30). The authors note that the globally recognized Magnum photographic agency is also a co-operative – and has been going strong since 1947.

While such collaborative initiatives are primarily driven by economic necessity, they speak to a deeper need for the communities of shared work that made journalism such an attractive area of employment. Fleet Street's famous three-hour lunches were not just for de-briefing contacts, but also for exchanging views and ways of work with colleagues. As one specialist correspondent said, 'you'd meet everybody from all the other newspapers' and 'get to bounce ideas off each other'.[22] That sense of common purpose, engagement in a worthwhile enterprise, infected the workplace, where people still talked to each other, rather than communicating via e-mail:

So you were given this story, and the more experienced reporters would come down and say 'oh I can help you with that, I know someone in this office, ring them, mention my name'. Because they were there for the good of everybody to make the paper be good, and I don't think that happens at all now, which I think is sad.

(Specialist reporter, freelance, interview conducted in 2009)

Conclusion

What is happening in journalism is symptomatic of a wider crisis in the nature of work. Individualisation has liberated the few to capitalise on their prominence, whether as bankers or broadcasters, and manipulate the market to drive up their income exponentially compared to the many they work with. Where only a generation ago senior executives earned a few times as much as those who did their work, now a hundred times is not unusual; even in the public sector, the Director-General of the BBC was found to be earning forty times as much as his assistant producers. This systemic inequality persists, even as competitive pressures force the job losses and increased productivity demands we have charted. In this combative culture, the journalist has lost the economic power of well-paid job security, the bargaining power of collective solidarity, and the cultural power of being socially valued and purposive. For all the claims of the technocrat zealots and benefits of digital technology, change has not ushered in the brave new world it promised. People in the UK work longer hours now than at any other time in the last half-century.

'Progress', once the most extreme manifestation of radical optimism and a promise of universally shared and lasting happiness, has moved all the way to the opposite, dystopian and fatalistic pole of anticipation: it now stands for the threat of a relentless and inescapable change that instead of auguring peace and respite portends nothing but continuous crisis and strain and forbids a moment of rest.

(Bauman, 2007: 10)

Journalists are being expected to be technically proficient individuals, capable of initiating and completing work autonomously, whilst retaining an unquestioning willingness to fit in with the systemic and economic dictates of organisations. Macho management culture imposes massive change, usually without consultation, yet expects acquiescence and adaptability from a workforce carrying a greater burden of productivity as a result, for lesser rewards and shorter terms of engagement. But there is a structural fault here in that such processes are linear and authoritarian, and the digital domain they seek to command is lateral and democratic. The internet was designed to be an open source, inimical to unitary control, and the next generation is educated in and wired to that lateral, multi-faceted orientation. Social networking, aggregation and increasingly sophisticated metadata will drive the future, whether traditional news corporations like it or not. It is for these organisations to adapt or disappear, in the same harsh way they now address their staff.

Individual journalists will invent new narratives of work, with many evolving the entrepreneurial skills and flexibility of the freelance. It is just possible to imagine news organisations ruing the day that they liberated their workforces from the slavish security of a permanent job and pension. Talent they need should be able to negotiate more favourable terms and conditions, just as leading columnists and popular TV presenters already have most profitably in the last 25 years; and genuine craft skills should attract a premium – by such market forces is Hephaestus triumphant. Were he alive a hundred years on, Robert Tressell would be astonished to find how well paid some tradespeople, even some decorators are today, relative to the average professional.

It will not just be the monetary value put upon the work. If journalists are no longer nurtured within the value systems of paternal employers, they will evolve their own codes of conduct and judgement criteria, as are the new collectives, inevitably less allied to the corporate goal. And in all of this journalism is not unique, its raison d'être being to reflect life at the moment, where work in many arenas is undergoing destabilising change. Quite apart from the economic recession and the decline of traditional industry, new technologies and corporate accountancy are transforming nearly every arena of employment. Arguably, journalism needed to experience that simply to continue to play a central role in reporting social evolution. After all, work itself, as Alain de Botton observes when concluding his *The Pleasures and Sorrows of Work*, can be seen as a fanciful illusion to give sense to our existence:

> The impulse to exaggerate the significance of what we are doing, far from being an intellectual error, is really life itself coursing through us ... To see ourselves as the centre of the universe and the present time as the summit of history, to view our upcoming meetings as being of overwhelming significance, to neglect the lessons of cemeteries, to read only sparingly, to feel the pressures of deadlines, to snap at colleagues, to make our way through conference agendas marked '11:00 a.m. to 11:15 a.m.: coffee break', to behave heedlessly and greedily and then to combust in battle – maybe all of this, in the end, is working wisdom. ... If we could witness the eventual fate of every one of our projects, we would have no choice but to succumb to immediate paralysis.
>
> (De Botton, 2009: 325)

Journalism has always seen itself as above that dystopian view of work as mechanical process, preferring the role of an original illumination of the world in which we live. But the combination of the demanding doxa of workplace and the restraining economics of contemporary practice has severely limited the expressive freedoms and the vocational ambitions of the journalist's work. The challenge for future journalists is to reinvent the means by which they may deliver those higher goals.

Notes

1 http://papercuts.graphicdesignr.net/ (accessed 13 July 2010).
2 Jon Slattery, in conversation with the author, 18 January 2010.
3 Robert Tressell, 1870–1911; Takiji Koybayashi, 1904–33.
4 As expressed by a regional newspaper editor, interview conducted in 2008.
5 President John F. Kennedy's Inaugural Address on 21 January 1961 contained the immortal line: 'Ask not what your country can do for you – ask what you can do for your country.'
6 Roy Stockdill, 'The Wapping cough', no longer available online, but see www.gentlemenranters.com/august_2010_256.html#rs158 (accessed December 2010).
7 Ann Leslie, speaking at Goldsmiths, University of London, 22 October 2009.
8 David Wade, *The Times*, 16 September 1970, quoted in Hendy (2007).
9 The *Daily Telegraph*, January 1972, quoted in Briggs (1995).
10 'Cocaine: Alex James in Colombia', *Panorama*, BBC1, 28 January 2008.
11 Section editor, national newspaper, interview conducted in 2008.
12 Interview conducted in 2009.
13 Interview conducted in 2008.
14 Roy Greenslade, talking to Publishing Expo event in London, 11 February 2009.
15 Guido Fawkes, talking at NUJ conference, 16 January 2010, reported by www.jonslattery.blogspot.com/
16 Greg Hadfield, talking at *news rewired* conference, City University, 15 January 2010, reported by www.jonslattery.blogspot.com/
17 Feature editor, regional newspaper, interview conducted in 2008.
18 Reporter, regional newspaper, interview conducted in 2008.
19 Anna Mainwaring, talking to the author, 17 December 2009.
20 Statement in freelance.org website, 4 May 2010 www.londonfreelance.org/fl/1005grab.html (accessed 29 July).
21 Mike Holderness, 'Bauer can't do this at home', freelance.org, 10 June 2010, www.londonfreelance.org/fl/1006grab.html (accessed 29 July).
22 Interview conducted in 2009.

3   Who guards the gateway?

Regulating journalism in fluid times

Peter Lee-Wright

It might be assumed that what journalists write is between them and their editors, mitigated only by what the market will wear. But the fourth force, largely unseen but no less significant, is the regulator. Every advanced media culture is subject to some form of regulation and – despite the increasingly global nature of modern media corporations and distribution – those regulators are overwhelmingly nation-bound (Freedman, 2005). Most regulatory systems claim to protect the public, protect rights owners, stabilise the system and (in democracies) ensure plurality, but they are also expressions of the matrix of power and culture prevailing in the particular country at the time of their conception. Early systems of regulation were essentially hierarchical but, in modern democracies, are giving way to what Thompson (2003) and others define as forms of market and network governance, i.e. driven by economic imperatives, or the pressures of hegemonic power. This reflects changes in the wider society – globalisation, liberalisation and strong deregulatory pressures from the market.

The classic purpose of regulation is defined by Abramson:

> Where policy sets out the state's role in bringing its preferred mediascape into being, regulation is the instrument through which the state supervises, controls, or curtails the activities of non-state actors in accordance with policy.
>
> (Abramson, 2001: 302)

This is sometimes interpreted as the censorious hand of an over-mighty state bearing down on free speech but, as we shall see, such simple dialectic is inadequate to describe the increasingly complex field of modern media and the many conflicting interests it serves. Liberal democracies and global corporations have increasingly favoured systems of self-regulation, in which the respective industry takes on the responsibility (and costs) of self-policing standards and behaviour. Freedman writes:

> The practice of industry self-regulation … demonstrates the possible independence of actors in the regulatory process, but those actors are still subject to the codes, laws and regulations drawn up in response to specific

media policy concerns and the ideological frameworks on which they are based.

(Freedman, 2008: 14)

This chapter will attempt to unpack those codes, laws and regulations within the various ideological frameworks they serve and look at the way they are adapting to the changing media landscape. In the first parts, I recognise that censorship and suppression are the objectives of some regulatory systems, but that the point where the dictatorial ensuring of conformity shades over into consensual democratic control is difficult to define. Then I review those democratic ideals on which many regulatory frameworks are based – to ensure pluralism and resist the establishment of media monopolies – and their sustained assault from the forces of global capitalism and media convergence. Thirdly, I enter the field of rights, from (relatively) recent legal proscriptions on derogatory representations of race, religion and identity, and legally contested definitions of privacy and libel, to consideration of copyright and ownership of material. Finally, I ask whether the systemic fluidity and free international flow of information we now have is amenable to the forms of journalism regulation that are, as I have said, still largely nation-bound.

Limiting free speech

Regulation, like all legislation, is a reflection of the culture and values of the time at which it is enacted, and operates within the wider frames of power and expediency. Throughout history, states have sought to control their populations through controlling information and the expression of ideas. The Spanish Inquisition and the McCarthyite anti-Communist purges in 1950s America tend to reappear in the rhetorical cloak of the day. When, nine days after the events of 9/11, President George W. Bush announced the appointment of a Secretary of Homeland Security, he advised both the US Congress and the world: 'Either you are with us, or you are with the terrorists.'[1] This did not overtly change the American system of media regulation, of which more later, nor repeal the Constitution's First Amendment guaranteeing free speech, but it did affect what it was deemed judicious to publish.

Four years later, a letter by Laura Berg, a nurse in Alberquerque, printed in her local newspaper, argued that, following the war in Iraq and the mishandling of the aftermath of Hurricane Katrina, people should 'act forcefully to remove a government administration playing games of smoke and mirrors and vicious deceit' (Allen, 2006). The US Department of Veteran Affairs, which ran the hospital where she worked, investigated her for *sedition*, the advocating of the overthrow of government (Associated Press, 2006). Although the US Sedition Act had been repealed in 1920, clauses within the 2001 US Patriot Act meant that the agency was, by its own admission, 'obligated to investigate' (ibid). Berg was exonerated, but a public sphere dominated by the right-wing fulminations of Fox News and the resurgent small-town nationalism of the Tea Party remains distrustful of dissent. All this occurs in an era where both the UK and the USA have seen fit to enact laws that restrict civil liberties for the assumed greater benefit of their so-called 'War on Terror'.

The UK abolished sedition and seditious libel as criminal offences only in 2009, and has a history of political imperatives that transcend the usual standards of free speech, from the General Strike of 1926, to the Second World War (1939–45). During the long war of attrition between Republicans and Unionists in Northern Ireland (1968–98), the most outstanding example was the then Conservative government's ban in 1988 on broadcasting the live speech of terrorists. For six years, British television could show interviews with banned parties' spokespeople, but not broadcast their synchronous speech, although a robustly non-compliant media routinely subverted the purpose by having actors dub the words. As an expression of Anglo-American solidarity, following a Trans World Airlines (TWA) hijacking in Beirut, Prime Minister Margaret Thatcher said, 'We must try to starve the terrorist and the hi-jacker of the oxygen of publicity on which they depend' (Edgerton, 1996: 115). This is frequently the objective of governments, to marginalise dissent by denying it the authority of a media presence; but, just as in Northern Ireland in the 1990s and now with the emerging orthodoxy in Afghanistan, settlements are rarely achieved without talking to and embracing the insurgent.

It is argued that the survival of democratic freedoms justifies the suspension of those same freedoms in the interim. During the Falklands War (1982), the very remoteness of the Falkland Islands and the limitations of communication had enabled a total military censorship of all journalistic media. In the Iraq war (2003–2010), embedding journalists with the troops and suborning the US media to the cause achieved the same effect. US mainstream news channels self-censored footage of a US infantryman's illegal shooting dead of wounded Iraqis in the Fallujah mosque, which was carried uncut through the rest of the world (Lee-Wright, 2010b: 43). This is what Danny Schecter calls 'selling, not telling', US disinformation and hi-tech war as 'militainment', 'the demise of democracy and discourse' (Schecter, 2010). This is also self-regulation, where news self-censors for political ease and economic gain. Within a state's boundaries, such spinning of the message is clearly still possible but, in the modern multinational digital domain, total control is inconceivable. That does not stop states trying to control the free flow of information.

Information control is power

Much of the discourse around the internet and its contribution to journalism centres on its relaxation of flow controls, the opportunity for individual voices and views, and the converse (occasional) value to news media of crowd-sourcing. UGC footage proved invaluable as the sole source of coverage of events in the 2007 monks' 'Saffron' rebellion in Burma and the so-called Green revolution on Teheran's streets after the 2009 Iranian presidential election. The view of the internet is that information is neutral and its transmission intrinsically benign, but its free availability does not mean that there are no impediments elsewhere in the supply line. When the Google-owned YouTube website launched a global call for footage to be shot on one day, 24 July 2010, Negar Esfandiary found that the claim to a global embrace was severely limited:

> It came as a slap in the face ... to read the FAQ on the Life in a Day website: 'Anyone over 13 years old can submit footage, except for residents and nationals of Iran, Syria, Cuba, Sudan, North Korea and Burma (Myanmar), and/or any other persons and entities restricted by US export controls and sanctions programmes.' The 'story of a single day on earth ... One world, 24 hours, 6 billion perspectives' is actively boycotting 1.5 billion of the 6 billion perspectives it pursues.
>
> (Esfandiary, 2001)

That Google has caved in to pressure in censoring material on YouTube is one issue. Another concern lies in the way in which the internet opens up opportunities for surveillance alongside its freedoms. Many of the Iranian dissidents who used new media channels to speak to the world found that the same channels were being used by the state to target dissenters, many of whom were subsequently arrested (Morozov, 2009).

China, for instance, with the largest number of Internet users in the world, employs over 30,000 people to police the net and eradicate any mention of forbidden subjects, such as Taiwanese independence or the 1989 student massacre in Tiananmen Square. The Open Net Initiative, based at the Harvard Law School, produced a comprehensive study of the effectiveness of the Great Firewall of China in *Internet Filtering in China in 2004–2005: A Country Study*.[2]

> China's Internet filtering regime is the most sophisticated effort of its kind in the world. Compared to similar efforts in other states, China's filtering regime is pervasive, sophisticated, and effective. It comprises multiple levels of legal regulation and technical control. It involves numerous state agencies and thousands of public and private personnel. It censors content transmitted through multiple methods, including Web pages, Web logs, on-line discussion forums, university bulletin board systems, and e-mail messages.
>
> (OpenNet Initiative, 2005)

Any internet company operating in China must be licensed and is subject to these far-reaching censorship laws. Companies are subjected to a barrage of instructions, such as this one from 2006: 'If reference is made on a forum to the news report, "774 ships of the Chinese fleet have sunk," suppress it immediately and step up monitoring' (Reporters without Borders, 2007). Over-zealous cooperation with the Chinese authorities, when Yahoo revealed e-mail details, led directly to the imprisonment of journalist Shi Tao in April 2005. He received a 10-year sentence for releasing the substance of one of these communications, about the dangers of celebrating the anniversary of Tiananmen Square, to the Asia Democracy

Foundation (BBC News Website, 2005). Yahoo CEO Jerry Yang was roundly condemned for this betrayal in a US congressional committee hearing.

Nonetheless, in January 2006, Google launched its separate China search engine Google.cn, which it had agreed with the Chinese government would abide by its censorship rules. Despite the company mission statement 'Don't be evil', Google was now well on the path to world domination as the lead search engine, and was willing to sup with the devil to achieve its commercial ends. It was willing to, and did, weather a storm of abuse from human rights supporters, until January 2010, when it announced that it would stop cooperating with the Chinese government's demands, after hackers persistently penetrated human rights activists' e-mail accounts. The criticisms duly declined, but Google was in fact negotiating a compromise where Chinese web traffic would be diverted to a 'landing page', which would give access to the freer Hong Kong site. In July that year, Google's lawyer David Drummond told the BBC in an e-mail: 'We are very pleased that the government has renewed our ICP [internet content provider] licence and we look forward to continuing to provide web search and local products to our users in China' (BBC News Website, 2010a).

In a book reviewing the countries which he has reported from, former *New Statesman* editor John Kampfner describes a global pattern of people prepared to abrogate 'freedom of expression for a very good material life' (2009: 5). 'This is the pact. In each country it varies; citizens hand over different freedoms in accordance with their own customs and priorities' (ibid: 6). Starting with the Singapore in which he was born, Kampfner reveals a society that enjoys great material comforts in return for voluntarily forgoing some liberty. Singapore residents have largely unfettered access to the internet but, if they exercise its freedoms in ways that criticise their system or its masters – what they denigrate as a 'Western mindset' – they can end up in prison, through a widely abused law of contempt designed to disable dissent. 'What does it say about the fragility of a regime if it goes into paroxysms of rage about any old blog?', Kampfner asks, and finds the answer that every business, government and Singaporean has a vested interest in the status quo (ibid: 39). This liberty-limiting compact he also finds not only in conventionally repressive states like China and Russia, but in the 'surveillance state' of Britain, where he points out that anti-terrorism and race and religion hate laws have effectively introduced the Orwellian concepts of speech crime and thought crime. In his bleak reading – not a majority view – journalism is more (self-)regulated by legal threat and cowardice than by any formal system.

> Much of British journalism has become supine in the face of intimidation from state organs and from libel and other laws. For some time reporters have complained that editors and proprietors are shying away from difficult stories for fear of 'getting into trouble': in so doing, Britain's once fearless press, is merely following a global trend.
>
> (Kampfner, 2009: 221)

Pluralism, democracy and regulating against monopoly

> If opponents of all important truths do not exist, it is indispensable to imagine them, and supply them with the strongest arguments which the most skilful devil's advocate can conjure up.
>
> (Mill, 1869: 37)

It is fundamental to democracy that no one person or party holds uncontestable and unaccountable power, and the job of the fourth estate is to ensure account-ability and enable the challenge of others. In most democracies the 'market place of ideas' was augmented by the rise of the printed press (Habermas, 1989) but, as monopolies started to form (Bourdieu, 2005), various interventions have been attempted to protect diversity. The problem of monopoly became particularly acute with the advent of first radio and then television beaming (initially) a single voice directly into every home. It was for this reason, and to provide a system to apportion the finite resources of the broadcast spectrum, that broadcasting has always been more closely regulated than print, notably in the UK. In Scan-dinavia and the Netherlands government interventions have been made to prop up the minority press (Curran and Seaton, 2009: 337). Laws have also been enacted to prevent monopolies forming and to prevent cross-media ownership in the UK and the USA but, as we shall see, the dominance of multinational media cor-porations exercises undue influence on governments, leading to regulation being softened to suit their commercial imperatives.

In the UK, broadcasting spectrum and diversity is organised through Ofcom (although the BBC is largely self governing through the BBC Trust). Ofcom is the independent regulator and competition authority for all the UK communications industries, with wide-ranging powers in radio and television licensing, compliance and complaint adjudication, research and policy analysis. For example, it oversees rules, such as that in which all broadcasters are under an obligation to represent the different political parties fairly and, at election time, political parties are apportioned airtime in proportion to their vote in the previous election. Broad-casters also have a range of public service obligations (for example, the provision of local news – although this is currently under threat) (Field Rees, 2009). Diver-sity is also dealt with under competition laws, both within the UK and under the aegis of the Europe Community, and by the apportioning of licences for terres-trial broadcasting.

The US broadcast spectrum is limited and regulated by the Federal Commu-nications Commission (FCC), an independent US government agency with direct responsibility to Congress. The FCC was established by the Communications Act of 1934 and is charged with regulating interstate and international communications by radio, television, wire, satellite and cable. But, as Pete Tridish of the Prometheus Radio Project explains, this was a market network stitch-up from the start:

> Herbert Hoover, the Secretary of Commerce in the 1920s, said that radio was the first industry he ever saw that practically 'begged to be regulated.'

The industry begged for regulation because the key players of the industry wanted the government to keep out any challengers to their oligopoly position in their markets. Their attitude was, 'We got here first, now protect us from anyone else that wants to set up shop.' This was all done, of course, under the rubric of 'protecting the radio dial from interference'.

(Tridish, 2007: 57)

The FCC has just five members, always appointed with a chair and majority to reflect the party of the US president in office. It has limited resources and powers, and its biggest sanction short of the courts is an $11,000 fine, whereas Ofcom has unlimited powers and, in May 2008, imposed a fine totalling £5.675m ($8,820m) on the main UK commercial television company, ITV plc 'for breaches in a number of programmes' (Ofcom, 2009: 20). However, officially politically neutral, Ofcom has been under threat from deregulatory imperatives within the UK coalition government, has had its policy recommendation powers reduced, and has been forced to move towards 'light touch' regulation, particularly of commercial channels' 'public service broadcasting' requirements. Similarly, as Tridish explains, there were 'public service rules' embedded in the original US legislation – that stations would operate 'in the public's interest, convenience, and necessity' – but most of these have been whittled away over the years, thanks to legal challenges based upon the First Amendment (Tridish, 2007: 57). There is no effective oversight of US content, as there still is in the UK, and the spectrum controls have been progressively relaxed.

Originally, no company could own more than seven AM and seven FM stations in the USA. Under the presidency of Ronald Reagan, this was raised to twenty of each. The Communications Act of 1996 abolished the cap, and by 2007 Clear Channel owned twelve hundred stations across the USA (since reduced to 900). As Freedman (2008) explores at length, this is part of an ideological deregulatory pressure in the USA, which has consistently fought for the relaxation of cross-media ownership restrictions, with a sympathetic FCC under George W. Bush, whose last chair, Kevin Martin, believed: 'that a robust competitive market place, not regulation, is ultimately the greatest protector of the public interest' (as quoted in Freedman, 2008: 113). Freedman shows how the FCC's 'Diversity Index' is a creative use of statistics, counting the voices heard, not the audience reached; the evidence tends once again to prove the Bourdieu (1998) maxim about competition producing uniformity.

This ideological belief in the discipline of the market and competition – initiated in the United Kingdom by the radical Conservative government of Margaret Thatcher and now rolled out across the world – has allowed transnational concentrations of power in all forms of utility, even in some nations' cultural heartland of broadcasting. France has made determined efforts to hold back the flood of (mainly American) material from overwhelming locally produced products. It imposes a strict quota on both television and cinema that allows a maximum of 40 per cent of programmes shown to be non-European in origin. France pressed for the introduction of the 1989 EU 'Television without Frontiers'

Broadcast Directive, which reserves a minimum of 51 per cent of TV broadcast time for European products (Ulf-Møller, 2001). In 1994, President François Mitterand signed the so-called Toubon law, endorsing the supremacy of the French language, not least because advertisers were using English words and phrases as signifiers of sophistication:

> Article 20–21. – The use of French is compulsory in all the programmes and advertising messages of radio and television broadcasting organisations and services, whatever their mode of dissemination or distribution, with the exception of motion picture and radio and television productions in their original language version.[3]

However, cultural determinism of this kind is strongly at odds with the globalising and monopoly-building tendencies of internationally traded media businesses. Even well-developed, decentralised systems, like the 'segmented pluralism' of Dutch, Belgian, Swiss and Austrian broadcasting, with stations catering to specific groups, are under threat from the fragmentation and consumerism of contemporary society: 'this collectivist political and civic organization that no longer meets, in the Netherlands and elsewhere, with the increasing individualization of postmodern citizens and society' (Bardoel, 2008: 218).

The German company RTL runs radio and television channels in ten European countries – eleven until it sold UK Channel 5 to Richard Desmond's Northern and Shell in July 2010 – and production companies in several more, including two of the UK's largest. In the UK just five media groups own over 60 per cent of local newspapers and News Corporation controls 37 per cent of national newspaper circulation, while BSkyB (part owned by News Corporation) accounts for 35 per cent of TV revenues (*Financial Times*, 2010). The European Union, with all its legal machinery outlawing monopoly, has made little attempt to intervene in commercial monopoly building (though it did rein back the BBC digital programming after complaints from commercial education companies).[4] Even the highly critical 2005 Council of Europe report on Italy's media duopoly has yet to have any effect (Hibberd, 2008: 195). Prime Minister Silvio Berlusconi owns the three commercial MediaSet channels and effectively controls the three state-funded RAI channels.

In 2005, the Venice Commission (the Council of Europe's advisory body on commercial law) called urgently for laws outlawing 'the conflict of interest between ownership and control of companies and discharge of public office'; ending 'political interference in the media'; and 'promoting media pluralism, both nationally and at the European level' (Venice Commission, 2005: 3–4). Five years of further deterioration led in May 2010 to the resignation of the presenter of Italy's leading news programme, *TG1*. Maria Luisa Busi's letter announcing her resignation claims that 'real Italy has been cancelled' and that *TG1* is now mostly 'a combination of infotainment (a mixture of information and entertainment) and of politically biased reporting' (cited in Giugliano, 2010). The unrestrained impact of the market creates monopolies profoundly incompatible with the plurality required for a functioning democracy.

In the UK the attempts by News Corporation to increase its share in BSkyB have been described as Britain's 'Berlusconi moment' (*Financial Times*, 2010) as, if allowed, it would increase the cross-media concentration in the UK in the hands of News Corporation. In its leader column in September 2010, the *Financial Times* alludes to the problem of 'Mr Murdoch's powerful grip on the UK media industry, and [it has] laid bare the extent to which British politicians are cowed by him and even fight shy from investigating alleged criminality. This is profoundly unhealthy' (ibid).

Roy Greenslade, writing in the *Evening Standard* (2010), distanced himself from these concerns, suggesting that the media storm about the imminent takeover of BSkyB was little more than 'sour grapes' from rival media companies. However, there has been enough evidence of the influence of News International on government to give some pause. During consultations before the Communications Act 2003, there were 22 major representations against relaxing regulations on cross-media ownership. Only News Corporation lobbied for it, and its auditors Arthur Andersen:

> Recent papers released from government archives reveal that the representatives of Rupert Murdoch's Sky Television met ministers six times during the short passage of the Communications Bill in 2003. They show that 'Mr Murdoch secured private reassurances from ministers during heavy lobbying that he would be able to buy Channel Five if he wanted to'.
>
> (Leigh and Evans, quoted in Freedman, 2008: 95)

Murdoch secured the cross-ownership relaxation but passed on acquiring Five, which was then bought by RTL. But the Murdochs ended up owning 17.9 per cent of ITV. Many of the deregulatory aspects of the 2003 Communications Act are widely seen as repaying a debt, as well as placating an assumed free market *Zeitgeist* which was itself stimulated by tabloid hostility to a 'nanny state' (Livingstone and Lunt, 2007: 20). In steering the Bill through the Commons, Tessa Jowell made much of its deregulatory impulse, but Ofcom research suggests that the majority of the British public are actually in favour of media regulation to maintain impartiality – 73 per cent (Ofcom, 2007: 65) – and to retain plurality – 80 per cent (Ofcom, 2007: 48). As Steven Barnett wrote in the *Observer* at the time of the Bill:

> With regards to broadcasting, experience suggests exactly the opposite (of the government's case): less regulation and more unfettered competition leads inexorably to a poorer service for consumers and an impoverished creative and cultural environment.
>
> (Steven Barnett quoted in Fitzwalter, 2008: 243)

This addresses the central dichotomy of regulation, with governments torn between the competing attractions of placating the electorate's desire for consumer protection and the industry's better-articulated demands for an unfettered free market.

Ofcom's statutory Broadcasting Code was formulated through 'extensive consultation with broadcasters, viewers and listeners and other interested parties' ... and so on. In the first two months of 2006 Ofcom had opened nine new consultations, and in the preceding year, 2005, it undertook 79 separate consultations.

(Collins, 2008: 297)

This consultative process, also recently adopted by the BBC, trades on the enhanced rights of, and consideration for, the views of the general public. Where once the public interest was defined by the media, there is now the discourse that the public, as 'stakeholders', must define their own interest and the media duly take note. However, there remains a tension between the public's interest and those more institutionalized interests of business; the 'public remains a largely passive force in the policy-making process' (Freedman, 2005).

As media converge and companies merge, the conventional lines of regulation have become entwined, making clear oversight difficult and rules regularly overtaken by technological change. The last (Labour) UK government produced a blueprint for 'Digital Britain' in 2009, which attempted a strategic overview for all the print, broadcast and new media, within the wider purview of data management and access. Part of a project called 'Building Britain's Future', this was an unusually holistic approach towards regulation, not just of allied sectors, but of the entire world of communication in all its many facets, especially with regard to its impact on education, employment and public information. Its prime author was Lord Carter, who enumerated the last of its objectives as:

A review of what all of this [catalogue of regulation] means for the Government and how digital governance in the information age demands new structures, new safeguards, and new data management, access and transparency rules.

(Digital Britain, 2009)

But the incoming Conservative government has cut back on Ofcom's policy role and repossessed some of its key duties, such as the five-yearly review of public service broadcasting, which some commentators see as a political power grab. Damian Tambini (2010) writes 'the reform of Ofcom is one of the gravest assaults on broadcasting freedom I have seen in the UK':

The basic organising principle of Ofcom is independence from government. That is the reason new members of the EU have to conform to this model of independent regulation: it is a key condition for the health of democracy. It is particularly important that regulation is independent from government in regulating issues such as media ownership, public broadcasting and commercial broadcasting.

(Tambini, 2010)

Policing content

A large part of media regulation involves state attempts to control media businesses – whether for the good of democracy or to enhance its own power – as I have discussed above. Another part of regulation and media law involves protecting individuals in an – what some might see as overly zealous – attempt to guard the freedom of the press. As philosopher Onora O'Neill observed in the *Guardian,* during the 2006 debate about the publication of insulting cartoons about the prophet Muhammad:

> A free press was then often seen as the champion of the weak, and as augmenting and giving voice to the powerless. Conferring the same freedom of expression on more powerful organisations, including media organisations, is now less easily justified. Once we take account of the power of the media, we are not likely to think that they should enjoy unconditional freedom of expression.
>
> (O'Neill, 2006)

This view is controversial among journalists, but laws have been enacted to protect minorities against racism, to offer protection to the victims of certain crimes, to protect minors, and to protect people against defamation and miscarriage of justice. As early as 1926, the Judicial Proceedings Act restricted salacious reporting of divorce proceedings in Britain, and the 1976 Sexual Offences Act introduced the right of anonymity for rape victims; but it was the Human Rights Act of 1998 that really introduced the notion of human, particularly privacy, rights (Frost, 2010).

There is no space here to comment in detail on media law, but one of the consistent factors faced by those like O'Neill, who favour increased regulation to protect the individual, is the way in which these laws are manipulated to damage and limit legitimate enquiry. One of the newer issues which has come into focus with the internet has been the way in which libel action can now be taken in countries which have tougher laws. The British courts traditionally favour the plaintiff, making London the libel capital of the world, as aggrieved individuals use the English courts to pursue offences committed elsewhere, but technically 'published' in the UK via the internet.

The English lawyer Geoffrey Robertson (2010) dubbed this 'libel tourism'. One case serves to illustrate. Khalid bin Mahfouz and two members of his family sued Rachel Ehrenfeld, an Israeli-born writer and US citizen, over her book on terrorist financing, *Funding Evil* (2003), which claimed that Mahfouz and his family provided financial support to Islamic terrorist groups. Her book had not been published in Britain, although 23 copies had been purchased online through web sites registered in the UK, and excerpts from the book had been published globally on the ABC News website. As an American, she claimed this action violated her First Amendment rights, but the British judge found against her, awarding costs and ordering the book be destroyed.

Laws intended to protect the individual are frequently used to constrain individual journalists from reporting on the powerful and wealthy. As leading lawyer Mark Stephens says: 'As the libel and privacy capital of the world, people are coming here [to London] to bully the media and NGOs into not reporting on their nefarious activities' (Robinson, 2009). 2010 saw the deployment of so-called 'super-injunctions' to protect the privacy of two adulterous Premier league footballers. Using expensive legal counsel unavailable to most, these not only prevented the media publishing the details of their sexual shenanigans, but prevented any mention of their names or the existence of these injunctions.

Confronted with hard economic interests, the law is not immutable. When Marks & Spencer sued Granada's *World in Action* in 1998 for defamation over allegations that the company was using goods produced by child labour, the court moved the goalposts in the way that it showed the programme to the jury. Previously, television journalists could reveal the facts, visual and verbal, and leave the audience to make up their own mind, inferences drawn being the responsibility of the viewer, as long as the programme made no unsubstantiated allegations. In the M&S case, the jury was asked to view the programme, consider what it believed to be the case, and the inference that M&S knew of this malpractice was accepted as *prima facie* defamation. It cost Granada £50,000 in damages, £650,000 in costs (Benady, 1998) and hastened the series' demise.

Laws are not necessarily the first line of defence in the protection against offence. There is, at least in Europe, notional support for regulation as a first court of appeal in protecting the individual against press abuses. However, the success of regulation depends on how it is used. In Germany, the self-regulating Press Council has seen a decline in complaints, Pöttker believes due to ignorance of the German Press Council (whose meetings are closed) and a loss of faith in the system. 'Press self-regulation rests on the assumption that the system itself is satisfactory but requires constant fine tuning' (in Pöttker and Starck, 2003: 59). He also suggests that a key driver of German self-regulation had been to forestall any attempts at political control of the media, reflecting a national desire not to repeat the horrors of the Nazi era.

In the USA, regulation is generally unpopular and unsupported. The US Council on Press Responsibility and Press Freedom – a self-regulatory mechanism reliant on the funding and co-operation of the press, like its UK equivalent Press Council at the time – survived only eleven years from its inception in 1973. 'Many news organizations simply refused to cooperate with and even ignored the News Council's efforts. This included such major media as the *New York Times*, *Chicago Tribune* and NBC' (Pöttker and Starck, 2003: 56). The First Amendment to the US Constitution is frequently invoked to assert the complete autonomy of the press: 'Congress shall make no law ... abridging the freedom of speech, or of the press.'[5] But, as the critic A. J. Liebling wittily observed, 'Freedom of the press is for those who own one' (quoted in Stephens, 1988: 211). Or, as Herman and Chomsky put it, 'The media are indeed free – for those who adopt the principles required for their "societal purpose"'(Herman and Chomsky, 1994).

Statutory regulation versus self-regulation

In the UK, regulation of content is largely enshrined in guidelines which, when it comes to legal contestation, must have been scrupulously observed if the media organisation involved is successfully to defend its case. Ofcom legally enforces codes in the broadcast media with significant sanctions, as we have seen; the self-regulator of the press, the Press Complaints Commission (PCC), is more of a law unto itself; while the BBC Trust sits at a difficult juncture halfway between statutory and self-regulation. (In an attempt to prove it is getting its house in order, the BBC's 2010 Editorial Guidelines are twice as long as the 2005 ones they replaced.) All guidelines effectively seek to demarcate the boundaries of social consensus. What is considered acceptable in the media changes with what consumers consider acceptable in their everyday experience, and adjudications can be adjusted to take account of this change. Bad language, nudity and explicit violence were all deemed inadmissible in most media forty years ago. The late theatre critic Kenneth Tynan caused a furore when he was, allegedly, the first man to utter the world 'fuck' on British television, in 1965.[6] By 2008, extensive research undertaken by the BBC Trust found viewers felt the licence of 'anything goes' had run too far, and the Trust instructed the BBC:

> the most offensive language should only be used in exceptional circumstances on BBC One between 9 and 10 pm. ... The BBC should not make programmes that celebrate or condone gratuitous, aggressive, intrusive, and humiliating behaviour.
>
> (BBC Website, 2009)

The increasing public importance of complaint is an expression of an evolving understanding that fairness and privacy are rights to which all people are entitled. Frost's survey of the two UK regulators' adjudications in this area in the years 2004–8 notes that the PCC does not include fairness as a criterion it covers:

> Although the PCC ... receives substantially more privacy complaints than Ofcom, the latter, through its Fairness Committee, adjudicates more than double the number of cases that the PCC handles and upholds an average 26 a year (14.5 per cent) compared with an average 12.8 (22.8 per cent) upheld by the PCC. It is clear that when consumers are really upset, the PCC receives complaints in the hundreds while Ofcom receives them in the tens of thousands.
>
> (Frost, 2010)

This reflects the very different policy that the PCC's composition brings to the table (and the relative size of audiences). Statutory regulation tends towards precise delimitations of proscribed territory, whereas self-regulation favours more nebulous boundaries. Two stories will serve to show those two contrasting systems in action in the UK.

On 7 November 2008, the avowedly right-wing 'shock jock' Jon Gaunt ran an item on his mid-morning current affairs radio show on the commercial TalkSport station about Redbridge council's decision to refuse smokers the opportunity to foster children in their care. In a live interview with councillor Michael Stark, Gaunt admits to 'losing his rag' as he hectored the councillor, calling him a 'health Nazi' and 'an ignorant pig'. He apologised on air later, but the station decided to sack him.

Fifty-five people complained about the broadcast to Ofcom, who subsequently found TalkSport 'in breach of broadcasting rules'. Gaunt, with the backing of civil rights group Liberty, decided to challenge Ofcom in the High Court on the grounds of the inhibition of free speech but, on 13 July 2010, he lost the case, with Judge Sir Anthony May saying, 'The essential point is that the offensive and abusive nature of the broadcast was gratuitous, having no factual content or justification' (BBC News Website, 2010b). Ofcom's chief executive, Ed Richards, in a statement released after the court's decision, said:

> We were perfectly happy for this case to be taken to court to review the way in which we interpret our statutory duties. … This is a thorough endorsement of our judgment in what was a difficult case.
>
> (Ofcom, 2010)

On 10 October 2009, the Boyzone boy-band singer Stephen Gately was found dead in his Mallorca hotel room, reportedly of natural causes. On 16 October, the day before his funeral, the *Daily Mail* posted columnist Jan Moir's comment on the newspaper's website under the title 'Why there was nothing "natural" about Stephen Gately's death'. Although this was amended to 'A strange, lonely and troubling death' in the print edition, the meaning was clear in the text with lines such as: 'Once again, under the carapace of glittering, hedonistic celebrity, the ooze of a very different and more dangerous lifestyle has seeped out for all to see.'[7]

By the following Monday morning, the PCC had received over 22,000 complaints, more than it had altogether in the previous five years. Gately's civil partner, Andrew Cowles, said he was disgusted by the article and claimed the *Daily Mail* had broken the PCC's code of conduct on three grounds, arguing that it was inaccurate, intruded into private grief and contained homophobic remarks. On 17 February 2010, the PCC ruled that to censure Moir would be 'a slide towards censorship'. The PCC's Director, Stephen Abell, said the article contained flaws, but the commission had decided: 'It would not be proportionate to rule against the columnist's right to offer freely expressed views about something that was the focus of public attention.'[8]

Both journalists were undeniably offensive, but it was the one who reached the much wider audience, occasioning a much greater tide of offended complaint, who was exonerated. The palpable incongruities between the two different systems reveal the imperfectability of regulation in consistently holding the media to account. In the criminal courts, those charged know they stand a much higher chance of being found not guilty by a jury of their peers than by a magistrate or judge, and so it is with the PCC.

The PCC is composed of seventeen grandees, of whom (at the time of writing) seven are active editorial figures from the press industry, but their job is to adjudicate on whether the industry's codes and standards are being upheld. These are drawn up by the Editors' Code of Practice Committee, which is composed exclusively of editors. As its website proclaims: 'The Editors' Code of Practice is the foundation stone of the UK press self-regulatory system. It sets out the rules that the industry itself has voluntarily drawn up and pledged to accept.'[9] Its powerful chair is currently Paul Dacre, Editor of the *Daily Mail* and Editor-in-chief of Associated Newspapers. In a long speech to the Society of Editors in 2008, Dacre poured scorn on the Human Rights Act and its wide-ranging interpretation by one particular judge, whom he accused of a one-man crusade to muzzle the press. He argued that a press accountable to its readers was a better upholder of civilised standards than a single judge.

> Since time immemorial public shaming has been a vital element in defending the parameters of what are considered acceptable standards of social behaviour, helping ensure that citizens – rich and poor – adhere to them for the good of the greater community. For hundreds of years, the press has played a role in that process. It has the freedom to identify those who have offended public standards of decency – the very standards its readers believe in – and hold the transgressors up to public condemnation. If their readers don't agree with the defence of such values, they would not buy those papers in such huge numbers.
>
> (Dacre, 2008)

This is the self-regulators' justification, of the market being a more democratic form of constraint than the hierarchical imposition of controls, which they argue are easily bent to the political interests of the master of the day. This implicitly questions the democratic credentials of laws passed by Parliament, which are notionally enactments of the will of the people. Yet investigations into the PCC have all complained of its failings. The late Sir David Calcutt, whose previous 1990 inquiry had originally recommended the establishment of the PCC, reported in 1993:

> The Press Complaints Commission is not, in my view, an effective regulator of the press. It has not been set up in a way, and is not operating a code of conduct which enables it to command not only press but public confidence. ... It is not the truly independent body that it should be. As constituted, it is, in essence, a body set up by the industry, financed by the industry, dominated by the industry, and operating a code of practice devised by the industry and which is over-favourable to the industry.
>
> (Calcutt, 1993: xi)

Calcutt recommended statutory regulation, which the government, and successive parliamentary inquiries, have continued to resist. Despite attempting to assuage criticism with amendments, the PCC was also roundly condemned by a Media Standards Trust (MST) report, published in February 2009, which found it 'unable to deal with the serious and growing threats to press standards and press freedom' (Media Standards Trust, 2009). The MST followed this in January 2010 with a raft of proposals recommending more transparency and accountability. Its Director Martin Moore stated:

> The public wants an independent self-regulator that, in addition to mediating complaints, monitors compliance with the code and conducts regular investigations. The PCC, as currently constituted, does not and cannot do this.
>
> (Media Standards Trust, 2010)

Although only 7 per cent of its public respondents said they trusted the press (less even than bankers), MST found that the public preferred an independent self-regulatory body (52 per cent) to a newspaper industry complaints body (8 per cent) or a regulatory body set up by the government (17 per cent). Their main demand was for a body monitoring press compliance to their code on behalf of the public (48 per cent), not mediating complaints (12 per cent) (Media Standards Trust, 2010). These findings suggest a more sophisticated public than the press or government seem to presume, one that values a media not controlled by government.

Escaping the net

When punishment as public spectacle was progressively replaced by imprisonment in the eighteenth century, the English philosopher Jeremy Bentham developed the Panopticon, a cartwheel-shaped prison structure which enabled the guard at the hub to observe all the prison wings, and to do so himself unobserved. This concept of supervisory omniscience pre-dates the surveillance society by over 200 years, and was picked up by the French philosopher Michel Foucault as central to his thesis of *Discipline and Punish: The Birth of the Prison*. Just as today's CCTV cameras can recognise faces and vehicle number plates and track them everywhere, Foucault writes 'the gaze is alert … visibility is a trap' (Foucault, 1977: 196).

Today the internet mega businesses Google, FaceBook and YouTube are being enriched, not by their apparently benign ability to create interconnections between users but by the resulting back-flow of information retrieval. The precious material being mined in this new extractive industry is about the consumer, not the content. Every time you make a Google search, you reveal commercially valuable information about your tastes and interests, around which data sophisticated algorithms sell advertising space. That is how Google makes its money. Lawrence Lessig explains how difficult this is to regulate:

> Every time you pick a result, Google learns something from that. So each time you do a search, you are adding value to Google's data base. The data

base becomes so rich that the advertising model that sits on top of it can out-compete other advertising models because it has better data. ... The potential here is actually that the data layer is more dangerous from a policy perspective because it cuts across layers of human life. So privacy and competition and access to commerce, and access to content – everything is driven by this underlying layer. Unlike the operating system, which couldn't necessarily control the content that you got.

(quoted in Auletta, 2009: 138)

Just as the commercial imperatives of Yahoo and Google ensnared them in doing a repressive state's dirty work for it, some commentators have seen journalism equally implicated in serving ends that serve needs other than the free flow of information.

As some of the biggest investigative stories of recent years have proven – from the *Daily Telegraph* scoop on British parliamentarians' expenses[10] to the Wikileaks/*Guardian* release of US Army Afghanistan war logs (Davies and Leigh, 2010) – data become a gold mine for the assiduous journalist with the modern tools of computer-assisted research (CAR). But as Andrejevic observes:

To the extent that the goal of journalism became, at least in part, to portray an increasingly populous and interdependent society to itself, it came to rely on strategies for tracking, describing, and categorizing the populace – strategies related to the disciplinary drive for monitoring and the incitement to self-disclosure. The rise, for example, of strategies for monitoring public opinion helps extend the role of journalism from that of monitoring the state to that of monitoring the population.

(Andrejevic, 2008: 609)

George Orwell in *1984*, written in 1949, imagined a future dominated by a totalitarian regime whose technology was all-seeing, retailored language as 'newspeak' and clamped down on 'thought-crime'. Just as Orwell foresaw the inevitability of widespread compliance, new technology is widely embraced as developmental, however invasive. Social networking sites such as Facebook and Twitter encourage a culture of self-revelation; personal privacy is now a commodity freely traded in return for 'friends'; and journalists are encouraged to follow these traces into territory that many believe to be their private domain (Phillips, 2010: 99).

There is by no means universal concern about this, nor consistency in people's reactions, and the recipients of media attention often feel more flattered than threatened by the personal targeting that data tracking involves. As the digital domain makes personal information all too freely tradable, the UK Data Protection Act 1988 sought to regulate the collection, storage and use of personal data and ensure the rights to privacy of the individual. But there is no privacy law as such in Britain and, when it was discovered that the *News of the World* was illegally tapping celebrities' and royalty's mobile phones, royal editor Clive Goodman and private investigator Glenn Mulcaire were jailed on charges of conspiracy, not data abuse (BBC News Website, 2007). As we go to press, following the arrest of two more senior *News of the World* journalists, 'News International has offered an unreserved apology and an admission of liability over the *News of the World* phone-hacking allegations. The global media giant said it had also instructed lawyers to set up a compensation scheme for a number of public figures to deal with "justi-fiable claims" '[11] Newly appointed News Corp heir James Murdoch told a Bloomberg PR seminar in New York that, 'It shows what we were able to do is really put this problem into a box',[12] which reveals more than probably intended about the company's attitudes to both regulation and the law.

John Kampfner quotes the UK intelligence and security co-ordinator, Sir David Omand, as admitting that 'application of modern data-mining and processing techniques does involve examination of the innocent as well as the suspect to identify patterns of interest for further investigation. Finding out other people's secrets is going to involve breaking everyday moral rules' (Kampfner, 2009: 222).

This amoral laissez-faire approach parallels the copyright issues that have exercised media companies since increased bandwidth allowed the free file-sharing of video and films, as well as music. While rights owners and distributors have seen some successes attacking piracy in the courts, the bigger move has been, as with journalism, to discover new business models that can monetise this new lat-eral form of distribution (see Chapter 1). Regulation is entering a new era where it will struggle increasingly hard to exercise control in a constantly changing mediascape, in which alternative routes will be found around the walls it builds. Just as alcohol prohibition proved ineffective in the 1920s USA in the face of public desire, like drug prohibition today, media regulation alone will never be able to deny the public what it wants.

One country has seen the potential benefit in taking the lead in such matters. Ironically spurred on by Iceland's failing banks' attempts to suppress reporting about them – through libel actions in London and injunctions against the national broadcaster RUV – on 16 June 2010, the Icelandic parliament unanimously passed the Icelandic Modern Media Initiative (IMMI). The government is tasked 'to introduce a new legislative regime to protect and strengthen modern freedom of expression, and the free flow of information in Iceland and around the world'.[13] Birgitta Jonsdottir, the chief sponsor in parliament of the IMMI proposal said:

> Iceland will become the inverse of a tax haven, by offering journalists and publishers some of the most powerful protections for free speech and inves-tigative journalism in the world. Tax havens' aim is to make everything opaque. Our aim is to make everything transparent.[14]

It is a brave attempt to adopt the open source principles of investigative journalism such as the Wikileaks website, offering such enterprises a sanctuary away from the all-points pursuit that powerful interests mount, when journalism dares to reveal wrong-doing. What we have yet to discover is how this laissez-faire approach will approach the very real issue of protecting the innocent from invasion of privacy while, at the same time, using the transparency of the net to pursue the guilty. However, as we go to press, the concerted attack on Wikileaks and its founder, by governments embarrassed by the continuing publication of secret documents, notably the USA and the UK, has included effective pressure on the internet service providers (ISPs) to deny the site a platform. Thus it is the self-styled liberal democracies who are now leading the field in attempts to regulate the web. ISPs' growing control of information flows and access, the walling-off of information within social network sites, and governments' invasive surveillance of data transfer have all been condemned by Sir Tim Berners-Lee, as threatening the essential principle of free access to information on which he founded the internet just 20 years ago.[15]

Conclusion

Regulation presumes an omniscient, multi-dimensional understanding of a society's needs in the control of information and entertainment flows, whereas it can never be more than the singular expression of the balance of power at the moment those regulations are drafted. Hence the widely criticised compromise that is the BBC Trust – part governance, part-regulator, the latter role part-shared with Ofcom – a creation of a constitutional crisis that set the BBC on a collision course with government and involved the fall of both its Chairman and Director-General Hutton, 2004. In the way that it is said that a camel is a race-horse designed by a committee, this two-humped beast would not have been born in more rational times.

Ofcom Standards Board member Anthony Lilley goes further and argues that the whole field of regulation is hobbled by both the questions it asks and the answers it frames being constructed in 'the unscientific language of economics'.[16] Just as economists were widely blamed for the sloppy thinking that led to the near collapse of the banking system and the subsequent recession, Lilley believes regulators claim too much and lead people to expect too much of an intrinsically narrow perspective. As Freedman writes: 'Media policy, the systematic attempt to foster certain types of media structure and behaviour and to suppress alternative modes of structure and behaviour, is a deeply political phenomenon' (Freedman, 2008: 1).

Consultation, as we have seen, is largely ineffective and the whole field of media policy has become too complex for most people, even its practitioners, to understand. Well-written codes of practice, properly communicated to journalists, cannot in themselves ensure ethics and standards, unless they are protected by employers as much as the public (Phillips, Couldry and Freedman, 2010; see also Chapter 8). Journalists are not just torn between the reassuringly hierarchical regulation of past ways of work and the individualized, entrepreneurial marketplace of today. They are also having to grapple with a polity whose principles and practices are changing as fast as the technologies they depend upon.

Throughout this book, we see how cuts impact on the quality of journalism, from the dumbing down of ITN to the much-diminished *Telegraph*, but there is no means of regulating that decline. Regulation manages public expectations through its complaints system, but – as Lessig (2005: xv) writes – its chief value to the industry remains to the powerful, in carving up the cake and ensuring competition operates only to their benefit, slowly eroding the real freedoms implicit in 'free speech'. The libertarian instincts of net journalists are laudable, but they do not extend to the protection of copyright for individual media workers. Determined governance of the kind that the Icelandic Modern Media Initiative promises may provide an effective opposition to state interference of the Chinese kind – but other nation states are only just beginning to find reasons and means to regulate ISPs or control Google. Yet people from all sectors of the political spectrum should be concerned about the extension of media monopolies, as was the late conservative American political commentator, William Safire:

> The concentration of power – political, corporate, media, cultural – should be anathema to conservatives. The diffusion of power through local control, thereby encouraging individual participation, is the essence of federalism and the greatest expression of democracy.
>
> (Safire quoted in Lessig, 2005: xv)

Notes

1 President George W. Bush, Address to a Joint Session of Congress and the American People, 20 September 2001, http://georgewbush-whitehouse.archives.gov/news/releases/2001/09/20010920–28.html (accessed 15 September 2010).
2 For a more up to date review, see http://opennet.net/sites/opennet.net/files/ONI_China_2009.pdf (accessed February 2011).
3 French Law No. 94–665 of 4 August 1994, www.dglf.culture.gouv.fr/droit/loi-gb.htm (accessed August 2010).
4 BBC Jam had spent half of its £15 million budget on this project before competitors complained to the European Commission and the entire project was cancelled, http://news.bbc.co.uk/1/hi/education/6449619.stm (accessed 26 September 2010).
5 Madison, J. *et al.* (1789), First (of 12) Amendments to US Constitution, originally adopted 1787, Philadelphia: Constitutional Convention.
6 Kenneth Tynan on 'BBC3', BBC1 19 November 1965, said: 'I doubt if there are any rational people to whom the word "fuck" would be particularly diabolical, revolting or totally forbidden. I think that anything which can be printed or said can also be seen.'
7 Jan Moir, *Daily Mail*, 16 October 2009 (article no longer accessible on website).
8 For full PCC adjudication, see www.pcc.org.uk/news/index.html?article=NjIyOA== (accessed December 2010).
9 Editors' Code of Practice Committee website, www.editorscode.org.uk/ (accessed August 2010).
10 MPs' expenses: Full list of MPs investigated by the *Telegraph*, 8 May 2009, www.telegraph.co.uk/news/newstopics/mps-expenses/5297606/MPs-expenses-Full-list-of-MPs-investigated-by-the-Telegraph.html (accessed September 2010).
11 'News International "Sorry" For Phone Hacking', Sky News website, 8 April 2011, http://news.sky.com/skynews/Home/UK-News/News-International-Offers-Apology-To-Phone-Hacking-Victims-At-News-Of-The-World/Article/201104215968901?f=rss (accessed 11 April 2011).
12 Andrew Edgecliffe-Johnson, 'Phone-hacking saga haunts Murdoch heir', Financial Times, 8 April 2011, http://www.ft.com/cms/s/0/61fcd11a-6212-11e0-8ee4-00144feab49a.html#ixzz1JEzOqQT1 (accessed 11 April 2011).
13 Icelandic Modern Media Initiative, www.immi.is/?l=en (accessed December 2010).
14 Ibid.
15 Tim Berners-Lee, 'Long live the web: A call for continued open standards and neutrality, *Scientific American*, 22 November 2010.
16 Anthony Lilley, in interview with the author, 9 September 2010.

Part II
Changing practices

4 Doing it all in the multi-skilled universe

Peter Lee-Wright and Angela Phillips

As technology has drawn the many different media technologies onto the single platform of the internet, the opportunity has been seized to try and mould journalists into multi-skilled workers, able to shift effortlessly from print, to camera work, to audio and back. Changes in work are already underway and they are capable of putting more control and creative power into the hands of individual journalists. That is not, however, the way it always turns out. As we will set out below, our research, as well as that of others, suggests that multi-skilling has too often been a convenient excuse for job cuts and centralisation of operations, which undermines individual agency and quality. In this chapter we consider whether a converged platform should automatically usher in multi-skilling, and the inevitable 'de-layering' of jobs that accompanies such change, or whether there are better ways of exploiting the undoubted advantages of new technologies.

Change in the field of journalism is nothing new, nor is the tendency for change to streamline the process of getting news to audiences. With each innovation, a layer of highly trained staff has tended to disappear. Sometimes redundancy, though painful, is inevitable. The jobs of typesetters and compositors have gone, along with many other craft skills that are no longer required since the advent of computer typesetting.

We refer in more detail in other chapters to debates on changing and fragmenting audiences, social attitudes and patterns of consumption, as well as business models which all play a part in driving change but, as Örnebring (2010: 58) observes, 'In the minds of journalists, many if not most of the changes taking place in contemporary journalism are essentially *technology driven*'.

The journalist crafts seem to have been suborned to the new technology and the resulting debate tends to obscure the complex interplay of cause and effect. There has too often been, Örnebring suggests, an unhelpful binary between those who decry all change as reductive de-skilling and those who see it as 'upskilling'. There has been a presumption that those who are sceptical of the need for full multi-skilling are also opposed to multi-media newsrooms or even to the introduction of new technology.

In order to wriggle out of this straightjacket of a polarised 'for' or 'against' debate, it helps to pause and take a look at what is really meant by multi-skilling. Clearly the existence of the single platform that is the World Wide Web demands closer integration between media specialisms; to suggest otherwise would be to ignore its potential for enhancing the work of journalism and the service that can be provided to audiences.

However, whereas computers actually did away with the need for compositors, the internet has not obviated the need for video, audio and text. Until the introduction of multi-media news hubs, these were all seen as separate crafts. There was no assumption that those with a particular flair for the written word would be equally adept at producing visually exciting material – or vice versa. The existence of a single platform need not necessarily change that assumption.

The so-far limited binary debate on the introduction of multi-skilling makes it harder to evaluate just which changes bring benefits and improvements to the work of journalism – and to the democratic process which journalism feeds – and which changes function merely to push journalism further in a commercial direction and towards greater homogenisation (see Chapter 5). The question which we address in this chapter is not what is *possible* for journalists to do, but what is *useful* for them to do, and how the possibilities of the new technology can best be harnessed to improve the work that journalists produce.

The seduction of technology

The introduction of new practices is often welcomed by new entrants (see Chapter 2), because these moments of transformation break down what are often seen as sclerotic terms of employment and the hierarchies they are usually constructed to protect. Indeed this is partly why Bourdieu writes that an influx of new agents into a particular field can have a transformative effect: 'It can be said of an intellectual that he or she functions like a phoneme in language: he or she exists by virtue of a difference from other intellectuals. Falling into undifferentiatedness … means losing existence' (Bourdieu, 2005: 40).

Benson and Neveu (2005: 6) suggest that changes in class composition can be such a source of 'dynamism in the field'. In the field of journalism one of the transformational moments was the influx of graduates into the profession in the 1970s and 1980s: 'Ivy leaguers (enamored with the excitement and Hemingway) replaced high school graduates (enamored with the excitement and the regular paycheck) on the White House beat, at city hall, and, soon, even on the police beat' (Stephens, 2010: 78).

They were looking for opportunities for independent working and they were conscious that new technologies would shorten the chain of interaction between reporter and audience, and provide them with far more direct control of their work.

In the USA, computer technologies started to appear in newsrooms in the 1970s. In the UK the process of change was held back by powerful print unions, who saw that computers would wipe out the need for all but a small handful of their jobs, so eroding their bargaining power.

As we saw in Chapter 2, when, in 1986, News International decided to move its entire print operation of the *Sun, News of the World, The Times* and *The Sunday*

Times into a new computerised complex at Wapping in East London, all the printers lost their jobs and a bitter dispute ensued. The printers fought against change because it meant the loss of their livelihoods. For most of the journalists, the adaptation required to work directly onto a computer was minimal. Many also made it clear that they were glad to see (what they considered to be) the stranglehold of the print unions broken, and welcomed the increased control it gave them over their work (Melvern, 1986: 101).

By breaking away from the printers, they could see the possibilities for greater flexibility, shorter deadlines, more opportunities, greater control and cheaper print operations. Soon other UK newspapers followed the lead of News International and typesetters were gone forever.

Similarly, many broadcast journalists and their producers welcomed the flexibility the new technology gave them – and the freedom from travelling everywhere with a very visible crew and up to twenty large silver boxes of film equipment. Smaller crews meant that sound recordists and camera operators had fewer opportunities for work, but reporters can now slip unnoticed into media-unfriendly environments – like Zimbabwe at election time – and broadcast live via a satellite phone. As BBC foreign correspondent and News Channel presenter Ben Brown says: 'There's nowhere we cannot go now.'[1] The technology is relatively easily managed, only problematic to the most technophobe of journalists. And the additional time spent on managing it, and the home studio links, is probably offset by the time not spent managing and socialising with the crew. Foreign correspondents and filmmakers find time spent alone on the ground gives them a unique access, through establishing personal bonds with their subjects.

Enthusiasts for new technologies are, inevitably perhaps, those who are most likely to benefit from them. Some are new entrants and see change as an opportunity to break through the existing hierarchies and job divisions. But most embrace new technology if it makes their jobs more productive or more creative. This has particularly been the case for journalists using the internet as a research resource, which is by far the most significant change brought about by the World Wide Web (Machill and Beiler, 2009; Phillips, 2010). Journalism is about finding things out, so the web's potential was very quickly exploited by journalists, eager to range across the world as well as down the road, as one specialist journalist remarks:

> Ten, fifteen years ago I would have had to [go] to the Committee and listen to him give evidence. Now I was able to get him to send his evidence direct to me by email which meant that process took, you know, fifteen minutes as opposed to arranging a meeting with him, for him to give me a paper, which may take him an hour to produce blah de blah. I could then, thanks to the new video part of the parliament website, watch [him giving evidence] from my desk.
>
> (Specialist journalist, national newspaper, interview conducted in 2008).

In our interviews we found that journalists were rarely resistant to trying new technologies as long as they were properly trained to use them. Their concerns were about the way in which change is being implemented and the uses to which the technology is being put.

Multi-skilling in television leads the way

Braced by the temptations of cost cutting and the committed support of a handful of enthusiasts, the first experiments in multi-skilling started in television. New cable companies proliferated in the 1980s in the USA and 1990s in the UK, operating without the massive advertising subsidies enjoyed by their networked cousins. They had to find cheap ways of producing usable video materials and that meant reducing crews to the bare minimum. The explosion of cable channels introduced the figure of the lone journalist setting up their own camera and doing their pieces to it in front of news events.

Conventionally hard-bitten news crews would soften at the sight of the inexperienced struggling and go to the aid of these invariably young reporters, helping them focus and check the camera's colour balance. Managements of mainstream broadcasters, though keen to cut the bottom line, saw other potential in these developments and the new generation of lightweight digital cameras being used. In Europe, videojournalism quickly moved into the mainstream, as recognised by the Belgium-based Concentra prize for videojournalism.[2] The Berlin-based international videojournalist (VJ) agency tiva.tv started up in 2006 and now offers the services of 1,153 VJs spread across 115 countries.[3] The BBC's regional news operation became the UK test-bed for an experiment with video-journalism, first trialled in Bristol in 1997 and then developed as a national training programme in 2001 (Wallace, 2009). The programme's inception was described by its project manager, Paul Myles:

> We had many cameramen and many picture editors and many journalists who all worked for those 15, 16 regional stations around the country and, as you can imagine, it cost a fair bit because to employ one person to do one job is an expensive way of working. The other thing, and the main reason that the BBC wanted to look at videojournalism, was that the content of what came up on the screen was something that was very dull and boring and formulaic.
>
> (Myles, 2008)

He does not deny that the first thought was the savings on progressively replacing costly camera crews, kit and editors with journalists who did it all on cheap cameras and laptops, but asserts that the principal gain was giving journalists more time to invest in their stories and get closer to their subjects, generating better work. Previously, BBC regional news centres had between four and six camera operators to cover everything. They would rarely spend more than an hour on any story, inevitably shooting it in the standard 'interview, cutaways, piece-to-camera' fashion. By 2008 the BBC had trained 650 VJs, who would normally have at least a day or two to commit to each story (ibid).

The majority of those trained were journalists, in need of the three weeks' technical training, but 10 per cent were former technicians: cameramen and sound recordists with no journalist training. This led to conflicts over whether conventional journalistic or technical standards should predominate. Wallace describes 'the strain that the introduction of new technology put on accepted definitions of journalistic professionalism as validated by professional competence' (Wallace, 2009: 698). Paul Myles, who was himself a cameraman, notes: 'This isn't a thing you can learn in three weeks. I mean you can learn a certain amount in three weeks but I'm still learning now six, seven years later on' (Myles, 2008).

Management enthusiasm for the VJ in UK television newsrooms was cautious. Some, among the ranks of middle managers at the BBC, who edited the local news magazine programmes, embraced this new way of work. Others were more resistant to change, arguing that the results were technically of lower quality and each piece absorbed the journalists, still mastering their newfound skills, for days rather than the hours it would take with technical back-up. When audited in 2008, more than half the nightly roster of packages on some BBC regional news programmes, such as Nottingham, were produced by VJs, whereas slow uptake in London, Scotland and Northern Ireland reduced the overall national average to a quarter, just two items in the average eight per half-hour (Myles, 2008).

A widespread editorial demand for personal narratives to illustrate every story can be well served by the intimacy of single video operators, but few of its practitioners are ready to take over the full panoply of craft roles in most news coverage. Hemmingway, whose research is based upon her own employment at the Nottingham newsroom, finds that videojournalism – which she refers to as personal digital production – does find the more engaging personal angles that its progenitors claim (Hemmingway, 2008). Wallace's more wide-ranging survey of the impact of videojournalism also found support for this view of increased synergy between form and content, but reports more critical judgements, including from VJs themselves:

> Videojournalism, it was argued, reduces its proponent's ability to conduct an in-depth enquiry, to unearth new information from its interviewees, and to ask challenging questions, because of the need simultaneously to concentrate on the camerawork. One conclusion, from a BBC VJ, was that videojournalism is 'just not good enough. It doesn't allow you to go for cross examination or complex interview techniques'.
>
> (Wallace, 2009: 695)

Interviewing is arguably the most complex and difficult skill, involving much more than putting pre-prepared questions. It involves encouraging or challenging interviewees, reading their body language as well as what they say and how they say it, establishing a rapport. All this is much more difficult to achieve with machinery interposed between the journalist's eye and their subject. An option some adopt is to set the camera on a tripod and lock off the shot, but that is sterile; the frame has to be wide enough to encompass unscheduled movement, and it loses the photographic sensitivity and reframing that best captures the moment.

Documentary camera-directors can offset these problems by evolving a modus operandi over extended time with their subjects, but it is rarely more than a compromise in the practice of everyday journalism. With limited time, the attention to technical detail, as well as the mentioned operational problems, diverts the reporter from focusing exclusively on the interview, making it more likely that the subject can escape penetrating interrogation. That's why, although Wallace argues that the control over the medium offered to VJs is liberating (Wallace, 2009), many feel videojournalism is limited and should not be overused.

Digital homogenisation

Ironically, as it turns out, single operator journalism does not necessarily equate to increased control over one's work either. Autonomous operators can too easily morph into lone operators. A broadcast correspondent is expected to fill an increasing number of news outlets, anchoring them to the news networks rather than releasing them to do original work in the field. The fetishisation of the live link sometimes seems to nail the poor correspondent to the same spot for days on end.

And while digital technology makes content capture easier, it also makes its centralisation, duplication and distribution easier. The material gathered is normally stored in a digital hub, to which everyone else within the organisation has equal access, and which they may use (or abuse) for whatever purpose and platform they wish. So journalistic work in which one might reasonably take a proprietorial pride becomes an 'open access' source to colleagues, raising issues of ethical responsibility parallel to the practices of unattributed sourcing we explore further in Chapter 8. The ubiquity of agency and pooled material, gathered in a similar fashion, frequently means the same shots accompany bulletins on rival news channels (Redden and Witschge, 2010), underlining and endorsing Bourdieu's comment about competition producing homogeneity (Bourdieu, 1998).

At the BBC, for example, everyone has access to pooled material, but it is precisely at this point that the potential for disconnect and demotivation sets in. If the journalist feels demoted to the level of 'mouse monkey', merely reprocessing other people's material, then however many skills they have, they feel relatively worthless. One online correspondent had a very good way of diagnosing this condition:

> Ask people what stories they did last week. If they're working on the process side, they won't be able to tell you. You know, they have forgotten what the stories are. But ask somebody who is a reporter what they did for the last six years and they can go back chronologically through every story.
>
> (Online specialist correspondent, national broadcaster, interview conducted in 2008)

Even the production people on BBC News feel some of this detachment, spread increasingly thinly over the output and rarely in a position to originate stories. Anna Mainwaring is a news producer and Mother of Chapel (union representative) in the National Union of Journalists (NUJ):

> Instead of having teams that have to go out and get stories, stories are coming to us. You know I went into journalism because I'm interested in people, I'm interested in getting stories, but when the stories are coming to you, and you've just got to process them and verify them, it's not as exciting or as interesting.
>
> (Interview conducted in 2009)

Another broadcast journalist at BBC News commented on how her role now embraces all stages of the production process, including the clerical functions previously performed by specialist bookers.

> We do everything ... we do the research, we write the scripts, we work with reporters on their reports, we find the pictures, we cut the pictures, we write the headlines, we cut the pictures for the headlines, we write the summaries, cut the pictures for the summaries, we find the guests ... we interview the guests to find out whether they're right, we then send a brief to the presenter ... we book the taxis, we book the lines, to make sure everything goes on air ... the whole nature of the job has changed.
>
> (Interview conducted in 2008)

The journalist craves autonomy, not the status of the automaton. While many accept the need to make cuts, this 'do it all yourself' approach shifts the emphasis from news-gathering to output production, a feature particularly regretted among online journalists. It is physically possible to cover all the bases and feed the machine, but time and focus needed to produce original, satisfactory journalism are inevitably diminished.

Online text production

In the early days of the 'net' most regular journalism online was simply uploaded onto the internet from the print version. Researchers referred to it as 'shovelware' (Thalhimer, 1994) to demonstrate just how different it was from what was considered the purer form of online journalism being produced by bloggers, usually writing about technology. Journalists working directly for the online versions of newspapers tended to be considered less important than their print colleagues and were often housed separately and paid considerably less (Paul, 2002). Like their VJ equivalents they were expected to do a number of jobs that had formerly been the province of several specialists. They had to write, and regularly update, stories (largely by keeping an eye on other online sources) and make hyperlinks so that they could link their stories to others (Fredin, 1997). They might also be expected to source and upload pictures onto the site. They then had to do the sub-editing jobs: rewrite headlines and introductions so that stories would be more easily picked up by search engines, break up text into searchable sections, introduce bullet points and in many cases sub (copy) their own material (Russial, 2008).

Asking reporters to act as sub-editors (copy-editors) was not a new idea. It had been tried in the early 1980s when computer typesetting came in. The idea was that, since it was so easy to correct on a computer, the journalists could do their own corrections. What seemed obvious to those trying to cut jobs and save money turned out not to be so obvious in practice. The job of a 'sub' is to craft, check and improve material that has been gathered by a reporter and the two separate skills of originating and editing stories may not always be available in the same person, as this sub-editor joining a much later conversation on the subject explained:

> I've certainly encountered them in my time in journalism. The brilliant news-gatherers who can get their foot in any door, collect all the facts, make the contacts – and are utterly incapable of turning the material they have gathered into a coherent piece of writing. Are their skills to be lost to the industry because there are no subs to do that for them?
>
> (Dusty, 2009)

The process of dispensing with sub-editors was soon dropped because of the effect it had on the quality of newspapers (Russial, 1998), but the inexorable logic of the bottom line does not always take quality into account. Online journalists have been managing without sub-editing, partly because of the greater possibilities for post-publication correction. As the distinction between on- and offline journalists has started to blur, there have been further moves to do away with subs entirely.

In 2009, Roy Greenslade, media journalist and blogger on the *Guardian*, became an unexpected advocate of shedding sub-editors in the UK: 'What we are doing, having eliminated the hot metal work-force in the 1980s, is eliminating another inessential layer in order to create all-round journalists – writers *and* subs – who are able to do everything for themselves' (Greenslade, 2009, emphasis in original). He suggests that this will be possible because of '[t]he inflow of a "new wave" of highly-educated, well-trained young journalists with digital knowledge' (ibid).

This suggestion comes at a time when some journalists are producing complex work, using several strands of copy as well as links and graphics, and others are working on stories in which a large number of writers may be contributing to a single, running, story which may not be published under their own byline. Many of those responding online to Greenslade's broadside pointed to the very real risk of errors going out uncorrected, as well as a deterioration in the quality and clarity of writing. Emily Bell, then director of digital content for Guardian News and Media, wrote in response to the debate that, rather than doing away with subs, she saw a future for an enhanced role for them:

Who better to curate, link, explain, contextualise and market than those with technical skills aligned to subbing? Until we recognise that the future is not just the processing of ever increasing text articles, subbing has a poor out-look, but as we evolve production tasks into more varied, involved and hopefully interesting work it should reinvigorate and redefine what copy editing really is.

(Bell, 2009b)

The development of such specialist production journalists with cross-platform editing skills, and basic knowledge of other online tools, cuts across the moves towards multi-skilling for all, and recognises that new specialists may be needed to manage the interactive and cross-platform possibilities that the web offers. It also recognises that the skills required for highly focused technical work are not the same skills as those required for gathering information and interviewing, or for filming or photography. All these skills are required but not necessarily in the same person. For those journalists who gravitate towards technical and produc-tion work, online possibilities could offer a very satisfying opportunity for job enhancement. For a reporter whose orientation is towards ferreting out informa-tion, hours spent fiddling with copy and links can be frustrating. The jobs have little in common and amalgamating them is unlikely to be the best solution.

Video moves on line

For the first ten years of the net, text continued to reign supreme. Then three things came to fruition simultaneously. Broadband with fast download speeds became almost universal in the developed world; mobile phone technology developed, allowing journalists to carry a video/still camera around in their back-pockets; and interest in video platforms such as YouTube demonstrated that audiences have an enormous thirst for video online (ComScore, 2008).

According to a US study (Madden, 2007), news is the most popular subject of online video for Americans over the age of 29 – and the second most popular for younger adults. This has not gone unnoticed by managements of commercial news outlets. In a 2008 international survey of newspaper editors more than 80 per cent expected that journalists would need to know how to produce video (and indeed content for all platforms) within five years (World Editors Forum, 2008). If people wanted video, then video must be provided. Some news organisations, and some journalists, took enthusiastically to the new mix of media.

Michael Rosenblum, the USA's leading proponent of videojournalism, commented in his blog how significant it was that the UK Royal Television Society's 2008 award for best international news went to a newspaper journalist, Sean Smith, who is a fulltime VJ for the *Guardian*: 'Increasingly, I am coming to believe that the future of television news will in fact be found as newspapers move aggressively to re-invent themselves and TV news crews tragically simply talk themselves into irrelevance' (Rosenblum, 2008).

The British academic and VJ David Dunkley Gyimah also suggests that 'it's the newspaper groups doing the innovating'.[4] He is employed as a videojournalism trainer by newspapers such as the *Financial Times,* and sees television as slow to adapt to the rich potential of the multimedia he practises on his own View-magazine.tv website: 'Devoid of any conventions, it's quite conceivable that print-based media could revolutionise story-telling with videojournalism. Unless, that is, they ape TV.'[5]

One of the most successful UK television VJs was a fortuitous recruit from newspapers. Sean Langan was a features writer bound for Kashmir when the first series of BBC2's *Video Diaries* gave him a video camera to see what might happen. What emerged was an award-winning film and a signature hand-held camera style that has seen Langan subsequently dig deep in some of the most difficult regions, from Iraq to Afghanistan. Langan freely admits that his film career was a happy accident, and his hand-held style a product of not wanting to lug a tripod around:

> What worked about it was because I didn't understand the form. I wasn't shackled. I didn't come from News, I was a Features writer and I hadn't been in TV. I was dealing with a very serious subject that would only normally have been covered by Current Affairs or News – human rights abuses in Kashmir, insurgents – and, because coming from Features, I was hopeless at filing quickly.
>
> (Langan quoted in Lee-Wright, 2010b: 79)

However, Langan's experience was quite exceptional and, as we explore further below, where journalists are being asked to 'multi-skill' it is most often where budgets are being heavily cut. Here journalists tend to experience a demand for increased productivity, even as they master an expanding portfolio of skills. Managers, noting that audiences seem content with very low-quality amateur footage on YouTube, too often make the assumption that low-quality video will be sufficient and that it can be provided, at very low cost, by virtually untrained print journalists using high-quality mobile phones. Whereas reporters would previously be accompanied by a photographer, now they have to whip out their mobile phone to take a still or a squirt of video while, at the same time, conducting interviews and taking notes.

On many sites video is simply used to provide a 'talking head', as this 'video trained' journalist explained: 'They'll say right, we want three sentences. Give me an opinion for three sentences, and that's what you do.'[6] We explore below the different ways in which news organisations are handling the tricky question of just how to manage convergence on the ground.

Merging news operations

The new opportunities for using different technologies in the same space have inevitably required new forms of organisation. Even in multi-media companies, text and VJs rarely met, now they were being asked to work together. Cultural change is difficult in any organisation and has to be managed carefully. The BBC transformed its TV, Radio and Online news operations into a multimedia news-room in 2008 not just as an appropriate modernisation, but also as part of a draconian cuts programme requiring many redundancies. However, it avoided labour unrest, not least through a process of consultation (Lee-Wright, 2010a). 'I am surprised by how much we got away with mixing the two messages', said the Head of Development at BBC News.[7]

A similar transformation of the UK *Telegraph* operation, including an office move and the retraining of journalists, was managed more brutally, as mentioned in Chapter 2. The *Daily Telegraph* and *De Volkskrant*, the Netherlands' leading newspaper, were among the first to use a 'hub and spoke' newsroom arrange-ment, with the desks of departments such as sports, features, foreign news and city news organised around a circular central news desk, where editors sit and organise material across platforms (Trends in Newsrooms, 2008).

At the *Telegraph*, the integration of video was 'spun' as the key feature of the move, but most of the video used on the site came from a deal with television company ITN. Journalists were indeed given some training but few of them used video very often. One said:

> That's sort of the irony really because they had to give us all these training courses and having talked about hubs and pods and things, but in reality say 95% of the job was identical to what it was two years ago
>
> (General reporter, *Telegraph*, interview conducted in 2008)

The major changes, it turned out, were not about multi-skilling at all but more a process of what journalists felt was 'de-skilling', as management demands for higher productivity took their toll. One former *Telegraph* journalist described the transformation:

> Now we sit in the office a lot, you know, we go out a bit but we just don't go out as much. And the internet's making it increasingly difficult because you constantly need copy and you can't write ... and get stories at the same time. In fact it's made it easier in some ways because the stories tend to be shal-lower, which is more words.
>
> (Interview conducted in 2008)

His job at the *Telegraph* had changed, not because of the internet but because of the way he was expected to use the internet. Trinity Mirror's Media Wales launched a multimedia newsroom in the summer of 2008. Once again, it turned out that this much-trumpeted multimedia newsroom was introduced as a cost-cutting exercise, in which reporters were mainly being asked to process material for what had, in the past, been a number of different local editions:

Journalists we spoke with quite reasonably complained of increasing work-loads, a lack of adequate time to produce multimedia web content, the fact they were inadequately trained to do new work such as video journalism, and the likelihood that this would result in the new content being of poor quality.

(Williams, 2010)

Editorial director Alan Edmunds robustly defended Trinity's new way of working and dismissed Williams' research.[8] At the multimedia newsroom's launch, Edmunds defined multi-skilled journalists as those 'who are able to write across all titles' (Stabe, 2008: 24). It is quite hard to see why this would be considered 'multi-skilling'. Learning to write for different outlets and audiences is absolutely standard for any journalism course and is increasingly mandatory for any news journalist but the pressures of the web to keep constantly up to date, and ahead of the competition, have produced additional constraints in many newsrooms. 'Our peak time is twelve o'clock. Twelve until two ... people who are in offices who are at their computers basically looking at the site', says one regional web editor, 'and then from four o'clock until about six o'clock, we have another little teatime peak.'[9]

To meet these deadlines, our research found that journalists are coming in earlier, with shifts starting at six, or seven, meaning some offices are half deserted in the late afternoon, when stories were traditionally being compiled for news-papers' over-night print runs, reflecting the working day of activities being reported. Shifts are also getting longer, as much as 15 hours, servicing both those online demands and the conventional newspaper production schedules. One senior specialist broadcast journalist working online admitted that journalists on a 10-hour shift may easily end up working 12 or 13 hours, but said: 'I would be disappointed if people would complain about it because I'd feel you are getting a much more nourishing experience on that particular day you come in to the office.'[10]

In our research of local and national news organisations (both broadcast and newspapers), we found little evidence of full integration or successful use of multi-skilling. The experience of the *Telegraph* and Trinity Mirror are not un-typical. Video and audio training is often perfunctory, and journalists are so rarely asked to practise their new skills that they rapidly forget what they have learned. With the best will in the world, not all journalists – recruited for their reporting and writing skills – are equally technically ambidextrous, and such skills take time and constant application to develop to a professional level. The online editor at one regional news site confirmed this was a systemic problem:

Although we've trained reporters to do video, they've all got other things to do, they're far too busy, they've forgotten how to do it, and they certainly won't edit it because they haven't got the software. They haven't got the software because the management have said we can't afford the software. So we've wasted a lot of people's time and money training these video journalists.

(Interview conducted in 2007)

In Spain, vertical integration of TV and print companies has offered opportunities for cross-media collaboration that are rare in the UK, where competition laws have precluded much joint operation. Research into national newsroom organisations in Spain (Avilés and Carvajal, 2008) compared those which emphasise multi-skilling with those that go for a more collaborative relationship, in which specialists learn how to work alongside each other, gathering a better understanding of what multi-platform working requires and how they might adapt their work to fit in a multi-platform environment. At *Novotécnica*, journalists were required to produce stories for print, radio, television, the internet and other platforms.

> Newsroom integration was quick: we announced the decision on a Friday and we moved to a single newsroom the next Monday. In this way, we invited everybody to join in, so that no-one would feel excluded from the project. I think it worked out better. Within a short time, the days of monomedia journalists were numbered.
>
> (Editor of *Novotécnica*, quoted in Avilés and Carvajal, 2008: 230)

La Verdad Multimedia, in contrast, had gone for a collaborative model and journalists worked across platform only if they were genuinely interested and showed some skill:

> Convergence is an adventure, in the sense that there are no previous experiences, so most times we are working by intuition. Nobody is able to predict what is going to happen and how the public will react in a few years' time. Therefore, we encourage reporters to make the most out of this multimedia structure they have at their disposal. But we cannot change those operations that already work properly in order to promote instead what it is still uncertain.
>
> (Editor of *La Verdad Multimedia*, quoted in Avilés and Carvajal, 2008: 232)

The researchers noted that those working in the fully integrated newsrooms were far more pressured. Journalists felt that they were not given enough time to do their jobs well and that this was affecting the quality of the final product (Avilés and Carvajal, 2008).

The one local publication in the UK that seemed to have made multi-platform work was the *Manchester Evening News* (MEN), which combined daily and weekly papers, and teamed up with Channel M cable TV and local radio. The newsroom was merged and video and print editors worked together, with a convergence editor making decisions about priorities and platforms. All print journalists were equipped with high-spec mobile phones capable of recording video. But they pretty soon realised that having the equipment does not, by itself, produce good journalism:

> Of course we've made some mistakes, as most people do by trying to ask reporters to do everything. I think that the early view of converging

multimedia journalism – get a reporter to go out with a video camera and a tape recorder and a pen and a camera and tell them that they've got to come back with the whole package by themselves. And of course they can't handle all those things. ... we thought that's what multimedia journalism was and so that gave convergence a bad name.

(Assistant editor, MEN, interview conducted in 2008)

Although TV and print editors worked together, important video stories would be identified in advance and specialist video journalists would be assigned to them. Journalists who specialise in text were trained with videophones to provide brief 'squirts' of illustrative material to use alongside work that was primarily text-based. As the editor explained:

The most success we've had is when we supplied about a dozen of them [print journalists] with high-quality mobile phones. And they just went out there and did bits of video.

(Assistant editor, MEN, interview conducted in 2008)

Video-trained print journalists enjoyed the fact that they could shoot video but were not expected to do so regularly, as one reporter explained: 'Occasionally I'll go out and cover a video story but we've got a TV company to do that, really.'[11]

The cognitive limits of multi-tasking

The reality is that highly skilled jobs require not only intensive training but also intensive practice. Really good video editors are working at their craft every day. Those who do the job only once a month cannot build on their expertise. They are simply not getting enough practice. When print journalists are trained properly to do video, and enjoy it, David Dunkley Gyimah admits that most eventually aspire to television, rather than knocking out a bit of video on the run and hastily constructing a sequence to fit into a text news story.[12]

In previous generations, skilled television craft workers would be offered the opportunity to diversify or progress, ideally to direct programmes. Some of the BBC's top cinematographers took 'attachments' as directors, only to happily return to the craft they knew and loved, unclouded by the conceptual and managerial distractions a director has to negotiate. Film editors made the transition more easily, despite having previously worked in the contemplative quiet of the cutting room, because their skill in welding disparate elements into an effective narrative is closer to the objectives and mindset of a director.

The preference to stick to the job you do best is not simply evidence of 'Luddite' thinking or inflexibility. Even where journalists have eagerly embraced new skills, they are unlikely to be able to exercise them equally well. Managers may argue that multi-skilling – i.e. having several skills – is different from multi-tasking – deploying them simultaneously. But that is precisely what is frequently demanded.

As we have stated, the craft of interviewing requires focus and interpersonal skills that are unquestionably impeded by the interpolation of a camera in place of direct eye contact. Concentration on technical requirements diminishes the time and mind dedicated to the editorial content, all the more so if the journalist is inexperienced and unconfident in the exercise of those techniques. Research suggests that very few people (young or old) can easily do more than one different task at the same time without losing concentration, and quality of output. Psychologists Jason Watson and David Strayer (2010) summarise the findings of numerous researchers looking into the ability of individuals to 'multi task'. They find:

> Nowhere are these limitations more evident than in situations where people attempt to perform two or more attention-demanding tasks concurrently. In these situations, a reciprocal pattern emerges wherein performance on one task prospers at the expense of the other ... Conventional wisdom suggests that people cannot multi-task (or 'time-share') without performance decrements on one or more of the constituent tasks.
>
> (Watson and Strayer, 2010: 479)

Watson and Strayer tested these findings and examine whether it is simply impossible to do two things well at the same time – or merely very difficult. They found that five in a test group of two hundred people did have an exceptional ability to multi-task with no loss of concentration – for instance being able to drive and talk on a mobile phone without the conventional dangers of distraction. That is only 2.5 per cent of the sample. But 'According to cognitive theory, these individuals ought not to exist' says Watson (quoted in Naish, 2010).

This would explain the capacity of multi-camera television directors, such as those who drive the news studios with their multiple inputs, to concentrate on all those inputs, plus live conversations and talkback information, while simultaneously cutting between the various sources. But once you extend a not dissimilar demand to the other 97.5 per cent not so peculiarly gifted, the results will be, to say the least, less good. Under these pressures, workers play safe by imitating standard formats, rather than exploring the dangerous possibilities of difference.

The economic limits of multi-skilling

In the end, the major stimulus for multi-skilling appears to be economic, but the major stumbling block is also turning out to be economic. As the managing editor of Bauer media pointed out, at a Periodical Training Council Meeting in London (June 2010),[13] something that might cost £40 to produce in print will cost £400 to produce in video. Journalists who are required to multi-skill find that their work rate slows down. It is far quicker to produce a text story using a telephone than to source, set up and go out to a shoot – and then come back and edit. Research released by the website Mashable in the summer of 2010 found that investment in online video was starting to diminish:

As far as how media outlets are incorporating digital formats, we're seeing more journalist-authored blogs and publication-run Twitter accounts, but these publications are pulling back from online video (which is typically more expensive to produce), white-label communities and/or forums, and podcasts.

(O'Dell, 2010)

The multi-platform operation at MEN, which brought together video and print specialists in a single newsroom, worked well, but dedicated video teams are expensive. As the recession of 2008 started to bite, profits plummeted from £14.3 million in 2007 to just £500,000 the following year. When the Guardian Media Group sold MEN to Trinity Mirror, Channel M was not part of the deal:

Not even Trinity Mirror wanted Channel M, the UK's highest-profile local TV channel, in with the bargain. It's no coincidence that GMG has moth-balled the channel down to four staff and repeats on loop – the chances of turning a penny in local TV are at least as unlikely as in local newspapers.

(Andrews, 2010)

Even the inflation-proofed BBC, not prey to the travails of its commercial com-petitors' dependency on advertising, cannot replicate its undoubted success in some of its web propositions across all its output. Despite the market dominance of BBC news online – with its peerless access to news video and audio – BBC Vision plans announced in 2007 to make all factual programmes '360° commissions', i.e. multimedia, were quickly dropped, when it was realised that the corporation had neither the editorial staff nor resources to achieve this. An economy-driven change of strategy in 2010 proposed closing half the BBC programme websites. So the up-skilling prospects for journalists in both print and broadcast may be more limited than might be imagined.

There is no doubt that the advertising downturn has had a profound effect on the way in which news organisations have been able to adapt to the technical challenges of the internet. The decision to move towards a far more expensive form of news-gathering (video), at the very moment when advertising revenues collapsed (see Chapter 1), resulted in the worst possible start for multi-platform news. News organisations need, however, to plan for the future as well as managing the present.

The future of multi-skilling

It is clear that new entrants to journalism need to understand how work can be used across platforms (Skillset, 2009). They need to understand how best to collaborate and that means understanding the technical capacity of the medium. All journalists need to understand how to research, link and source material on and off-line, they need an understanding of social media applications and how they work. Text journalists also need to be able to write fast and compelling copy to different lengths and for different audiences, they should have a clear sense of what works in which environment and the place of search engine optimisation. They should also be able to source, and if necessary produce, simple images (both still and in video).

Video journalists may well be required not only to shoot and edit but also to summarise a story in text and work within a text environment as well on TV bulletins and longer features. Radio journalists are already expected to produce written bulletins summarising their stories, and increasingly radio and video are being brought together (although they are very different media). There are a plethora of additional skills that can be added to this basic skill-set and soon there will be many more possibilities.

These necessary adaptations require news journalists to be far more technically adept than in the past. For new entrants to journalism, already used to the environment of the internet, many of these adaptations come easily. However, it would be tragic for the future of high-quality journalism if the assumed requirement for multi-skilling on low-budget news operations starts to militate against the training and employment of the specialists who are preferred on most of the higher quality operations.

The larger operations are taking a cautious approach to multi-skilling. Magazine and newspaper editors still require new entrants who understand the basics of print journalism and long-form writing (Skillset, 2009) and increasingly see the value of using visual specialists for visual work. Former Director of Nations and Regions at the BBC, Pat Loughrey, suggests that three-way skilling (video, text and audio) is not really possible[14] and ITN Managing Editor Robin Elias sees a mixed economy for the foreseeable future, cutting back on the numbers of crews and craft editors, but not expecting reporters to do it all. Nor does he expect specialist crafts to disappear:

> Some of our well established big beasts, if you like, are actually loving the liberation [of being able to edit their material themselves]. Not shooting their own stuff, I think that's a different step, but being able to get back. … and doing a rough edit and then giving it to a craft editor to finalise and make look lovely with mixes and treatments etc.
>
> (Interview conducted in 2008)

The idea that a new standard one-size-fits-all form of multi-skilled multimedia journalist will emerge, fit for all purposes, has not happened in practice and is unlikely to emerge, even as new generations, seeped in computer technologies, come into the industry. No vehicle is equally suitable for all journeys. Journalists generally do need to have a wider skill set than previously, and a familiarity with the audio-visual tools of the trade, but that flexibility needs to be reflected in the ways in which they are deployed, with individuals playing to their strengths, and knowing their limitations and where supplementary effort is needed.

Even though many documentary filmmakers seized the camera with delight when union restrictions were abolished, others committed to forensic interviewing realised camera operation would dilute their particular skill. Similarly, a good print journalist may be able to take an adequate photograph of an interview subject, but they cannot all be Sebastiao Salgados.[15] One indisputable fact is that the victors will be those media outfits that emerge with the most clearly distinct propositions, which can attract sufficient interest to sustain a viable business, whether that is the TV news report with something unique to add, or special interest fan sites such as MirrorFootball.co.uk. To that end, the wise editorial management will continue to employ and support the journalists best able to serve their brand, be it forensic or fluffy, and use the skills that best suit it.

Multi-skilling, it would seem, is at best 'work in progress', with the shape of employment yet to emerge from the technical, economic and organisational transformations ongoing. At worst it is merely a cover story for vicious cutbacks in staffing levels, which tend to result not in the multi-skilling of journalists but rather in their de-skilling. As we have shown, the new technology is capable of enhanced journalism, and cannot be held responsible for its misuse. It is a digital world but, as Brian Winston observes, 'the digital is just an encoding system'.[16]

Notes

1 Interview conducted in 2007.
2 www.theconcentra.org/en/nominees/2010/ (accessed February 2011).
3 www.tiva.tv/ (accessed July 2010).
4 www.viewmagazine.tv/videojournalism/VideoJRevolution.html (accessed December 2010).
5 Ibid.
6 Specialist reporter, national newspaper, interview conducted in 2008.
7 Interview conducted in 2008.
8 Alan Edmunds, quoted by Roy Greenslade in blog, 21 July 2010, www.guardian.co.uk/media/greenslade/2010/jul/21/trinity-mirror-wales (accessed 29 July).
9 Interview conducted in 2007.
10 Interview conducted in 2008.
11 Specialist reporter, MEN, interview conducted in 2008.
12 www.viewmagazine.tv/videojournalism/VideoJRevolution.html (accessed December 2010).
13 PTC training day, Bauer Media, 23 June 2010.
14 Private conversation in 2010.
15 The Brazilian Sebastaio Selgado is one of the most renowned and revered photojournalists and documentary photographers.
16 Brian Winston, speaking at Media Futures conference, Alexandra Palace, London, 20 June 2008.

5 Faster and shallower

Homogenisation, cannibalisation and the death of reporting

Angela Phillips

News journalism has always put a premium on speed. Indeed the definition of news is contained at least partly in the word itself. It is the description, in words, sound or pictures, of something new, and the word carries within it a certain imperative. Many scholars (Galtung and Ruge, 1965; Tunstall, 1971; McQuail, 1994; Harcup and Neill, 2001) have attempted to describe and define the news agenda but, whatever constitutes 'news' content – from stock-market information, or a pre-arranged press conference, to a cup final – two attributes are unchanging. Information, however important, will not become news until it is transmitted to a third party (Gans, 1979: 80), and once it has been transmitted, its value drops (Picard, 2006). Thus the speed of transmission is a factor in the trading of news as a product.

The competition between news sources for first place in the news delivery race has had, and continues to have, a disproportionate effect on how we access news and what news we access. This post from the BuzzMachine blog demonstrates just how fast the news machine is currently spinning:

> anybody happen to be online at around 7pm a week ago sunday? (that's the time the bear stearns deal was first announced).
>
> i was.
>
> within 5 minutes it was everywhere … bloomberg, cnn, msnbc, AND the stock message boards were humming all night long.
>
> news is instantaneous. and since we're learning it is a process rather than a finished product appointment newscasts and dead tree editions are past the borrowed time thing.
>
> (tdc on the BuzzMachine, 27 March 2008 at 3:06 pm)[1]

It would be wrong to suggest, however, as tdc apparently does, that speed is the only factor in play. After the initial 'hit' audiences often want to hear more and they want different versions of the same news (hence the enduring popularity of the Monday sports pages which chew over news which everyone heard on Saturday). If tdc is to get what he apparently wishes for, fast news will grow, pushing out more considered news and the Monday sports pages will be a thing of the past. This chapter considers the impact of speed on the content and diversity of news journalism over time and asks whether speed really is more important to audiences than depth, expertise and proportion. In running faster are we losing site of the broader view?

The speed premium

We all want to know what is going on in the world but the news that matters most has always been information that people can act upon. A death may be only an event to mourn, or it could concern changes in power relations, movements of money, evidence of a crime. The kind of news that can affect markets and governments has always had a special importance. Being first with this kind of news could, literally, make fortunes or save lives. It was the interests of business that created pressure (and opportunities) for an organised news service, and the very first ones were organised for merchants exchanging hand-written newsletters across Europe to provide information about market opportunities (Habermas, 1989; Bakker, 2007). These services were very costly and those using them would not have wished to waste precious space and copying time on information that was not directly relevant.

Printing, which arrived in Europe in the mid-fifteenth century, with the invention of the Guttenberg press, allowed for easier, faster, copying. It didn't take long for printers to recognise the importance of a business audience and to coordinate printing and distribution in order to take advantage of their particular requirement for fast regular news services (Conboy, 2004). But most news still moved only as fast as the fastest means of transport. So information about an event in a far place might take months to find its way back home. Napoleon died in prison on St Helena on 5 May 1821, but news of his death was first published in *The Times* (London) two months later (Hohne quoted in Rantanen, 2009: 12). Nevertheless, it was still news when the information arrived because those at the receiving end had no other, faster, means of finding out the information they sought.

For business, there is always a value in getting news earlier than anyone else. Profits lie in the differences between prices in different locations. Entrepreneurs buy cheap in one location and then sell dear in another. When places were geographically separated, people on the ground were unable to tell whether they were undercutting or being undercut. Nor could they tell whether they could buy the same thing cheaper down the road. Those with access to transport, and to reliable sources of information, had always had knowledge denied to those who stayed in one place and were less well informed (Carey, 1992). So it is not surprising that businesses were the chief subscribers to *The Times* (London), which started a pigeon post in 1837 to speed up the movement of information from European stock markets back to subscribers in London (Bakker, 2007: 7). In America at that time, fast boats went out to meet ships as they entered the harbour. So valuable was early information that, according to one account (Standage, 1998: 145), editors were prepared to pay a substantial premium for news arriving just an hour ahead of its rivals.

The coming of electric telegraph in the mid-nineteenth century (Carey, 1992: 226), changed the way in which newspapers – and capitalism – worked, by altering the relationship between time and space. With the telegraph, those in the cities could collect a wealth of price information without having to move from their offices and they could then bargain for goods on the basis of that knowledge. The telegraph started to equalise the knowledge inequalities associated with geography and replace it with inequalities related to time (ibid: 235). To be involved in business it was necessary to keep up with the fastest. The owners of the telegraph technology were in a very good position to monopolise time-sensitive information and to sell it to the highest bidder (Bakker, 2007: 30).

The internet now allows everyone to compare prices, as long as they know where to look, but in the nineteenth century access was limited, and in Europe governments stepped in to nationalise telegraphy, in order to prevent monopolies in business information developing. In Britain the telegraph was nationalised in 1870, in the USA those trading in news demanded a freeing up of competition as a means to the same end. But, by equalising access to news, the telegraph opened the door to a different kind of monopoly building by news organisations carrying information to the public. We discuss this in more detail below.

Agencies and the birth of vanilla news

Even before the invention of the electronic telegraph, a number of companies had been set up to feed the voracious appetite for business information. The news agencies Havas (founded 1832), Wolff (1849) and Reuters (1865) entered the frame in Paris, Berlin and London, as the first truly global media businesses. Havas started just before the telegraph arrived and Wolff and Reuters initially worked for him (Rantanen, 2009: 30), before starting out on their own as the new technology opened up opportunities. In the USA, Associated Press was established in 1846, by newspaper companies. In the UK the Press Association, a similar cooperative agency specialising in home news, was set up in 1868, jointly owned by British national and provincial newspapers.

The agencies provided a more efficient news service, at a lower price than the haphazard methods of the past, and editors could now rationalise news-gathering (Silberstein-Loeb, 2009). However, they also fundamentally changed the form and content of news coverage and set the scene for greater consolidation, not only of news-gathering but also of news outlets. This 'industrialisation' of the news process relied on the development of two kinds of news: routine and exclusive. Routine news became increasingly the preserve of agencies, producing a vanilla content service available to all subscribers, which newspapers could then spin and colour for their particular audience.

Agencies had to write neutral copy that could then be used by newspapers of any kind or political leaning, and for countries that might be at war with one another. They could not be seen to be biased, if they wanted to retain clients.

Objective reporting as a concept is very much the child of the agencies. They also established a subsidiary group of reporters whose job was to feed journalists with 'bits' of knowledge which they could incorporate in their work. The technology itself brought about a change in the way in which journalists wrote. News sent by telegraph became short and terse because it was paid for by the word. Gone were the old flowery circumlocutions that characterised the earlier period; in came a new form of news speak. Indeed, according to Carey (1992: 231), 'The spareness of the prose and the sheer volume of it allowed news – indeed, forced news – to be treated like a commodity: something that could be transported, measured, reduced and timed.'

Reporters began to take over from journalists. The distinction is subtle, and the words are often taken to be synonymous, but there is a difference. Journalist (from the French word *jour*) means some one who writes about daily events, and there is an expectation that a writer maintains some responsibility for the authorship of their work. Reporters are people who record and transmit facts, which can be collated and shaped by others. Their responsibility is to check the evidence and tell what they see/hear. They were no longer always responsible for writing their stories, merely for providing the information with which the stories could be reconstituted. A new category of news worker emerged: the sub (or copy) editor whose job was to shape and rewrite copy and add headlines.

Routine news spewed out into newsrooms in the form of agency news-wire machines which rattled and clicked, providing an endless stream of news reports which then needed to be read, organised and either passed on or 'spiked' by copy tasters – the news 'gate-keepers' (Gans, 1979) – who decided what was likely to make it into the paper. Agency copy would be handed over to the reporters who could follow up with their own additional calls. The information was fed into every newsroom but it was taken apart and put together again by other journalists who added detail and inflection.

It was the agencies themselves that created the first monopolies, by establishing a cartel and dividing the world up into segments, so that each could supply news for its clients without competition (Herman and McChesney, 1997: 12). They provided a steady stream of information, produced according to methods that were agreed and endorsed by the newspapers that either owned or contracted them. It is not possible to measure the amount of shared material used by newspapers in the mid-nineteenth century, but it was likely to have been considerable, given the difficulties (and therefore expense) of travel. The agencies improved the flow of basic information across the world, but they also made services more similar to one another – the first step towards the system we have today, in which most major news organisations provide a similar range of stories (Davies, 2008). In the fifty years following the establishment of the agencies, and the electric telegraph, printing processes also changed. Presses became more efficient, but also more expensive, squeezing out smaller, and often more radical, voices in favour of the bigger and more establishment ones (Curran and Seaton, 2009: 27).

Making 'instant' news

Anthony Smith said of the invention of the telegraph: 'Henceforth daily journalism operated within a new tense ... of the instantaneous present' (Smith, 1978: 167). Well not exactly. Information could be transferred from telegraph office to individual subscribers but, in order to get out to the world, it was still necessary to print it onto paper and distribute it (using horse-drawn transport and trains). The instantaneous present had to wait until 1884, when some enterprising telegraph operators pre-empted by several decades the arrival of radio sports broadcasting. One watched a baseball game in Chattanooga and telegraphed each move to his colleagues, in a hired hall in Nashville. He then relayed the information to the audience and re-enacted each move using name cards on a simulated field. The audience, according to a contemporary account, 'was wrought up to a very high pitch of excitement' (Marvin, 1990: 60) Where enthusiasm goes, enterprise is never far behind, watched over by big business, ever hungry for a money spinning idea. Within three years, the Cleveland telephone company was luring subscribers with the promise of a baseball score service, not unlike the text information offered to fans on their mobile phones today (ibid).

Even with the arrival of radio, and then television, the instantaneous present required organising. Early radio and TV news events had in common the fact that they were predictable, and allowed the cumbersome technologies of the time to be trundled into place and hooked up to existing transmission equipment, so that recordings could be made. Where possible, news came to the news organisation under its own steam, in the form of interviewees and presenters. Organisations responded by synchronising news events to tie in with artificially produced 'deadlines' and organised bulletins (Murdock, 1974: 210; Bakker, 2007: 21). For those who were listening or watching, news programmes appeared to provide an immediacy that newspapers couldn't rival, slowed down as they were by the time it took to set up pages, print and distribute the final product. In reality, broadcast news was managed news. News time became TV time.

Where the telegraph allowed for the synchronisation of news supply, radio, and then television, created the synchronisation of news-gathering and distribution and the creation of a whole industry to organise this synchronisation: public relations. Public relations specialists catered to the need for television to have visual events and readily available commentators to help them create the illusion of spontaneous, instantaneous news (Bakker, 2007: 21). Politicians and other people with sufficient clout and organisation could now speak directly to the people, via a TV channel. A decisive change had taken place in the relationship between journalists and their sources (Schlesinger, 1978). Press offices started to take charge of the relationship between organisations of any size and the press. The number of people employed in public relations rocketed. Between 1979 and 1998 the corporate PR sector increased eleven fold (Davis, 2003: 30):

41% of press articles contain PR materials which play an agenda-setting role or where PR material makes up the bulk of the story. As we have suggested, this is a conservative, baseline figure. If we add those stories in which the involvement of PR seems likely but could not be verified, we find that a majority of stories (54% of print stories) are informed by PR.

(J. Lewis et al., 2008: 20)

What started as a service to television and radio became a way of managing, channelling and controlling the news flow. As television took centre stage in the delivery of news to people across the developed world, press and public relations professionals became the mediators and their messages helped to standardise yet further the kinds of knowledge that are presumed to be news (Schlesinger, 1978). Far from diversifying news, the addition of television as a news source tended to speed up the move towards oligarchy, with an every decreasing number of organisations involved in news delivery. TV news was expensive to produce. It required investment in technology, as well as large numbers of people, most of whom were not engaged directly in journalism. In the early days, 'spectrum scarcity' meant that there was not room for more than a handful of channels. Only very large organisations, or organisations with state support, could afford even to enter the market. The inevitable oligopolies were controlled by legislation to ensure that they did not abuse their position in relation to the distribution of news (see Chapter 3), but the legislation didn't stretch to cover the other media which broadcasting also impacted.

Running in TV time

In the USA, the combination of telegraph and geographically dispersed centres had already encouraged the growth of a regionally based press, fed by highly lucrative local advertising. The arrival of television as a mass-market medium, did not compete directly for the same advertising, but it did erode audiences. Evening newspaper circulations in the USA were particularly badly hit. Readership was 34 million in 1955; it peaked in 1973 and then dropped rapidly, as cable TV spread in the 1970s. By 2000 it was down to only 9 million (Newspaper Association of America, 2009). Many provincial newspapers continued to provide news much as they had always done – but to a smaller audience (see Chapter 1).

Paradoxically, even as circulation stagnated, family-owned newspapers grew fat on easily available local advertising. They were then gradually gobbled up, and consolidated, by companies more concerned with profit than with local democracy. The remaining papers gradually became the monopoly suppliers of local advertising – and news. Similar consolidation was taking place in the maturing TV industry. The proliferation of voices necessary for a healthy functioning democracy (Herman and McChesney, 1997) was eroding and, by the 1990s, 98 per cent of US cities and towns had only one newspaper (or none at all). Eighty per cent were no longer independent, but were owned by chains who could cut costs by syndicating news and features, further eroding diversity (Bagdikian, 1992: 119; Baker, 1994).

In Europe, this tendency towards monopoly was ameliorated by a variety of different pressures acting within the journalism field. In southern Europe (and the UK), serious news has never been wholly commercial, and has often been loss-making. It has, at least partly, been a vehicle for social and political advancement and debate, subsidised by political parties, or cross-subsidised by other businesses, or by wealthy proprietors with an interest in maintaining their position at the more autonomous end of the journalism field, where they might hope to influence governments. Times Newspapers, for example, made losses in five of the years between 1995 and 2004, and was propped up by the substantial profits of the *Sun* newspapers (Lewis *et al.*, 2008: 8). In Scandinavian countries there has been a history of direct or indirect government subsidy to ensure diversity of news supply (Hallin and Mancini, 2004). Current policy in Sweden, for example, subsidises the 'second' newspaper in any town (Curran and Seaton, 2009: 377). For more on this, see Chapter 1, but the overall impact of instant TV news was to increase competitive pressures, and decrease the number of newspapers available.

Two-speed news

Since the dawn of the agencies, daily newspapers ran yesterday's 'vanilla' news, inflected to appeal to their own readers. Readers were loyal as long as all the news arrived at the same time. But, once TV became established, yesterday's news seemed old, because everyone had already seen or heard it the previous evening. There was some scope for tweaking late front-page news, but if they didn't want to look stale on the breakfast tables, print journalists needed to find a new way to be needed.

One big advantage of print was that news-gathering required no technology heavier than a notebook and pen, or a lightweight camera, and printing methods were improving so that pictures (particularly in weekend supplements) were becoming more than just smudges between the lines. It was photojournalists and print reporters, for example, who provided some of the most memorable documentation of the Vietnam War. Their equipment was light, they could work alone and go where the soldiers went, providing pictures for the weekend papers, while the evening TV news mostly had to make do with maps. In 1967 even Lord King, proprietor of the British, mass-market, popular tabloid, the *Daily Mirror*, proclaimed: 'Popular newspapers will follow their present course of becoming increasingly intelligent and less ideological' (Engel, 1996: 193).

These publications had always relied heavily on the news agencies for routine information; now they could maintain relevance and differentiation from other news sources, with a steady throughput of exclusive material. Indeed the idea of journalists as investigators, rather than merely reporters, probably reached its zenith in this period, after the launch of TV, but before the spread of cable. In the USA, the *Washington Post*'s Watergate investigation was credited with bringing down President Nixon, and the creation in the UK of *The Sunday Times* 'Insight' team produced a string of investigations (including the uncovering of the 'Thalidomide' scandal[2] in September 1972) many of which took months, and many people, to produce (Melvern, 1986: 96).

Editors did other things too. There was a massive increase in 'life style' pages, which were rather more popular with the advertisers than pictures from the battlefront, and brought with them a new female readership.

So, in the environment that emerged in response to the growing centrality of television as a news medium, we now had two-speed news: breaking news, much of it PR driven – referred to as 'stop-watch' journalism by Schlesinger (1978) – and the slower, often deeper news produced by newspapers and magazine programmes, as well as specialist and 'life style' news. Much of this was material that would not make it onto the tightly organised evening bulletins, and it was often produced by freelance contributors. This differentiation allowed media to co-exist, providing differentiated audiences for the growth of advertising.

Global companies and conglomerates moved into the news business, seeing chances for amalgamation and snapping up (and often closing) businesses in order to consolidate advertising income. At this point the entry into the UK market of Rupert Murdoch's 'Soaraway *Sun*' in 1969 had the effect of pushing UK print news media further towards what Bourdieu (2005) refers to as the 'heteronomous pole' within the field. Murdoch told the new *Sun* staff that the paper was going to provide 'Sex, sport and contests' (Engel, 1996: 252). This it did, fast overtaking the more serious, popular tabloid – the *Mirror* – in terms of readership. News International had opted out of the basic newspaper compact that assumed news comes first and entertainment is merely the icing on the cake. With the *Sun*, Rupert Murdoch had turned the formula on its head. He was selling entertainment with a little bit of news mixed in – and people liked it.

Serious newspapers maintained some degree of autonomy from the market until News International took over *The Times* and *The Sunday Times* in 1981, pushing them in a far more commercial direction. Within two years the investigative 'Insight' team was abolished (Melvern, 1986: 97). Hugo Young, then political columnist for *The Sunday Times*, wrote of the Murdoch takeover: 'The investigative tradition, which depends on detachment and irreverence as well as professional competence, has been all but abandoned' (Davies, 2008: 303).

The two-speed formula was still in place at *The Times*, but 'life-style' journalism was proliferating, spilling over into special supplements, tempting new readers, and with them new advertisers. Competing proprietors were forced to take notice as *The Times*' circulation soared (helped by price cuts and new printing technology). By the end of the decade, British newspapers had been redesigned, bringing in more pictures, bigger headlines and lighter stories. Circulations in the UK began to creep up. This move towards commercialism within the newspaper field provides the background to the next major technical shift: the arrival of digital communications (Franklin, 2009).

Going digital

The 'instantaneous present' finally arrived with digital. It was now genuinely possible to 'be there' as news was breaking and transmit it instantly, rather than 'producing' it on location or bringing the news into the studio to record it. Radio news now operated with regular hourly updates and 24-hour TV news came into its own but, barring the occasional live news events that demanded continuous coverage, for the most part, bulletins supplied brief bursts of information, that were recycled and updated every hour. As Lewis and Cushion found:

> The rush to be seen covering more breaking news stories combines the frenetic with the banal. It takes place largely in the studio, as routine stories delivered by news agencies and releases are hastily processed, broadcast and tagged as breaking news. Unlike its predecessor, the 'scoop' or the 'exclusive', breaking news has become a kind of breathless routine, a form of predictable punctuation marking out a news day.
>
> (Lewis and Cushion, 2009: 316)

Digital was also changing newspapers. By the mid-1980s, the speed of production meant that whole newspapers could be produced in a matter of hours. Newspapers still came out with news that everyone had seen the evening before, but digital drove everything faster – not because it had to be faster (or even because there was any premium in being faster), but because it could be faster. Formerly the features had been laid out and typeset days before the news sections. Now it was possible to turn around a feature at the same time as the news.

Depth requires time but, increasingly, a thoughtful feature, produced three days after the event, started to look stale. The division between spot news, and in-depth reporting, began to collapse. Features pages started to fill up with opinion pieces (often written by freelance journalists), which could be commissioned and then written between the morning news meetings and the early evening feature deadlines. Whole pages could be cleared, late in the day, to make room for a big breaking story. Journalists could watch the evening news and rewrite stories to incorporate quotes from TV interviews.

It was also now easier than ever to steal an exclusive story from another news outlet. The early editions of rival newspapers would be read hot off the press. Anything really important could be shamelessly rewritten and fitted into the pages. Editors with a good exclusive took to holding back for their own late editions, to be sure that they could still dominate the news stands for the whole of the following day. Newspapers, forever watching their rivals and desperate to be seen to be ahead (or at least up in the front row), were running faster and working harder.

Serious newspapers in the UK maintained, or even increased, circulations through the 1980s and 1990s and several new national newspapers, including the *Independent*, entered the market. In the following decade *The Times* doubled its circulation (by cutting its cover price) and the *Guardian* dipped but then strengthened again (Franklin, 2008a: 8). The number of pages in each edition increased (Franklin, 1997: 90), paid for by buoyant advertising on the back of life-style features. There were complaints of 'dumbing down' from those who found it hard to understand why personal stories should find their way into newspapers which had, previously, reported only the lives of important people (Franklin, 1997). Others saw this as a welcome adjustment and democratisation (Fiske, 1992; Phillips, 2007), which opened them up to new readers.

By the end of the 1990s, the celebrity, sex and scandal formula that had made tabloids so popular could now be found on TV, and that was having an impact on the popular dailies, but serious newspapers looked in reasonably good shape (outside the USA, where circulations across the board were in decline). They had found a formula for existence, alongside the instant broadcast news. Circulations in this sector were holding up and advertising was buoyant. In the UK, advertising accounted for some 60 per cent of daily paper revenue in the mid-1980s (Meech, 2008: 236). In the USA, advertising revenue accounted for 80 per cent of news-paper revenue as late as 2007.

News was still produced on a daily cycle, relying on a mix of agency copy, public relations hand-outs (now delivered by fax rather than by mail), other media and the work of their own staff to follow up routine stories, consider specific 'angles' and audiences, and ferret out the exclusives on which reputations (of individuals and publications) depend. The amount of comment material had risen exponentially, facilitated by faster computerised printing processes, and encour-aged by competitive pressure to ensure that, in every edition, comment reflected the fast-moving news agenda of the day. The number of political columnists, virtually unknown in the 1970s, had ballooned to around 600 a month by 1998 (McNair, 2000).

This could have been an opportunity for democratisation and diversification – allowing non-journalists such as academics to write for newspapers. However, the acute deadline pressure and the need for writers to fit into the style of the newspaper meant that the space was increasingly taken by specialist journalists, groomed to write for the comment pages (Wilby, 2006). Speed and style outweighed knowledge and experience.

News cycles faster

It was against this background that news was confronted by the challenge of the internet. The delicate balance between electronic and print media, which allowed each to take its share of audience attention, was thrown into disarray, when newspapers found themselves sharing a platform with radio and television and operating within the same time frame. Digital had dragged video into the 'instantaneous present'. The internet had the same effect on the news-papers. To start with, newspapers merely played with the new medium. They started by uploading the print edition of the newspaper onto their websites, and they enjoyed the benefits the web and digital technology provided for better research:

I mean if you're out on the road you'll see the likes of myself sitting there on the mobile phone to the researcher while I'm on the internet doing my own research. I'll take a laptop but that will get me the wires, it will get me emails, somebody can send me the Electoral Registers on there, and then I can cut and paste it [the result] into my satnav and it will take me there in my car. It's wonderfully Batman.

(General reporter, national newspaper, interview conducted in 2008)

In the USA some regional newspapers were experimenting with writing directly onto the webpages, and using the possibilities that the internet offers for adding photo galleries and video (see Chapter 4). Newspaper journalists were used to spending hours on the phone to contacts, going out to meet people, attending press conferences and then writing two or three pieces a day. The internet made research easier and more efficient and gave journalists access to material that, in the past, would have taken days or weeks to find.

This could have been the opportunity for a renaissance in investigative journalism. Instead, the advantages the web offer for more depth were squandered in the desire for more speed. Print journalists joined what Schlesinger (1978: 48–49) described as the 'stop-watch culture' of TV.

The purchase of the *Telegraph* newspapers by the Barclay brothers in 2004 had a similarly electrifying effect on the field as the takeover of *The Times* had had in the 1980s. The Barclays decided to take these august, conservative newspapers, with a reputation for solid, thorough reporting, and turn them into a 24-hour, web-first, news operation, adding video through a tie-in with Independent Television News (ITN).

The *Telegraph*'s web readership rocketed overnight. Soon the other newspapers felt obliged to follow suit by going 'web first'. Now text journalists could 'be there' and get their thoughts to the public just as quickly (often more quickly) than video journalists. Soon they were adding Twitter feeds, fed directly onto their website, usually producing a kind of inane and shapeless babble of unedited material. The effect of all this on news reporting was not at first recognised, in the excitement of realising that newspapers could beat TV and radio in the one place where they had always had the advantage: speed.

News journalists found themselves caught up in what often felt like a hamster wheel. The age of the 24-hour news cycle has created a medium that privileges immediacy over more traditional forms of reflection (Lewis and Cushion, 2009: 305). Research by Lewis *et al.* (2008) found that the average daily output of stories among journalists canvassed was 4.5. One young reporter said he had written thirteen stories the previous day:

We do these stories in 15 minutes. I mean we've got so much work now. You're given six or seven stories a day, you don't have time to do much with them. But I added a bit at the end, you know, I try and put a bit of context.

(Reporter, national newspaper, interview conducted in 2008)

The job of the copy-taster changed:

> Nowadays what they [copy-tasters] spend most of their time doing is looking
> at other newspapers' websites, like the *Daily Mail* website, and the *Daily Mail*
> website's looking at our website, and the number of times we're told to look
> at this and it's just come from the *Daily Mail* website, and they look at *The
> Times* website and they're – it used to be they just looked at the 'wires'
> (agencies) but now I reckon they spend just as much time looking at other
> people's websites.
>
> (Reporter, national newspaper, interview conducted in 2008)

It was no longer just a question of nervously watching rival publications just to
ensure that you hadn't missed anything. Now editors were reading stories the
minute they went up on other sites and asking reporters to copy them. The odd
paragraph might be re-arranged and maybe an extra phone call would be made.
The focus on keeping up with what other publications were doing began to get in
the way of their own reporting.

> There are times when you could have done something the day before and
> things have even been filed, and then it's been decided that that won't go in
> the paper, and then the next day it's in other papers. So you're told to write
> a story based on what another paper's written about something that could
> have gone in our paper the same day.
>
> (Reporter, national newspaper, interview conducted in 2008)

Research produced in 2008 found that 30 per cent of articles from a British
newspaper sample came entirely from 'wires or other media' and a further
19 per cent came 'mainly from wires or other media' (Lewis *et al.*, 2008: 15). In
our research the same year this cannibalistic culture was more entrenched at one
newspaper (the *Telegraph*) than at other newspapers investigated. Reporters were
questioned in detail about the source of recent stories. Nearly one third of the
Telegraph stories originated in other media, and only a handful resulted from a
direct tip-off. Of a similar number of randomly selected *Guardian* articles, only one
originated from another newspaper and more than half were original stories.
(The interviews were carried out in 2008 before the *Guardian* went entirely to 'web
first'). The impact of a news-desk driven culture and radically increased speed of
production was clearly taking its toll. Reporters found ways of coping by making
use of more PR material:

> [W]hat we really rely on now is people just emailing us with comment. You
> know, people who are ahead of the game and they know judgements are
> coming and it helps now when someone says: 'By the way, if you're doing
> this story today this is a comment from an analyst'.
>
> (Specialist reporter, national newspaper, interview conducted in 2008)

Throwing reporters in at the deep end is not unusual in journalism. General reporters routinely cover stories about which they have little background knowledge. Part of their training is aimed at learning where to find the person who does know. But they are increasingly tied to their computers, performing what Nick Davies (2008: 60) refers to as 'churnalism'. German research into the re-use of copy from other media found that the youngest journalists were twice as likely as their older colleagues to use other media as the major source for story ideas (Reinemann, 2004).

Homogenising the news

The tendency of the news media to move towards concentration and homogeneity has long been a subject of scholarly debate (Bourdieu, 2005; Powell and DiMaggio, 1991; Herman and McChesney, 1997). Bourdieu, for example, pointed to the 'paradox' that, as the number of different news outlets grows, so the competition for the biggest audience means that each of them has a tendency to copy the leader:

> Competition, which is always said to be the precondition of freedom, has the effect, in the fields of cultural production, of producing uniformity … [It] tends not to differentiate them but to bring them together. They steal each other's front page stories, editorials and subjects.
>
> (Bourdieu, 2005: 44).

Our research suggests that 24-hour news coverage and the move to the internet was speeding the tendency towards concentration. Journalists complained that it was increasingly difficult to do original reporting. There was a sense that everyone who was not at a computer was probably not working. Even an experienced senior reporter at one of the national newspapers was interrupted several times, during a one-hour interview, by agitated texts and messages from the news desk at the same paper, wanting to know where he was. Another experienced general reporter, also on this newspaper, said that he had recently been 'let out' for ten minutes to go down to reception and interview a woman who had just travelled for four hours from the depths of the country to tell her story. He wasn't even given the time to buy her a cup of tea. On television, Lewis and Cushion found similarly: 'The focus on breaking news means, in practice, less independent journalism, fewer stories on location and a more limited range of sources informing the news' (2009: 316).

In the year after the start of the 2008 recession, the US advertising market declined by 18 per cent (Newspaper Association of America, 2009). The much hoped for move of advertising from print to web was delayed (or may have been still-born). In the USA, 11 per cent of journalists' jobs disappeared in 2008 and, as journalists jobs are lost, those who remain at their desks are being required to work even faster. Frank Schirrmacher, the publisher of the second-biggest German newspaper, *Frankfurter Allgemeine Zeitung* (FAZ), said in an interview in the *Guardian* blog, PDA:

Today, the factors that are important in journalism are still speed and automisation – factors, by the way, that were responsible for starting the financial crisis. Now, it makes a big difference if you have 30 seconds to make a decision or a tenth of a second. The path we face in journalism is one in which there are fewer humans and more machines – and if you look at all the inaccurate news reports already, that is grotesque.

(Schirrmacher, 2009)

The speed and ferocity of the 2008 recession could not have come at a worse time. News organisations had been happy to play with the new medium while advertising was buoyant. The assumption was simple: build an audience and the advertising will come and fund it. No one had factored in the possibility that advertising would disappear leaving news organisations high and dry (see Chapter 1). The response to the sudden and precipitous loss of income has been to lay-off journalists, just at the very moment when more people than ever before were needed to feed the hungry acres of internet sites. The response has been a massive effort of 'rationalisation', wrapped up in debates about the advantages of 'multi-skilling' (see Chapter 4). Far from multi-skilling, the new regime is de-skilling journalists.

We don't go out because there's not enough of us to fill all the holes in the website and the paper so it just becomes a sort of vicious circle I think. The sources become ever fewer sources and more and more outlets for them ... Everyone, that's every newspaper, every newspaper would be like that.

(Junior reporter, national newspaper, interview conducted in 2008)

It has been suggested that all this destruction is not a problem because, as old newspapers die, alternative news sources are rising to take their place. The assumption has been that the web would counteract the growing concentration of news ownership and the homogeneity of the news would break down and a multitude of voices would be heard and then amplified (Rheingold, 1994). In fact the reverse has been the case. Research by Joanna Redden and Tamara Witschge (2010) investigated stories online and in newspapers across a number of different official and unofficial sites, and found that there was little difference in subject matter between them. Online news sources did not appear to be creating their own 'news agenda'; rather they were borrowing from mainstream news organisations. Research from Pew found similar results:

More than 99% of the stories linked to in blogs came from legacy outlets such as newspapers and broadcast networks. And just four – the BBC, CNN, the *New York Times* and the *Washington Post* – accounted for fully 80% of all links.

(Pew Project for Excellence in Journalism, 2010c)

The problem lies in the fact that it is the most popular sites that always rise to the top of the search engines. A system that always selects information of mass appeal, above information of niche appeal, will inevitably narrow rather than diversifying information (Hindman, 2009). Even the more established aggregators and web-only news-sites such as the *Huffington Post* and *PoliticsHome* are showing few signs of being able to replace the news-gathering of the old news media (see Chapter 1). The problem is partly one of scale. In 2008, the *Huffington Post* had 46 full-time employees (and a large number of enthusiasts who contributed material unpaid). The *New York Times* had fifty times as many (Alterman, 2008). One alternative suggested (see Chapter 1) is 'trust funded' websites that can specialise in the investigative reporting that 'Old Media' are abandoning in the scramble to be first with whatever is the popular news of the moment. One such is *ProPublica* which, in its statement of aims, attests to the problem it is seeking to solve:[3]

> It is true that the number and variety of publishing platforms is exploding in the Internet age. But very few of these entities are engaged in original reporting. In short, we face a situation in which sources of opinion are proliferating, but sources of facts on which those opinions are based are shrinking. The former phenomenon is almost certainly, on balance, a societal good; the latter is surely a problem.

When news organisations banded together to fund news agencies, so that they could rationalise news production of the most routine (or difficult to reach) stories, they still used their considerable staff to add to the news pool. The aggregators such as Google News (one of the most popular news sites) are making use of the combined efforts of the newspapers and the agencies, but they are themselves adding very little indeed to the news pool in terms of original reporting. Since they depend for their existence on the free circulation of material that has been paid for elsewhere, they are in fact undermining the funding base of the very organisations they depend upon for that material. Janine Gibson, director of digital content of the *Guardian*, is critical of the contribution made by Google:

> Google awards the latest – not the original – it awards quick hitters not originators. They deny it and say their algorithms take into consideration originality. But, in the end, do they really care about who originates stories? It is a distributor – unlicensed – it has no remit to benefit its suppliers. It is not compelled to maintain content.
>
> (Gibson, interview conducted in 2010)

Where people in the early nineteenth century were disenfranchised by their distance from sources of information, people in the twenty-first century are in danger of being disenfranchised by lack of time (or the ability to pay for time) to search for the kinds of information that news organisations bring together, organise and analyse. Much of the necessary information may indeed be 'out there' on the web but the time involved in accessing it is still considerable. While some people may well enjoy spending their days trawling websites for information, the majority still access news via 'newscasts' (Ofcom, 2007) and of those accessing news on the web the majority still make use of websites produced and (at this point) subsidised either by 'dead tree' publications, news agencies, TV or, in the UK, the BBC licence fee payer (House of Lords, 2008).

Deeper and slower

The electric telegraph didn't destroy the press (as some had predicted), but it did shift the balance away from individual voices and small organisations towards business and large organisations. The broadcast media, with their high cost of entry and narrow news agenda, further consolidated news, but left open opportunities for organisations interested in investigation and commentary. The internet could be a means of increasing diversity and improving the depth of reporting rather than chasing the great god of speed.

News organisations that find their own stories and release them in their own good time are still capable of making real contributions to democratic debate, which resonate far beyond the momentary high of hitting the top slot on Google for an hour. While *Guardian* journalists were busy tweeting from the Globalisation protests in April 2009, a man died. A tweet mentioned it in passing.[4] It was reported in the newspaper the following day. A week later a video emerged, taken by a member of the public. It was this video that established what had really happened. It wasn't available instantly, its authenticity was checked and it was published on the website in the fullness of time. The fact that it took a week to emerge did not in any way impair the information it contained, nor the ensuing debate on police tactics in demonstrations. The use of new technology does not have to be about doing things faster. It can provide opportunities for doing things better.

In early 2009, the *Daily Telegraph* purchased a computer disc containing details of expenses claimed by members of parliament; it did not simply publish 'web first'. Instead, it used old fashioned 'slow news' techniques, using up to 25 reporters to trawl through the material and drip feed the information out via the newspaper, so that no other publication or news outlet could get hold of it earlier. For the whole period of the campaign the *Telegraph* led with new information taken from its treasure trove of facts. Within weeks, the Speaker of the House had tendered his resignation and the entire British political class was in uproar. The story raised the circulation of the paper by 14 per cent on some days (Wilby, 2009), demonstrating that readers are willing to pay for news which is not just the same old stuff recycled. Speed undoubtedly has an important place in news reporting but, when time and research is invested in news, the dividends are far greater – for the organisations involved as well as for democracy.

The worry is that the *Telegraph* scoop may be a one-off – a last blast for old, slower news media; and the *Guardian* video will not be seen as an argument for slowing down and thinking, merely as a triumph of new technology. On the other hand, the current collapse in advertising revenue could hasten the start of a rational debate about a viable future for real, in-depth news-gathering. Emily Bell, at the time *Guardian* director of digital content, and long-time enthusiast for web journalism, had this to say in her column (Bell, 2009c): 'Perhaps the biggest mistake of the past 10 years has been the idea that digitisation is an invitation to do more, when it is in fact an opportunity to do less, but better.' She went on:

> The light at the end of the tunnel is the possibility that, when all of the current attrition is over, there will still be enough revenue from advertising to support the very best of the content. Shrinkage is the new black, even the stylish Lygo can see that. The war against too much stuff has officially begun. The challenge is to make sure we are left, when the gloom lifts, with the right stuff.
>
> (Bell, 2009c)

If news organisations are to survive they will need to invest in this kind of 'slow news', which cannot simply be skimmed and recycled for free. The *Guardian* policy seems to be turning in this direction. Janine Gibson, editor of *Guardian online*, said:

> We have stopped rewriting PA copy unless we are adding value. If it is 400 words that the agency has done then we just publish it. Having someone in the office rewriting PA isn't worthwhile – its more a question of what do we have to add to it.
>
> (Gibson, interview conducted in 2010)

A look at the newspaper reveals that Press Association stories are now used with the Press Association byline (presumably unedited). The *Daily Mirror*, with a very different audience and a very different place at the popular end of the field, is also moving carefully down the path of creating its own brand and building its own audience, rather than merely 'following the leader':

> Since launching, only 15 per cent of *MirrorFootball*'s traffic comes from search engines and 60 per cent of its online audience comes from within the UK. Only 9 per cent of 3am.co.uk's traffic is driven by search; while UK visitors constitute 65 per cent of its audience.
>
> (Oliver, 2009)

The internet provides exciting possibilities for diversity, but only if news organisations find some way of resisting the death pull towards monopoly and increasing homogeneity.

In a time-pressured world, in which few people really have the time to source their own news, journalists and news organisations must continue to have a role. It seems unarguable that a well resourced newsroom is better able than an individual blogger to afford the cost of employing journalists who can spend time verifying information and following up sources. If the news base is to be broadened, it has to be possible for a mixture of large and small organisations to co-exist because, without companies sufficiently well funded to put 12 journalists onto a single story in order to find out what really happened, all news organisations, and the public, will be the poorer.

Notes

1 www.buzzmachine.com/2008/03/27/the-news-will-find-us/#comment-372167 (accessed December 2010).
2 Thalidomide was a drug prescribed to pregnant women which resulted in their children being born with missing limbs.
3 www.propublica.org/about/ (accessed February 2011).
4 Paul Lewis via Twitter at 4/1/2009, 22:58:47, http://twitter.com/paul–lewis/status/ 1434743855 (accessed December 2010).

6   The 'tyranny' of technology

Tamara Witschge

This chapter discusses how the development of new media technologies is appropriated in the discourse on the future of news. New media are mythologised as the answer to dwindling audience figures, and an idealised notion of new media is proffered, as a way to put into effect changes in news production and to solve a myriad of problems that are seen as a threat to the future of news.

This discourse presents new media as the solution to the problems in journalism, and creates a situation in which there is very little ground for working journalists to challenge the introduction of new technologies and their consequences for the practice of journalism. Most working journalists themselves feel trapped by technology, a situation that forecloses any critical debate on forms of implementation.

By critically interrogating this discourse I aim to show how this coupling of concepts operates on a discursive level, producing an environment in which managers and editors have been able to employ a number of (mostly economically motivated) changes while encountering very little resistance from the people affected by them. Also, with the employment of this discourse a very specific type of role has been attributed to the audience in the news process. In this chapter, I focus on the role new technologies play in the changing news environment on the output side (presentation and dissemination), not so much their role in the production of the news (see Chapter 4 for the changing news production practices as result of multi-platform working). The next chapter will further consider the changes in audience participation through new media technologies.

Technological determinism

Analysing the way in which journalists report on new media technologies, Curran found that they display a 'taken-for-granted belief' that 'new technology would prevail, and determine outcomes' (Curran, 2010: 31). Örnebring, when describing the role of new media within journalism practice, found a similar rhetoric on the role of new media technology:

> When asked to reflect upon the changes taking place within their profession and the world of news media in general, journalists frequently invoke technology as a self-sufficient explanatory factor. Journalists in general seem to

view technology and technological development as inevitable, impersonal forces that directly cause many of the changes taking place within journalism. ... In the minds of journalists, many if not most of the changes taking place in contemporary journalism are essentially *technology driven*.

(Örnebring, 2010: 58, emphasis in original)

Our interviews show a very similar result. However, it is not just technology that is discussed in such deterministic terms; of particular force is its connection to the declining (and fragmenting) audience. New media technologies are seen as *the* way to respond (and find their way back to) the changing audience. Moreover, technology is presented as the *only* way out of what is perceived as a 'crisis' in journalism. Different, very powerful, arguments underlie the implementation of new media technology. First, there is an imminent threat to journalism – or, as an article by the *Guardian*'s editor, Alan Rusbridger (2009: 19), phrased it: there is a 'wolf ... to be kept from the door'. Second, the audiences are going online (and journalists need to chase them). Third, moving into new platforms and 'embracing' new media technologies are the only ways to follow the audiences.

Örnebring suggests that concepts such as 'commercialisation', 'professional socialisation' and 'organisational structure', used by academics to explain the changes in the field of journalism, are too 'abstract' and thus journalists make sense of the changes in their everyday work environment by focusing on factors such as new media technologies, which have become ubiquitous (Örnebring, 2010: 58). I would like to suggest another factor. The great managerial 'campaign' to implement organisational change in the newsrooms has successfully coupled technology to progress, and moreover expressed it as the only way to survive, in the industry. In this way, economically motivated reorganisations have been employed without much resistance. My aim is not to judge the validity of the arguments used in this discourse, but rather to examine how this discourse functions and has created an environment where, for journalists and editors alike, 'possibly everything's changing'.[1]

The audience that is no more

In the debate on the challenges that face journalists and the future of news, one of the main factors that constantly recurs is the changing audience, in particular the decline in audience figures. One of the main concerns in both academic debates and the debate held within the news industry, it is also one of the main issues raised by our interviewees. There is no doubt that people are using media in different ways and certain news outlets face considerable changes in consumption. Of note, however, is the remarkable resilience of traditional news organisations in maintaining their audiences for news. The vast majority of UK adults still turn to the TV for news: in 2007, 67 per cent of adults; compared to a mere 6 per cent that listed the internet as their main source of news (Ofcom, 2007). Of course, TV itself was a new, game-changing technology half a century ago, and newspapers had to adapt to its entry into the news field (see Chapter 4). Nevertheless even TV executives regard the relative decline in audience figures with a rather dramatic view of the literal death of the audience: 'Our loyal viewers are actually leaving this earth and dying and we're not replacing them with younger people.'[2]

So even though there are considerable masses in traditional markets still to be found, and online traditional media are establishing oligopolies (Ofcom, 2007) – as they have always done in the field of news – there is a perception that mass media are no longer able to attract the masses. And without these masses they will fail to attract the advertisers they need to sustain news production:

> [Unilever and Proctor & Gamble] want mass markets and it's becoming increasingly difficult in the UK to buy mass market because of the fragmentation of various forms of media.
>
> (Finance director, national newspaper group, interview conducted in 2008)

It is not just the discrepancy between the considerable size of news audiences across the news industry, and the portrayal of a doomed genre, that is of importance to note here. Another notable feature of their portrayal of changes in audiences is the benchmark to which they compare: in arguing that the mass audience is no more, the interviewees refer to a time in which there was a 'stable', 'homogeneous' audience that was genuinely interested in news for its own sake. Back in the 'good old days', the audience was easily reached, according to this view, with a 'newspaper seller outside the factory gates' delivering the newspaper and 'you knew where your readers were, and they had very fixed lifestyles'.[3] This audience has a clear news consumption pattern: 'You sit down, you might be a retired person, you might be a business person, but what you're going to do, is you're going to sit down at nine o'clock, eight o'clock, and you're going to read the paper.'[4] There is a clear idealisation implicit in the narratives of the former audience:

> You know, in the old days, when I first joined, it was very much about: you write your news and people are going to buy it because they want to know what's going on in their area.
>
> (Features editor, regional newspaper, interview conducted in 2007)

Forming a mental picture of the audience serves to shape newsroom practice and provides guidance while producing media content (Ettema and Whitney, 1994). However, in the current situation, the idealisation of the old audiences, in combination with the mystification of the new (online) audiences, serves to create a sense of urgency, more than is warranted, obscuring the reasons for and impact of implemented changes.

New entries to the field always provide a challenge to existing practices (Bourdieu, 2005), and as such produces a certain amount of anticipation and fear. Introduction of new media entering the field of news is bound to lead to some fragmentation of audiences, but this time around – with the internet – new media technologies created a different challenge according to our interviewees. In this case, they argue, a new audience has 'sprung up', which coexists next to the traditional audience.

With media convergence, existing outlets operating on separate platforms now compete for the same audience on the same platform, whereas there used to be a separation of press and broadcast media. Moreover, traditional news organisations not only compete with one another, but also with new players. Thus interviewees are worried that any audience that they fail to attract will be lost to some other online organisation. The online audience has become a source of both expectation and fear, particularly as it asks for a new set of skills and a change in mindset:

> Obviously we want to serve our traditional audience but there's a whole new audience out there and this is the kind of news that they expect packaged this way, presented this way, presented at this pace. So I think it's a type of expertise, there is a certain skill in doing this and a sense of how the internet is a different medium and the people who consume news on the internet have a different expectation than our traditional newspaper audience.
>
> (Digital editor, national newspaper, interview conducted in 2008)

The focus on attracting audiences can be found specifically with regard to the young. Young people are seen as the audience of the future, and there is a belief that capturing this audience is vital to the long-term viability of news businesses. The above noted fear and expectation apply particularly to young audiences. Journalists maintain that what works for other audiences does not work for them. Or, as one of our interviewees states: 'If you ask a 16–24 year old what media do they prefer to get their news from, they all tell you the web.'[5] Finding them is deemed worth any change in news (both in content and delivery mode). As a regional editor explains, 'We're always chasing the younger reader because the advertisers are the Holy Grail.'[6] The promise of a young audience in particular proves to be an important justification when explaining the rationale behind change, as their demands need to be catered for, altering the news world and introducing new features online:

> Video is rapidly becoming a key part of it [a richer experience on demand] – to get more of that younger audience to come to us and to spend longer with us.
>
> (BBC News executive, interview conducted in 2007)

Thus, the bid to attract new audiences, in particular the young, is proffered as a reason to implement change in the news environment. Interestingly, research conducted at the same time as the interview quoted above shows that, even among the young (16–25 year olds), an actual 59 per cent name TV as their main source of news (Ofcom, 2007). However, this portrayal of a 'crisis' in audience figures and need for change, serves an evasive purpose. By employing the rationale that audience demands drive the implementation of change and the employment of new media technologies, journalists, editors and managers distance themselves from the responsibility. Going online is not so much presented as a preference by most of the journalists questioned, but rather as a 'necessity':

> You have to follow where the customers go. So if the customers were perfectly happy sitting down watching TV, that's where we'd be.
>
> (Finance director, national broadcaster, interview conducted in 2008)

Again the responsibility for change is denied by the interviewees. Rather, any change is presented as an essential move motivated entirely by external forces, such as the need for 'eyeballs'. The news industry is chasing the audience, by going to the spaces where they are (or are thought to be), such as Facebook, Twitter, YouTube and other social networks. This is where the audience can be found according to our interviewees: '[they are] not on Channel 4 and they're not on channel4.com but they are in social networks'.[7]

For the journalists moving to online platforms, using new ways of connecting to and engaging that audience are the only way to hang on to audiences, to have competitive advantage and ultimately to survive. The internet and other new media technologies are celebrated as *the* answer to a myriad of issues that the news industry is faced with, not least the decline in 'offline' readership:

> And, you know, in the intervening years we've moved right the way through to new technology, no printers, the advent of Internet – a brilliant research tool. [We have also seen] the loss of newspaper sales, but then copy sale was replaced by audience figures and, of course, therefore, we're now looking – thanks to our good website – at growing audience figures, even though the copy sales are going down.
>
> (Editor, regional newspaper, interview conducted in 2007)

Faced with a declining audience in the traditional media, the promise of the web is widely celebrated and offered as a way out of the situation in which news organisations find themselves. Presented as a crisis situation, the internet 'provides news organizations with a wonderful opportunity to engage new audiences in the hope that they may somehow compensate for declining ratings and advertising' (Freedman, 2010: 43). Contrary to the doom-laden pictures of declining audiences and the loss of the masses, however, we can certainly find dominant players online with a considerable market share, and considerable audiences (Ofcom, 2007). The real issue with the changing audiences is the problem of redirecting the revenue stream (see Chapter 1), which has still not been solved. Even so, the promise of an online audience is used to promote change that is not always in the best interest of either the news producers or the audiences.

Seducing the audience

An embattled market has fetishised audience demands; there seems considerable willingness to amend practices to audience desires; audience demands are 'a top priority'. This is no surprise, but the level to which the interviewees are willing to accommodate audience demands is notable. One of the interviewees, for instance, reflects on the role that blogging can play, and suggests – contrary to the notion of professionalisation and established journalistic style and culture – that when this is the style the audience wants, journalists should provide it:

> I mean newspapers have declined in sales over the last 10-15-20 years, it's a real issue, and it's something that needs to be addressed. And if the style of blogging and if what bloggers are doing is interesting to our readers, then why not? I'm all for it.
> (Specialist reporter, regional newspaper, interview conducted in 2008)

At the same time, while expressing a willingness to embrace certain elements introduced by new entries in the field, such as bloggers, there is resistance to these same new entries. The style may be adopted to accommodate to the audience, but on a more fundamental level we see that journalists actually vigorously try to set themselves apart from bloggers and other online players. So, whilst maintaining that change is necessary and certain features of the online world need to be embraced, the interviewees at the same time argue that professional journalists and their practices are different and need to be different for them to survive (Fenton and Witschge, 2010).

Furthermore, even though managers and editors may believe that blogging can be easily incorporated into news practices, our research found that journalists themselves find it difficult to adapt to the new style of writing. Blogging more often than not increases the workload of journalists, as the writing of a blog is routinely done on top of existing work, requiring journalists to work extra hours to fit all their work in. However, in chasing the audience, journalists and editors are willing to incorporate different methods, and extra work, not least because it is presented as the only way forward. And so, to reach the audience, as one manager argues, 'you do almost everything', including:

> Extending the kind of content you do, improving its quality, making sure you've got [the news] available to people wherever they are or what they are doing. So if they want a holiday, they can get a holiday. If they want news, they can watch video as well. Of course it's in print, of course it'll be on mobile, you know, and all these various places.
> (News executive, national newspaper, interview conducted in 2008)

The fact that news is available on different platforms is almost taken for granted, presented as a given. This convergence may seem obvious to us now, but up until recently media were hesitant to cross over to a different platform. Now, the move to different platforms and incorporating a multi-media approach is presented as inevitable. To reach the audience is only a matter of getting the news on the right platform, as this BBC news editor explains: 'The content you can shape; what you need is to get that content to people in a way that they welcome.'[8]

Focusing on the technology of delivery diverts attention away from the actual quality and content of the news. By wrapping up questions of content in debates about technology, and presenting technology as progress, it is hard for journalists to protest about any dilution of quality that may come with these changes (see Chapters 4 and 8). Portraying the problem of news as a mere question of 'getting the platform right', makes the coupling of new media technology to the future of journalism a very powerful rhetorical tool in pushing for change. Likewise, the perceived splintering of news audiences is deemed grounds on which to spend less on certain productions, as a specialist correspondent explains: 'People [are] consuming news in lots of different ways, and as it splinters it means we can't spend as much money on a big news programme.'[9] All in all, 'the internet features as an increasingly significant factor in the "restructuring" that is occurring throughout the news industry' (Freedman, 2010: 41). This restructuring goes beyond the realm of technology, but is successfully 'sold' under the banner of essential evolution.

Technology is the future

The central contradiction in the 'new technology' discourse is that, even though some news sites attract much larger audiences online, none of them is able to sustain the same advertising revenues as offline. New media technologies, in particular the internet, are presented not only as the future but also as the *solution* for the news industry, in spite of the fact that, as yet, the internet has not provided a funding basis which could (using current funding methods) actually sustain the high cost of producing original journalism. The challenges faced by the employment of new media are then also viewed differently; low audience figures online or low uptake of certain content and tools, are not seen as a crisis but as an 'opportunity':

> And although our online audience is growing and growing pretty strongly actually it's not matching the decline of our traditional audiences in numbers. So there are big opportunities for us on the Web.
>
> (BBC News executive, interview conducted in 2007)

Even though the figures on news consumption presented earlier in this chapter do not suggest this, the interviewees assume that everyone will be 'tuning into the internet for everything', and it will soon be immensely more popular than TV, radio and newspapers.[10] The internet is different, the journalists argue. As one interviewee puts it: 'It's a different animal; it's a different vehicle; it's a different platform.'[11] As it is all-pervading, journalists 'have no choice but to work with it'.[12] Here again, the technological determinism becomes clear. However, there was clearly an element of choice involved by editors who embraced it:

> We've maybe been forced to or maybe chosen to open ourselves to it and have to embrace it because it is all-pervading, far more so than any of these

previous forms of media in terms of what they can deliver to the end audience I suppose.

(Finance director, national newspaper group, interview conducted in 2008)

Of course, the question lies exactly in the hesitation this editor expresses. Have we been forced or have we chosen to open ourselves up? In the latter case this would mean alternative routes are available and not all changes pushed through would be necessary.

Most journalists, however, do not talk about it as a choice, but rather view it as necessity, as expressed above. While it is presented as the only way forward, any arguments against it are dismissed and those who question its central focus are branded as Luddites (see also Chapter 4). Any doubts remaining will naturally disappear, it is argued – a further indication of how new media are considered the only way forward. Those who have not shared this uncritical embrace of new media technology are considered 'slow in coming round to this way of working.'[13] Moreover, the way in which the interviewees present news organisations suggests a fundamental shift in the media products offered, the ways of working and the audiences served: 'It is very much that we no longer own regional newspapers, we own regional media businesses.'[14]

Managers are pushing for the convergence of newsrooms, the employment of new media technologies across the board and, most of all, pushing for change, and there is little tolerance for a slower pace of change:

> Because I was saying: look, you're not pushing hard enough on the interactive stuff, you're not pushing hard enough into where your audiences are, you're not pushing hard enough into challenging your internal assumptions about how you tell stories in this landscape.
>
> (Managing director, Interactive Media Company,
> interview conducted in 2007)

Lying behind this discourse is a sense of superiority, of knowing the 'real' situation and not being 'stuck' in old habits and practices; there are those who 'see' it and those who don't.[15] Thus to move forward, the 'doubters' have to 'see the light', it is argued by the 'believers', and see that online news is the future (and the only possible route). So powerful is this idea of the all-pervasive technology, that it is 'unnecessary to convert everybody';[16] the push of technology is so strong, it will sort itself out. Even so, there is a project going on within newsrooms to change those who are not 'on board' yet. The strong push creates a situation in which those who do have their doubts are hesitant to express them. Even though reluctantly, they too argue that it is a necessity to move online and abandon 'old' technologies, adopting the hegemonic discourse that change is necessary.

In addition to the powerful coupling of technology to the declining audience figures, and the downplaying of any concerns as Luddite, new media technologies are coupled to efficiency – a discourse that further limits the range and effects of alternative, more specifically, critical accounts of new media. Multi-platform production is presented as a way of doing more for less, at a time in which news organisations struggle (see also Chapter 4). So journalists are told that they have to move to multi-platform working in order to create efficiencies and save money. At the same time, they see that the act of moving online – where their work is consumed for free – appears to be creating the very crisis that multi-skilling is claimed to solve.

This powerful presentation of new media technologies as providing progress, efficiency, and the future of news makes it difficult for anyone to successfully challenge their implementation. A journalist explains how this worked in his newsroom:

> I mean this is it, the editor came in and said: you're all doomed, it's all going wrong, you're dead in the water, newspapers are over, they'll be finished in two years and look, I've saved you with the internet. You've got the oldest readership and people kept saying, well if we've got the oldest readership, surely that means we're more immune to the internet than anyone else. We've got [a] much larger readership than anyone else. Surely we should be using our strengths but no, no, no, we're naïve, we're stupid. You've got to be with the internet. If we don't do it, we're dead.
>
> (General reporter, national newspaper, interview conducted in 2008)

The enhanced link to the audience

The strongest rhetoric surrounding the employment of new media technology is the renewed connection to the audience that is claimed through going online. Not only does it provide a way of reaching the audience, but the connection that is made with that audience is much closer, according to the interviewees. Here too, however, there is an idealised version of its role, and a more sceptical version of the story.

Our interviews with those in the news industry, as well as other research, suggest that there are a number of different discourses on the changing relationship to the audience that new media technology gives rise to. They include those reasons – in line with hopes invested by many academics in new media technologies – such as 'increasing accountability towards the public', 'democratisation of the news process' and 'allowing the user's expertise to find its way into the newsroom'.

Most prevalent, however, in describing the perceived benefits of employing new media technology are commercial reasons, such as monitoring the audience's interests so that their needs can be better met (and thus increase audience numbers). Here I focus on the audience-related reasons and perceived effects for using this new platform of delivery of news. In the next chapter I will discuss the implications for the role of the audience (and that of the journalist) in the news production process.

Increased accountability

New media technologies are considered by many to open up the news process (see, for instance, Beckett, 2008). The increased access for the public to news producers and insight into the process of news making are often quoted in this respect. Journalists themselves refer to the benefits of new media technologies as allowing them to 'get closer to the audience' and to give them 'a look in'. Using blogs and podcasts and other tools 'gives our readers a chance to understand more about us', as well as the opportunity to interact, both of which are 'absolutely vital',[17] it is argued. Here, too, the sense of inevitability when describing the employment of new media technologies comes to the fore. It is not a matter of choice: journalism has to 'open up'. There is a 'need to re-engage with our audiences', and new media technologies allow journalists to be 'always plugged into our audience directly'.[18]

Moreover, new media technologies allow for a way of 'public scrutiny', according to the journalists, tapping into the debate on the lack of trust currently held in British journalists by the public (see, for instance, Barnett, 2008). As such, the internet is heralded 'as a vehicle for genuine accountability, for when you get your facts wrong'.[19] Contact details and bylines in the online version of news outlets are seen as evidence for a more accountable journalism by our interviewees.

Of course, requesting feedback from the audience when they find factual errors can similarly be seen as a cheap way of subbing, such as an earlier experiment of the *Telegraph* (Oliver, 2008); and, as Domingo *et al.* point out, it is hard to consider this request 'as a real opening of the news-editing process' (Domingo *et al.*, 2008: 338). Likewise, the insistence on bylines and phone numbers does not square with the dominant practice of working without bylines online, where articles stemming from agency copy are recycled and updated – often by a team of people, rather than one author – and more often than not without documentation of the history of the process (see also Chapter 8).

It becomes clear from the interviews that the 'new reality' of online publication is still in flux, and that journalists do not yet know how to accommodate to this new environment. The following quote shows the tension between the internet's forte, of having a more direct connection to the audience on the one hand, and the traditional notion of the journalist as a neutral, distanced, reporter on the other:

> [The internet has] opened up the channels of communication between the reader and the journalist, which I think is a really interesting aspect of it because it holds the journalist immediately to account and enables there to be lots of different views expressed rather than just one – although this journalist is not really meant to express a view unless it's comment anyway.
> (Online journalist, regional newspaper group, interview conducted in 2008)

The internet has, according to journalists, altered the relationship with the audience, and this informs other newsroom practices as well. The internet, they say, functions as an 'accountability mechanism', and is viewed as a reason to scrutinise the news production process and hold editors 'in check'.[20] In a similar vein, newsrooms are opening up to their audiences by providing access to the physical space, which they would never have done three years ago, as one editor explains, but now, with the new media tools of 'transparency', 'newspapers are changing their methods'.[21]

The afterthought of this editor, who reflects on the new openness of the news process – 'newspapers are always trying to find ways of making themselves more interesting to their readers' – shows again the dual function of these new practices of 'accountability'. For the interviewees, these broader cultural changes are all based on developments of new media technologies. They view the 'new' relationship between audiences and professionals as firmly established in new media practices, and in doing so they forget the cultural, economic and social contexts. They do not consider the broader cultural change that may be the basis of this, as has been outlined by Turner in his notion of the 'demotic turn': 'the increasing visibility of the "ordinary person" as they turn themselves into media content through talk radio, citizen journalism, news blogs, reality TV, celebrity culture and the like' (Turner, 2009: 390; see also Turner, 2010).

This relation between new media and the audience, as reported by our interviewees, is consistent with O'Sullivan and Heinonen (2008: 365), who found, in a survey among European journalists in eleven countries, that two-thirds of the respondents appreciated the benefit that online journalism brings to connect to their audience. However, more than half of the respondents disagreed that 'online journalists are closer to their audience' and 36 per cent disagreed 'with the statement that the Net's interactivity makes journalism more accountable to the public' (ibid: 364–67). These differing opinions suggest that there is no unequivocal embrace of the accountability that could result from new media technologies. Our research shows that, more than accountability, commercial advantages are proffered as reasons for celebrating the closer connection to the audience which new media technology enable.

Commercial advantages

The following quote puts the expectations surrounding a more direct link with the audience well. The journalist in question talks about how the organisation tries to make the process 'more collaborative'. It becomes clear, however, that this is not an aim in itself; it is a means to an end, the end of commercial advantage of getting more viewers:

> I think we've moved away from the stuffy, tablets of stone kind of news journalism; that's what's happened in the last few years. … It's crediting the audience with more; it's saying: 'this is what we know, we're not 100% sure but come with us on this and we'll follow it through together'; and it's trying to be a more collaborative process and I guess the idea is that that will engage younger viewers, hopefully.
>
> (BBC News presenter, interview conducted 2007)

Similar to our finding, that connecting to the audience is mainly based on these economic motives, Hermida (2009: 11) found that within the BBC, blogs and other tools notionally employed to get a 'greater degree of transparency of the journalistic process' are more 'a way of reconnecting with audiences, than as a means of having a dialogue with readers' – a way of 'gauging audience reaction' to journalistic content.

Similarly, our research shows that the tighter relationship and possibility for feedback allows for the monitoring of audience reaction, which in turn has commercial advantages. 'Enabling comment at the bottom of the story … [means] you get a heck of a lot of clicks if somebody's going to go back and find what people are saying about his comment.'[22] Audience responses through e-mails and texts, as one interviewee puts it, 'makes you very aware and responsive to what the audience are interested in'; you know whether the audience is interested in a topic 'within seconds'.[23] Another editor explains how they 'encourage everybody to read [the inbox for viewers' e-mails] all the time' so as to get 'instant feedback on what we're doing'.[24] In other words, the changing relation to the audience is primarily because it provides 'business value' (van Dijck, 2009: 46). Given the commercial environment that most news organisations operate in, this of course does not come as a surprise. However, the packaging of the move to closer audience connection at times obscures these more economic motives, as well as disregarding the implications of the changes for news quality and the position of journalists in the news production process.

The effect on the news agenda

One of the consequences of this 'renewed responsiveness' is that the news agendas are informed – if not formed – by the constant user feedback available to journalists and editors alike. The constant feedback is not limited to the 'in-house' audience responses, but is very much taking place outside of traditional newsrooms, whether it is on Facebook, Twitter or other social (networking) sites. One such social news site is Digg, where audience postings and ratings of stories provide an alternative, 'collaborative' news agenda. As one correspondent explains, sites such as Digg can drive traffic to news sites and determine popularity of news stories:

> You might write something that you think is really uninteresting but someone thinks it's interesting and *diggs* it and *diggs* it and *diggs* it on Digg, and then suddenly it's a really important story. Is it important because people like it, or is it important because boring people in suits think it's interesting?
> (Technology correspondent, national broadcaster,
> interview conducted in 2007)

Such a shift – where the audience can become the filter for news, can highlight stories and determine the news agenda – has significant ramifications for the way in which news is accessed and the role that editors play in this. Whereas the traditional role of journalists was to decide and provide the 'whole' news picture of a day, now individual articles lead a life of their own. The news agenda becomes atomised and audiences collaboratively construct an alternative conception of the 'news of the day'.

This shift can also be found on more individual levels, where new media technologies allow users to develop their own news diet, by personalising search engine settings, accessing 'multiple stories across a diverse range of news outlets on individually chosen topics' (Carlson, 2007: 1014). Rather than accessing one main news outlet which provides a 'purposefully arranged, delimited news product' (ibid), with search engines users are not limited to one provider, but rather can access a myriad of sources, the news hierarchy determined by the search engine logic.

In Chapter 1 we discussed the problematic relation of news producers to search engine sites with regard to advertising. While traditional news providers see their revenues being sapped by these intermediary sites, they try to regain control by playing the search optimisation game and increase their visibility through them. As Machill, Beiler and Zenker note, an 'entirely new economic sector concerned with the optimization of pages in order to achieve better rankings in the results lists has sprung up around search engines' (2008: 596). News organisations, like every other business, try to optimise the results so as to draw readers to their sites and regain the advertising revenues.

Of course, journalists have always paid attention to audience demands but, as the *New York Times* notes, audience data have 'never been available with such specificity and timeliness' (Peters, 2010). Now, companies argue that they can provide newsrooms with exact information on 'how much money – down to the penny – each of its articles online was making when readers clicked on ads' (ibid). Journalists' responses have been varied to these new developments. Some have responded with 'fear and mockery' to the idea that the 'need for human editors is declining' (Carlson, 2007: 1024). This responsiveness to (parts of) the audience is seen to challenge the core of the news process, where it is not the editors deciding, but rather the audience who gets a direct voice, as an editor explains: 'If the audience have the opportunity to interact and tell us how to shape our news agenda, then our news will change'; the audience will even get to say 'Yes, go and send a crew.'[25]

Even contributions in the form of user-generated content (UGC) – discussed more thoroughly in the next chapter – are seen mainly as a tool of tapping into consumer interest, where 'if a lot of people have been sending in [UGC on a particular topic] ... that might make you inclined to [run] one story over another'.[26] This constant monitoring and the inclination to adjust the news agenda to audience feedback does, however, receive some criticism. A BBC News executive stated that they had 'probably lowered the bar a bit too much',[27] suggesting that putting the editor or journalists back in charge produces better quality.

Finding a balance between this direct audience input and editorial values is a struggle that seems prominent in journalistic practice now. Is it positive that the news agenda is informed by audience feedback (whether audience figures or audience feedback through comments and e-mail)? A BBC presenter wonders how representative the audience feedback is that informs the decision on which stories to run and the prominence given to them: 'How reflective are the e-mails of our audience?'[28] Research by the OECD (quoted in van Dijck, 2009: 44) into the role of audiences as producers of content suggests that this is a legitimate concern; only a small part of the audience 'participates' in production of content and 'over 80 per cent of all users are in fact passive recipients of content'.

Moreover, as several journalists point out, there is an issue that most feedback is negative. And, as some maintain, when there is too much of it, and too much of it is negative, journalists start to ignore it. They become 'less forthcoming' with the audience and when they become used to the fact that their name is on 'all of these hundreds of e-mails', 'it stops mattering.'[29] As another editor puts it (a bit more bluntly):

> You haven't got to let it affect what you do because it's a wider problem they've got in their own heads, and you've just got to thank god you're not married to one.
>
> (Section editor, national newspaper, interview conducted 2008)

Journalists find ways to guard themselves from this constant input and reaction to their work. The increase in audience feedback is furthermore downplayed by the view that online feedback is less valuable than offline equivalents, such as letters to the editors. E-mails cost less time to write, are far easier and thus less substantial, according to the interviewees. It is assumed that, unlike letters, communications via online posts, texts and e-mails do not require a response by journalists.[30]

Conclusion

The 'long tradition of millenarian prophecy in relation to new media' as noted by Curran (2010: 19) is strongly present in relation to the 'newest' of new media – the internet, mobile phones and other digital devices. Not denying the role that technology plays in journalism (as it has always done), it is important to note – in response to the technological determinism present in media practitioners' accounts of the current state of journalism – that 'technology is not a force "in itself". It is adapted and implemented according to already existing value systems, and these value systems have cultural, social and economic roots' (Örnebring, 2010: 68).

Here I have outlined the extent to which the coupling of 'dwindling' audience figures with the progressive force of technology, masked, at least to a certain extent, the motives behind the employment of new media technology. Cuts have been made, workloads increased, news agendas altered and content changed, all under the banner of the inevitability of 'going online'. Presenting new media technology as the future of journalism has made any critical stance by journalists virtually ineffectual. Moreover, packaging the economically driven employment of technology as a way of getting closer to the audience proves a very powerful rhetoric, safeguarding changes in the newsroom from any criticism.

This technological determinist narrative present in newsrooms not only stifles criticism but also closes off a number of paths that could be taken in the news industry to make use of technology in more progressive ways. Suggesting that newspaper audiences are lost because of the rise of the internet is obscuring the fact that there has been a steady decline of news audiences since the late 1950s (Curran and Seaton, 2009). Suggesting they will all be won back by 'going online' damages the news quality, if this is done to decrease investment in quality journalism. Implementing managerial change and moving towards converged newsrooms may make for better, more accountable journalism when the technological tools are used properly. Implementing such change to install new and cheap forms of 'cut-and-paste' journalism and unreflective capture of and response to audience sentiments does nothing to ensure improvements in journalism that are much needed in the changing mediascape.

The technologies available to journalists and audiences alike have much promise to reflect an open, ethical and reflective news practice (see also Chapter 8). On the whole, however, our research contradicts expectations or presumptions that the 'new digital environment has jolted traditional journalism out of its conservative complacency; [or that] news operations are much more responsive to their empowered and engaged audiences' (Bird, 2009: 295). The commercial considerations weigh more heavily than any ethical issues in the new relationship between the professionals and the audience.

Erjavec and Kovačič (2009: 161) correctly point out that audience participation in a capitalist social order 'has social significance mainly because it is about using (and exploiting) new media for commercial purposes'. So far, news organisations are struggling with finding the means to commercialise this audience; but it is the intention behind the idea of audience empowerment that needs to be critically interrogated – the focus of the next chapter. What role do professional newsmakers see for the audience; and how does this reflect on the relationship between them and the audience?

Notes

1 Technology correspondent, national broadcaster, interview conducted in 2007.
2 Head of technology training, regional broadcasting, interview conducted in 2008.
3 Editor, regional newspaper, interview conducted in 2007.
4 Web editor, regional newspaper, interview conducted in 2007.
5 Ofcom senior adviser, interview conducted in 2008.
6 Editor, regional newspaper, interview conducted in 2007.
7 Editorial director, *Illumina Digital*, interview conducted in 2008.
8 Interview conducted in 2007.
9 Technology correspondent, national broadcaster, interview conducted in 2007.
10 Television presenter, regional news media group, interview conducted in 2008.
11 Web editor, regional newspaper, interview conducted in 2007.
12 Finance director, national newspaper group, interview conducted in 2008.
13 Online journalist, regional newspaper, interview conducted in 2008.
14 Finance director, national newspaper group, interview conducted in 2008.
15 As noted by a journalist working on the online community team at a national newspaper, interview conducted in 2008.

16 Digital editor, national newspaper, interview conducted in 2008.
17 Specialist reporter, regional newspaper, interview conducted in 2008.
18 Digital editor, national newspaper, interview conducted in 2008.
19 Ofcom senior adviser, interview conducted in 2008.
20 Editor, national newspaper, interview conducted in 2008.
21 Web editor, regional newspaper, interview conducted in 2007.
22 Trainee at a national newspaper, interview conducted in 2008.
23 BBC news presenter, interview conducted in 2007.
24 Deputy editor, national broadcaster, interview conducted in 2008.
25 Technology correspondent, national broadcaster, interview conducted in 2007.
26 BBC news presenter, interview conducted in 2008.
27 Interview conducted in 2008.
28 Interview conducted in 2008.
29 BBC Online News executive, interview conducted in 2008.
30 Editor, BBC Radio, interview conducted in 2008.

Part III
Changing journalism

7 Changing audiences, changing journalism?

Tamara Witschge

The relationship between the producers and consumers of news, some argue, has been fundamentally changed by new technologies. With audiences increasingly becoming part of the process of journalism, the different constituencies in the world of news – journalists and audiences – are said to blur into each other (Gillmor, 2004). Moreover, 'technologies of news relay broaden the field of who might be considered a journalist and what might be considered journalism' (Zelizer, 2004: 23). Audience participation in the news process challenges the traditional relationship and distinctions between the audience and professionals and shifts the power from the journalists to the audience, it is argued.

This chapter questions assumptions that a 'more reciprocal relationship between reporters and their audience' is developing and a more 'participatory journalism' is coming about (Domingo *et al.*, 2008: 326). It critically examines the way journalists view their audiences, asking to what extent the relationship between audiences and journalists is significantly changing, and how this impacts on the so-called democratisation process within media. Is there a shift of power from the news producers to those traditionally known as consumers, and how does this reflect on journalism as a profession?

The changing role of the audience in the news process has been a major focus of academic research. O'Sullivan and Heinonen (2008: 368) wonder whether the profession of journalism can 'shift from its traditional role towards a more democratic community and public debate-oriented ideal heralded since the earliest days of Internet news'. Others argue that we are already there:

> Greater public participation, for example, is generating more useable so-called hyperlocal news, which is reported increasingly via crowdsourcing and instant messaging by local residents intimately familiar with what they are reporting. … The trend is realtime, participatory, engaging and growing.
>
> (Russell, 2009: 366)

Initially wary of this vociferous and often strident audience, the news media have since grown to embrace this promising amateur workforce. Inspired by the success of open-source models in other areas, organizations are beginning to recruit their newly empowered readers for newsgathering and analysis.

(Muthukumaraswamy, 2010: 48)

Not everyone is unequivocally positive about these trends. Turner (2009: 309) views professional journalism as one of the 'casualties' of what he labels 'the demotic turn' in popular culture – 'the increasing visibility of the "ordinary person" as they turn themselves into media content'.

Beyond binary distinctions

The current debates, both within the profession and within academic circles, on how the relation between newsmakers and the audience is changing, provides interesting insights into what journalism is considered to be and who can do journalism. The academic focus on *change* in this debate implies that there used to be a very clear and stable definition of journalism and those working in it, such as Brain McNair, for instance, suggests:

> The dominant model for journalism in the 20th century was a trained professional delivering objectively validated content to a reader (or viewer, or listener). There was also room for a journalism of analysis and opinion delivered by an authoritative public voice, where authority was determined by consensually accepted forms of organizational, professional and cultural status.

(McNair, 2009: 347)

Similar to the mythification of the audience addressed in Chapter 6, this homogenised characterisation of the journalist does not do justice to the diversity in the field. As we discuss in Chapter 2, journalism in the UK has only recently become a graduate profession and, in most contexts, entry into the field has been rather flexible, and thus we see that journalists still come from a variety of backgrounds and perform journalism in many different ways.

An equally simplistic notion has developed of a unitary audience engaging in activities such as 'citizen journalism' and producing something called simply user-generated content (UGC). In reality, users engage with technology, with news organisations and with journalists in a myriad of ways, and have done so in the past to varying extents (see, for instance, Phillips, 2008). Van Dijck (2009: 41–42) points out how the debates around the current state and future of journalism suggest a simplified relationship between newsmakers and its audience, with the new hybrid terms of 'produser' or 'co-creator' implying a bipolar distinction between two categories, which in fact does not reflect the complexities of the relationship. As she argues, 'we need to account for the multifarious roles of users in a media environment' (ibid: 42).

In the main, the audience relationship with news has not changed. Most people still 'consume' news via a 'one-way' relationship with a few main news providers, whether through television (the majority), newspaper or online (Ofcom, 2007). According to an OECD survey of users of UGC sites, only 13 per cent are 'active creators' and produce online material, such as blogs or upload videos or photos. Over 80 per cent variously collect URLs, or read or view the work of others (OECD report quoted in van Dijck, 2009: 44). There are few publicly available sources of information about the behaviour of news audiences, but a *Guardian* technology correspondent suggested that about 10 per cent of those reading online interact with news in whatever form, and an even smaller number do so on a regular basis (Arthur quoted in van Dijck, 2009: 44). By focusing on these numbers, I do not mean to suggest that only 'creation' amounts to 'participation'. This is, however, how the current debate has framed the 'democratisation' of the news process. It is this active (or potentially active) audience that produces material with which this chapter engages – the so-called user-generated content.

There is another group of contributors to the news process, who are often referred to as 'citizen journalists' – although this term is not uncontested (see, for instance, Couldry, 2010). They are more often than not conflated with the above group, and incorrectly categorised as part of the audience. Their role is much more akin to that of the alternative press. Operating independently of the mass media, they seek to offer an online alternative to mainstream press (see, for instance, Atton, 2004). Some do so in an amateur, part-time capacity without expecting to profit from their work. The more successful bloggers are able to fund their operations and work effectively as small businesses. An example in the UK is the political blogger Guido Fawkes. Journalism is still a porous profession, and different voices contribute in a myriad of ways. Viewing those alternative voices from the audience perspective does not allow us to grasp the dynamics of the field of journalism in the current digital environment. As mentioned, in this chapter, I focus on journalists' changing relation to the audience and hence do not include the role of independent bloggers as a part of the audience (but see Chapter 1 for some reflections on these new online voices).

Even without the complicating status of independent bloggers in the field of journalism, it is not possible to talk in simple terms of the journalist–audience relationship. Expectations that the new environment is 'blurring the line between news producer and news audience' (Bird, 2009: 293) need to be interrogated. Similarly, we need critically to challenge claims 'that the internet allows a change in the relative position of journalists and audiences, from a one-way, asymmetric model of communication to a dialogical kind of journalism, through which news production becomes a collective endeavor' (Mitchelstein and Boczkowski, 2009: 573).

To avoid falling into the trap of simply celebrating new media technologies for their democratising nature, we should examine to what extent there are meaningful ways for the public to be involved in the news process. To what extent is the public involved in 'the origination and extension of content' (McQuail, 2009: 387–88)? In asking that, I focus on 'the extent to which news organisations are willing to "open the gates"' (Lewis, Kaufhold and Lasorsa, 2010: 165–66), and also whether this is the way that journalists and journalism should go.

This analysis is aimed at critically interrogating this claim of democratisation. Given its prevalence in the debates on journalism, I examine the implications of the discourse that connects 'public participation' in the news process to 'democratisation', and examine journalists' views on the role of the audience. It is more than 'scholarly curiosity about whether institutional journalism empowers and engages citizens in public communication with newly available means' (Domingo *et al.*, 2008: 327) which informs this chapter. These discourses have very real consequences in terms of managerial change in the newsrooms, even if they do not lead to a democratisation of the role of the audience. It is these consequences that we need to consider.

The discourse on the 'democratisation of news media'

Under the banner of the democratising nature of new media technologies, a lot of commentators as well as those working in the news industry argue for an embrace of new technologies – the precise details (and merits) of this democratisation in news media often left undeveloped and unchallenged. As Rebillar and Touboul (2010: 325) point out, in the 'libertarian-liberal' model currently dominant, 'views of the Web 2.0 associate liberty, autonomy and horizontality'. The rhetoric surrounding new media technology is powerful. How could one argue against more equality and democracy? But it conceals some of the more pressing reasons for which new media technologies are employed in the news industry.

In this chapter, I problematise these views of new media technologies as bringing democracy through participation by conducting a critical analysis of the views of newsmakers on the role of the audience in the news process (as expressed in interviews conducted in 2007–9 with people in the news industry including editors and journalists working in regional and national news journalism, broadcast, print and online). Our interviews with those in the news industry, as well as other research, suggests that the dominant discourse on user participation does not value audience contribution in the news process as a great democratising feature. It furthermore challenges the 'newness' of audience participation in the news. These findings call into question the great disruptive force new media are said to be, with regard to the relationship between the audience and the journalist. However, given the strength of the rhetoric surrounding new media and democratisation, there is very little discussion – whether within the profession or in academic circles – about what alternative, meaningful ways of public participation in the news process could be deployed.

Outside of the profession, among academic and other critics of journalism, there has been very little questioning about what the role of journalists would be if they were to allow the audience equal (or simply more) access. If the defining characteristic of being a journalist is determining 'what publics see, hear and read about the world', and their main sense of purpose has traditionally been 'their control of information in their various roles as watchdog, gatekeeper, and guardian for society' as Lewis *et al.* argue (2010: 165), can we expect them to forgo these roles lightly? And, more importantly, do we want them to?

In Chapter 1 we argued the need for professional journalists, precisely because of the added value they provide to the news realm (of course we are talking about journalism at its best here): the ongoing process of checking, collating, presenting and interpreting information that is in the public interest. In asking for a critical examination of what we mean by 'democratisation of news media' and a greater participatory role for the audience, I do not mean to suggest that the status quo should be unchallenged. However, instead of simply asking for more participation, we need to consider what kind of audience participation is required (and what kind of participation is currently allowed for by journalists). Currently, the unreflective promotion of new media under the banner of democratisation is used to put into place changes that may actually harm rather than improve the news process. In this chapter I challenge the idea that such democratisation has already taken place, by presenting the views of journalists on user participation. A next step would then be to discuss what type of meaningful participation we do want, if we are not moving towards a process of journalism where journalist and audience are equal participants in terms of their direct, 'active' role in the production process (it is important to note that the audience has always played a role in the news process, whether directly or indirectly).

The added value of user participation

One of the contested issues in the debate on the changing role of the audience in journalism is what they contribute. Many journalists, when discussing audience participation, reflect on the type of contribution they deliver. Even though frequently applied, they do not consider the term 'journalist' to be appropriate – even if preceded by 'citizen':

> Well they're not a reporter, but they're a viewer or a listener or a consumer of news, and they can be a source of a story or they can be a source of an opinion or they can just be a source of a feedback but they have a role.
> (Online journalist, national broadcaster, interview conducted in 2008)

> We don't really call it citizen journalism. You might call it citizen newsgathering.
> (BBC News executive, interview conducted in 2007)

Journalists are understandably eager to establish the difference between professional content and user-generated content and return to traditional values of the journalistic 'profession' to argue why user contributions are not journalism (see also Fenton and Witschge, 2010; O'Sullivan and Heinonen, 2008). The distinction made by one of the interviewees between 'produced' and 'un-produced' content reflects this focus on the difference in contribution.[1] Journalists are protective of their 'craft', even though most of our interviewees acknowledge that journalism as it is currently performed is not at its best. In their reflections they show they have high standards for professional journalism and actually find it difficult to come to terms with the fact that they cannot practise journalism to those standards most days. But inspired by their ideals about journalism, they then do argue that what the audience does (apart from some exceptions) is not considered journalism or news: 'In fact, most user-generated stuff is conversation.'[2]

Affected by the changes brought about with the coming of new media technologies, newsmakers are trying to find ways to organise, respond to and incorporate audience participation. Even though everyone in the news industry is soliciting this type of contribution, it becomes clear from the interviews that many journalists only provide the space for users out of necessity. This is the way you do things now (as mentioned in the previous chapter) or, as one editor puts it, 'everybody has jumped on the user-generated concept or straight citizen journalism bandwagon'.[3] One journalist reflects on how, at the moment, user participation is seen as compulsory, rather than done in 'good faith' and that journalists have to find out 'why they're doing it' and why users should take part in the website.[4]

The dominant view on continued, 'everyday' participation of the audience in the news process is rather sceptical of its value; that view reflects the above analysis: many view it as a necessity, and see no higher aim for public participation. This becomes apparent in this web editor's response to the question about what UGC contributes:

> It contributes to the idea that the visitor, the community, is able to make a contribution to the website. And in that respect, okay, that's fine, and I'll happily make it available because it's no skin off my nose if they do it. I don't have to do it, somebody will do that. And also in many cases it will be automated anyway so there's not going to be that much time wasted looking after them. Quite what it contributes, I'm not sure, and what its value is, I'm not sure. Other than, we're reaching into the community and giving them access.
>
> (Web editor, regional newspaper, interview conducted in 2007)

The above quote shows how an instrumental view of giving the audience access is considered to be a possible reason to provide ways for the public to participate. Journalists are not necessarily convinced of the value of user participation, as is indicated in the way they talk about it – 'I like a picture of a duck on a pond as much as the next man'[5] – and there is a very limited idea of what it can actually contribute:

> It's probably the future. I think it's pointless and meaningless, in journalistic terms it's just meaningless, it's your family photographs, what's it got to do with me?
>
> (Specialist correspondent, working freelance, interview conducted in 2007)

A regional news editor states she would 'ban user participation completely', adding: 'But then I'm not after hits which other people are',[6] again emphasising that the only valid reason to pursue user participation is based on economic advantages that might result from it. We see here that both arguments prevalent in the previous chapter about the implementation of new media technologies come to the fore here too. Again, UGC, like new media technologies, is the 'future', and may bring us economic benefits. So, even if journalists have their reservations, they are hesitant to express them, as they cannot provide a real challenge to the idea that this is the future and the saviour of journalism.

The sceptical attitude of journalists[7] towards user contributions also comes to the fore in other research (see, for instance, O'Sullivan and Heinonen, 2008). However, given the strong drive to incorporate user contributions, connecting UGC to the future of journalism, and lacking any real possibilities to challenge this UGC trend, our research concludes that journalists are trying to find ways of incorporating these contributions without conflicting with their journalistic values, which they consider almost diametrically opposed. Hermida and Thurman, in an examination of British newspapers, likewise, found hesitations to embracing user participation and found that 'news professionals were still working out whether and how to integrate user participation within existing norms and practices' (2008: 350). It would be too easy, however, to downplay these hesitations as a lack of democracy within the news process; we need to ask whether the standards journalists are arguing they wish to protect are actually worthwhile upholding to ensure the public-interest function of news. This does not mean, though, that we cannot at the same time critically examine the discourse used by journalists on user participation, as well as journalistic practices more broadly.

A qualified use of user contributions: the journalist as expert

In trying to find out how to incorporate user participation, journalists focus on their own role in the news process; user contributions can be valuable, but only if processed by journalists:

> In order for [UGC] to get into the newspaper or even onto a website of a newspaper we have to do something with it. ... If it's going to become mainstream news it has to go through the process. ... it is important that people have a way of getting any sort of information out there, that's important to any sort of democracy. But I think it's also important to any sort of democracy that you have rigorous and professional journalism.
>
> (General reporter, regional newspaper, interview conducted in 2008)

For the interviewees, it is not only that UGC needs to be filtered by journalists, it is also seen to clash with journalistic values – with the ethical values and news values that guide journalistic practice (see also Fenton and Witschge, 2010). Moreover, one of the main concerns of the journalists in providing a space for the audience is their legal responsibility for the material – many news organisations are still struggling to find a good way of dealing with this issue, and have (temporarily) closed their forums to avoid litigation.[8]

In itself UGC is not seen as having much value for journalists, and yet it is invited by almost all news organisations, following the latest trend. Given the low value of UGC as perceived by the interviewees, they argue that it should only be used if you have nothing better: 'you should only run them if you've got nothing else'.[9] It is then up to the editors and journalists to make sense of user content, to edit it, and add value to it. Some interviewees argue for 'framed' user-generated content, where journalists ask only for user content related to a particular topic.[10] In general, the areas in which journalists consider user contributions to have any value are very limited and mainly refer to the sphere of entertainment. One of the interviewees, in reflecting on UGC, argues that – if it is to be allowed at all – it should be allowed only in limited domains:

> The classic example is the humour out there. ... we've got some little video clips from the football fans who do things, you know, they've got nothing better to do while they're studying or whatever. And it's great fun, and that's user-generated content, which, all right it doesn't add anything to the great scheme of things but at least it makes you smile, and that's good.
>
> (Web editor, regional newspaper, interview conducted in 2007)

Likewise, journalists often view UGC as limited to pictures that can be sent in by the audience. Another local web editor also focuses on pictures when reflecting on the added value of UGC, and explains how competitions are the most popular (asking people to send in pictures of their pets), and that it is in this area that user participation really works.[11]

Örnebring (2008: 783) similarly found that UGC is limited to particular areas of news: 'the overall impression is that users are mostly empowered to create popular culture-oriented content and personal/everyday life-oriented content rather than news/informational content'. Providing the users with this type of space, a playground where they are free to roam, is of course a 'safe' way of introducing user participation in the news arena. We see that when it is about serious news coverage, journalists are very hesitant to give access to the news process. The extent to which UGC can be used is limited, interviewees argue: 'Some of that kind of citizen journalism stuff can help you, but only so far. You still need reporters to go out and find stories and, you know, work them hard.'[12]

Journalists are understandably defensive of the work they do in a time where it is argued that anyone can be a journalist, and this could well be a major reason for journalists to downplay the role of the audience. However, our interviewees also show a major concern for the product they put out. There is a strong sense of public-service purpose amongst the journalists interviewed. If they protect areas of 'serious' news, it may not only be to defend their professional identity but also to protect the quality of the news – even though, as I mentioned before, they do not feel they can always live up to the standards of quality themselves in the current news environment. And so we can observe a tension between the public interest journalists wish to serve and the commercial interest of allowing more audience participation.

The view of the journalist as expert is very much dominant in news organisations. For journalists there is still a strong division between the role of the amateur – the audience – and the role of the professional – the journalist – countering the expectations that with new media technology these categories blur into one another. The journalist clearly retains the expert position and knows better than the audience how to package, form and present a news story. And in many ways, knows better what the audience needs and wants, as found by Erjavec and Kovavic (2009: 154): 'Journalists are convinced that they know better what the audience wants, and they prefer to rely on their indefinable "journalistic instinct".'

In his ethnography of online newsrooms, Domingo similarly found that journalists regarded users 'as a rather passive audience, consumers of the stories' (as quoted in Mitchelstein and Boczkowski, 2009: 573). As mentioned earlier, research has found that it is only a small part of the audience that actually contributes (van Dijck, 2009). Moreover the contributions that do come in are not all perfect pieces of journalism that can be used un-altered and concerns regarding quality control and costs are pressing (Soun Chung, 2007). The fact that a considerable team of trained journalists is hired at, for instance, the BBC, to trail, edit, moderate and follow up on UGC is not out of mere vanity on the side of journalists – sourcing, researching and presenting quality news involves considerable time, costs and skills.

UGC as competitive advantage: the role of the public as news gatherers

This is not to say that journalists do not think user-generated content has value. Examples such as the coverage of the election protests in Iran (2009), the Burmese protests (2007), and the 7/7 bombings in London (2005) show how important user contributions are in news production. However, the number of examples that people give when discussing the value of user contribution is limited – they are exceptional cases of events such as protests or natural disasters. Moreover, even in these cases, there is a limited role ascribed to the audience; their contribution is contained to a specific phase of the news production process, namely the news-gathering phase. Or, as one journalist puts it clearly when reflecting on user participation, 'it's not someone writing the story for us'.[13] UGC can have value, but even the most avid proponents of UGC consider its advantage limited to the 'news-gathering potential'.

Above all, UGC provides a quick way of getting to information:

> User-generated content with stills and video is tremendously important now for any 24 hour news operation to have that kind of relationship with its audience, because if you want speed of reaction, then of course the first people, they are the public, and if you can get them to send you their video or stills or whatever, then that gives you competitive advantage as a 24/7 news provider.
>
> (Deputy editor, national broadcaster, interview conducted in 2008)

UGC in this way brings a new element of competition between news media. Now news organisations are not only competing with one another for people as audience, but also as news providers: 'you're in competition to bring people in and use them as a form of information, because people have phones and they take pictures and are more likely to be at a spot than a journalist initially'.[14] Or, as the BSkyB chief financial officer notes, 'UGC can be a differentiator in terms of our ability to get stories on air faster. ... So we're in a competitive race, both technologically to make ourselves easy to send images to and also rhetorically with other organisations.'[15]

Another way in which using UGC is considered to provide competitive advantage is through 'adding colour to stories'. UGC, as one editor explains, provides 'access to people who have had personal experience of news stories'.[16] Thus, journalists argue, UGC provides a way of tapping into 'reality': 'the organisation that [manages UGC] best is unbeatable, because you're tapping into reality'.[17] The web, as another journalist argues, 'is a great aid to some sort of authenticity'[18] and by drawing on the experiences shared online, journalists can 'make real the fact that we're not making it up' as well as give 'an impression of mood'.[19]

Using UGC for the competitive advantage of news organisations is of course highly understandable in light of the economic imperatives of these organisations. As a finance director of a national newspaper group notes: 'we can't afford to have reporters in every single village in the whole area [that we are operating in]'.[20] However, particularly as we are viewing these practices in light of the promise of democratisation, this does raise the question to what extent using UGC is just another measure to cut the budget and a way of employing cheap labour. See also our discussion in Chapter 1 about the proposal to use volunteers in local news production (Parry, 2009). This is an ongoing debate in which the outsourcing of salaried work to unpaid amateurs is critiqued (see, for instance, Deuze, 2009b). As one editor remarks:

> Bizarrely, people were sending us the pictures [of the Glasgow bombing] and then running back to the scene of the fire to send us more, and they weren't even being paid, how utterly bizarre.
>
> (Editor, BBC College of Journalism, interview conducted in 2008)

It is important to note, however, that even though UGC may provide cheap(er) forms of news-gathering, managing UGC is far from free and, as Hermida and Thurman (2008: 352) point out, news organisations struggle 'to balance the resources needed to control – editorially – UGCIs [user-generated content initiatives] with the commercial potential of user media'. As outlined above, journalists use UGC only in a filtered edited form. Moreover, only very few stories are actually sourced through UGC (Phillips, 2010). Thus:

> To really create something from it you have to have community managers, you have to have a moderation policy, you have to have a platform that

supports it, you have to have something that scales, and none of those things are particularly cheap.

(Online news executive, national newspaper, interview conducted in 2008)

In their struggle to on the one hand take part in the trend of user participation and on the other to maintain standards and protect their professional identity, news organisations provide possibilities to participate, overseen by journalists. Domingo *et al.* (2008: 337) question whether this provides audiences with any access to the job of selecting or filtering news stories, which, they contend, remains the sole province of journalists. They suggest this demonstrates that user participation does not put more control in the hands of the audience – a finding that is in line with the ways in our interviewees report on user participation in their newsrooms.

User participation is 'nothing new'

Even so, as argued in Chapter 6, users do have an influence on agenda setting via new media technologies, which are employed to monitor audience interest. These two roles of the audience in the news process – as sources of news through various forms of 'witnessing' and as a factor in determining the news agenda – have always existed. In this light, journalists rightly challenge the newness of UGC that is implied when it is presented as a disruptive democratising force. The audience has always participated in the news process, particularly at the news-gathering stage, and even though the technology has changed (and thus perhaps the frequency with which the audience participates), the nature of the process has not changed:

> I think this is like a re-labelling of the wheel, in that people have always interacted with news stories, people have always provided pictures, there wouldn't be any stories otherwise, would there? Okay, now it's easier and I think the digital tools have made it more noticeable.
>
> (Web editor, regional newspaper, interview conducted in 2007)

The journalists argue that UGC is not new, even when the term is, and thus it is nothing revolutionary that may fundamentally change their role. The following quote does state that there has been a change in the amount of user participation, but no change in the nature of the participation. Moreover, the value of this is again brought back to the economic advantage, not to the democratising potential of UGC:

> User-generated content is a big thing for us now. ... I think they've just given a new name to an old term because we've always relied on people bringing us stories. But it's just the way that they bring us stories that has changed. ... I think it's good [that it's increased] because people sell news-papers. So, the more stories we can get in from people, the more important it is.
>
> (General reporter, regional newspaper, interview conducted in 2007)

Some of the interviewees argue that not even the difficulties with UGC, such as its reliability, are specific to new media:

> It's nothing new. We've always had reliable eyewitnesses and unreliable eyewitnesses. It's part of a journalist's role to pull the facts from the fiction and make a judgement what they believe is right and true.
>
> (BBC News executive, interview conducted in 2007)

We see that even as a news-gathering tool, to which its use seems to be limited, the role of UGC is restricted to providing 'fill up' for existing stories. In the interviews only one example was provided of a 'good story' that came out of UGC; most of the UGC is not productive they argue, which, according to one of the interviewees, 'is supported by the fact that most of it's ungrammatical, unpunctuated nonsense'.[21] In commenting that they 'have always done it', BSkyB chief financial officer reflects on the fact that the current practice of his organisation is perhaps not really 'proper' UGC – 'it's not people making their own news stories, but it's image collection'.[22]

Whether this is because of an aversion by journalists to UGC or the economic reality of how costly it is to process UGC, it is difficult to imagine in this environment how new media will 'allow the average person to contribute to the democratic process in meaningful ways' (Muthukumaraswamy, 2010: 48). For journalists user participation does not mean more control for the public in the news production process.

Of course, it is beyond doubt that this is an ongoing development and, as noted earlier, the news organisations are still trying to find ways of dealing with the potential that new media bring for the role of the audience, as is illustrated by the following:

> It's fledgling, it's new and I suppose we're going to have to adapt as we go along learning to trust the public. We do need to open up. We do need to democratise and we do need to capitalise on the expertise that is out there. ... We do want to open up so it's not just us reaching out; it's a two-way process. At the same time we've got to protect our brand and protect other people who use the site from some of the sick people that are out there.
>
> (Sky News executive, interview conducted in 2007)

Changing role of audiences, changing role of journalists?

Mitchelstein and Boczkowski identify three key issues on which studies of 'professional and occupational dynamics' have focused:

> [i] the identity of journalism as a profession or occupation and its continued relevance in a networked society; [ii] the self-reflection of journalists about possible changes to their professional identities; and [iii] the challenges posed

by user-authored content to the jurisdictional space that news workers occupy as gatekeepers of information.

(Mitchelstein and Boczkowski, 2009: 570)

We have at different places discussed our findings with regard to identity (see, for instance, Chapter 1 in this book) and self-reflection (see, for instance, Witschge and Nygren, 2009, as well as Chapter 2 in this book). In this section I focus on the challenges and examine the reflection of journalists on their position as gatekeepers of information and the way in which they feel new media technologies have impacted on this position.

The interviews, while asking how journalists view the role of the audience or the amateur's contribution to the news process, provide a lot of insight into how they view their own role in this process. As the above sections showed, where the role of the journalists starts is where the role of the audience ends. Even though interviewees are very reflective on their role in the news process, 'traditional' values dominate in their thinking about their role. In an environment where they feel they are less and less able to produce 'proper' journalism (Witschge and Nygren, 2009), they struggle to uphold the professional values of journalism. Even so, they maintain that these values set them apart from citizens who contribute to the news process and argue that this role of the journalist is still needed in society. Accordingly, there is a strong belief that traditional journalism will survive, with the journalist as expert sticking to their traditional values. (The role of traditional journalistic ethics as a response to new media technologies is discussed in Fenton and Witschge, 2010.)

We find that the public-interest notion of journalism is still very much alive among journalists – which does not suggest that journalists are not aware of the commercial realities of their news practice:

> You know, there could be stories which are very important, which people might find even boring ... it could be the thing that destroys our financial system, so there's some things that you have to take a judgement about and say this is really important and [you have to] try and make it at least clear and engaging but [you can] not think oh well people are more interested in [stories such as] 'Beckham not being picked for England'.
>
> (BBC presenter, interview conducted in 2008)

That journalists do not feel there is a real threat to their position is also found by O'Sullivan and Heinonen, in their survey among European journalists: two-thirds of the questioned journalists do not consider amateur contributions to the news a threat to the role of newspapers (2008: 364). The authors conclude that 'the social institution called journalism is hesitant in abandoning its conventions' (ibid: 368). Similarly, Domingo *et al.* find that the traditional, and core role of journalists as gatekeepers 'remained the monopoly of professionals' (2008: 335).[23] Even though now both news sources and amateurs can potentially reach a wide audience without the journalists as intermediary, our research found the view of journalists as gatekeepers to be dominant. The word gatekeeping, though, was not explicitly mentioned by the interviewed journalists; it remained 'an implicit thread running through much of their reasoning' as was also found by Lewis *et al.* (2010: 175).

Thus, the journalistic tasks remain with the journalists. As discussed in the above, even those advocating a close relationship with the audience emphasise the role of the journalist in adding value to audience contributions, as this editor's view illustrates:

> That kind of relationship with our audience or people who've actually really got some important bit of information to tell us, which we then need to go away, investigate, check, corroborate, etc, etc, is really vital to our kind of journalism.
>
> (Deputy editor, national broadcaster, interview conducted in 2008)

Lewis *et al.* (2010: 169) similarly found that a large part of the people working in the news field 'make a clear distinction between professionally trained journalists and everyone else, and they see journalism as the business of professionals only'. The trained professional remains an indispensable actor in the news process according to our interviewees:

> I don't think you can replace journalists with the public effectively. You know, I mean they can provide material. ... You can make spaces within the news organisations as a platform for their ideas, and obviously as a journalist you should be aware of not just assuming a kind of an authority. But at the end of the day they're not trained journalists, they don't know what they're doing a lot of the time, so it's not right that they should – I don't think you can replace one with the other really.
>
> (Online journalist, national broadcaster, interview conducted in 2008)

Before dismissing this as a sign that journalists are 'stuck' in their traditional ways of thinking, we need to consider whether we want to let go of the journalist as expert, adding value. Recent times have seen many a budget cut in the field of journalism, with a considerable cut in the number of specialist reporters, foreign correspondents and others who are so very important to the diversity and quality of media content. The homogeneity in content that results from heavily relying on press releases and agency material is a serious threat to the public-service function of news media. Before dismissing the view of journalists that their training and experience allows them to make a difference, we need to consider what we take issue with. If the current practices of journalism are not up to scratch (which journalists acknowledge), we need to consider why this is the case, and try to find ways of supporting journalists aiming to perform their profession to their standards, rather than asking them to further negate their professional values. (See Chapter 1 for a discussion of possible models of sustaining public interest journalism.)

There is very little actual insight into what the audience wants in terms of user participation. According to the interviewees, not all members of the audience are interested in citizen-led journalism:

> A lot of the feedback [on a trial on Newsnight for the audience to decide what the news is] was: 'You do your own job, I spend all day at work, I come home and I want to know what the news is, don't expect me to do your job for you.'
>
> (Editor, BBC College of Journalism, interview conducted in 2008)

> There is a limit to how much popular input you can take, and I have heard there is something of a backlash from people saying: 'We pay the licence fee for you people to do the work: stop asking us to do it for you.'
>
> (BBC News executive, interview conducted in 2008)

Thus, as a BBC News executive puts it: 'Among all the untrustworthy news we have a role to stand out'.[24] So what then sets journalists apart? What makes them stand out in this world of ever increasing numbers of producers of content? One of the interviewees nicely summarises his thoughts, and they voice the view of a large number of the journalists interviewed:

> I think that what sets journalists apart is the ability to communicate, the ability to distil, the ability to aggregate lots of different content sources and make sense of them, and crucially access [news sources].
>
> (News executive, national newspaper, interview conducted in 2008)

Does content remain king?

Largely then, the interviewees consider the role of the journalist unchanged. There is, however, one area where we can see a debate springing up: is journalism an act of 'creation' or of 'curation'? Does the journalist create news, content and analysis, or is the role of the journalist increasingly that of an editor of content provided by others (especially with the increasing amount of amateur contributions through media technology)? Even though this distinction is to a large extent analytical – the straightforward answer would be: the journalist does both – I will discuss this debate here, as it provides an interesting reflection on the role of journalists in the news process. There are only a few (all of them new media proponents) who are pushing for the role of the journalist as curator – in our sample only two argued for this role of curation – but they have growing cultural capital in the news organisations for which they work.

With the increased amount of user-generated content, for a number of journalists (in particular online) their task consists of sifting through the pictures, videos and text produced by amateurs. However, only a few would argue that this is also ideally the only task that journalists undertake; the journalists whose job consisted of this work solely all felt that what they were doing was not 'journalism', was not what they had been trained to do. Equally, few interviewees in describing the role of journalists focus on their role as filter for, or as editor of, material they have not created themselves. Of course, these positions assume UGC to be unfinished material, something that needs attention and work from the journalists. In this view, though, user contributions are secondary to, or at best input for, journalistic output. One journalist, however, puts user contributions central to the news process, and argues that more and more the journalist's job is to respond to what the audience brings them: they can 'pick out a really good [user] comment and go and write their next article in that vein'; and 'the other thing that journalists are useful for is filtering and curating stuff'.[25]

An online news executive at the same organisation similarly argues that journalism is increasingly 'an act of curation rather than act of creation'.[26] Accordingly, she speaks of a 'comment organisation' (instead of a news organisation), where the news is the 'context' in which the users operate, and where the users are offered 'data' and 'immersive experiences' rather than traditional news and commentary. News, in this view, is not the core of the organisation, but user participation is. Thus, and provocatively, the news executive maintains she does not 'believe in the holy power of original content creation and by-lines'.[27]

This type of fundamentally alternative view of journalism and news organisations remains rather marginal. Some may acknowledge that new media technologies allowing user participation affect the role of editors and journalists, but very few are actively trying to push more and more control to the users. Even the view that social networking and crowd-sourcing tools may impact on the journalist's role – such as is expressed in the following quote – is still marginal among those working in the news industry (see also Chapter 6 for a discussion of how these new media technologies have impacted on the practice in journalism):

> The power of something like Digg and social bookmarking and tagging means that actually what people consider to be relevant news is in a sense no longer decided by us in the media.
>
> (Technology correspondent, national broadcaster, interview conducted in 2007)

Conclusion

I started this chapter by summarising the expectations that exist regarding the democratising effect that new media technologies are considered to have on the news process. Authors such as Muthukumaraswamy maintain that a 'significant accomplishment of the new media world is a shifting of power from publishers and advertisers toward the people' (2010: 50). In this chapter, rather than assuming this democratisation process to be a *fait accompli*, I have asked to what extent we can see a transfer of control from the traditional gatekeepers in the field of news production to the audience. To be clear, I do not argue that such transfer is necessarily desirable. Rather, the argument of this book is that there remains a specific role for journalists to play in the changing mediascape (see also Hind,

2010). However, given the rhetoric of progressive change that underlies a lot of the employment of new media technologies in news organisations and beyond, we need to consider its consequences.

I have argued that journalists and editors have not embraced the assumed potential of new media technologies in providing a considerable role for the audience in the news production process. To be sure, every journalist acknowledges the current necessity of user participation. However, the way in which this is employed and viewed suggests that a 'minimalist' view of participation dominates in news organisations; the endorsed forms of participation are those that 'do not touch the core of the power relations of the social systems that might be organizing or facilitating these practices' (Carpentier, 2009: 417). Thus, even though participation is a concept that is 'deemed socially and politically beneficial' (ibid), and most importantly – as our research showed – considered to be of economic benefit, the public has a 'rather limited potential to "wrest power from the few"' (van Dijck, 2009: 42).

It is important to acknowledge, though, that there is an ongoing process of change in the news field, and journalists 'live out in their everyday practices a tension between tradition and change' (Mitchelstein and Boczkowski, 2009: 575). Journalists are continually responding to the changes in their field and there is a constant quest for 'differentiation'. Key questions for the future remain: what is the position that journalists will take in the field of news? What is their cultural capital in the news process (Kunelius, 2009: 343)? Change does take place, 'but as an element of the perpetual development of capitalist production relations' (Webster quoted in Conboy and Steel, 2008: 655).

On this critical note, we should also consider that – although there has not been a transferral of power to the audiences – this does not mean that there has not been 'wholesale redistribution of agency away from those who tend to crave only one thing: creative and editorial autonomy' (Deuze, 2009b: 317). If creative and editorial autonomy does not currently lie with the journalists, we need to ask where this does lie. At the moment, it seems that the economic imperatives have considerably weakened the position of journalists, and this seems to be an ongoing process (as also discussed in Chapter 5). We need to consider which of the professional values held in high esteem by journalist are worth saving and investing in, before assuming that the public can and should take over any of the journalistic tasks. The next chapter focuses on the new ethical practices that should become commonplace for journalism in the changing mediascape.

Notes

1 Online News executive, national newspaper, interview conducted in 2008.
2 Managing director, Interactive Media Company, interview conducted in 2007.
3 Deputy editor, national broadcaster, interview conducted in 2008.
4 As noted by a journalist working in the online community team at a national newspaper, interview conducted in 2008.
5 Web editor, regional newspaper, interview conducted in 2007.
6 News editor, regional newspaper, interview conducted in 2008.

7 Interestingly, local journalists are even more dismissive than journalists working for national media, even though the added value of user participation is considered to be highest for hyper-local initiatives. It remains a question whether this is because they feel more threatened by the trend of user participation, or whether it is because local newspapers are 'behind larger organizations in Web sophistication' in general, as was found to be the case for the newspapers in the research conducted by Lewis *et al.* (2010: 166).

8 Yahoo for instance did not allow comments after 2006, and only opened up this possibility in March 2010, in response to a 'very strong desire from the audience ... to interact with the news site at a much more profound level' (Tartakoff, 2010).

9 BBC presenter, interview conducted 2007.

10 The term framed UGC was introduced by a web editor of a regional newspaper (interview conducted in 2007).

11 Web editor, regional newspaper, interview conducted in 2007.

12 Editor, BBC Radio, interview conducted in 2008.

13 Online journalist, national broadcaster, interview conducted in 2008.

14 Online journalist, national broadcaster, interview conducted in 2008.

15 Interview conducted in 2008.

16 BBC News editor, interview conducted in 2007.

17 BBC News executive, interview conducted in 2007.

18 News executive, national newspaper, interview conducted in 2008.

19 Editor, BBC Radio, interview conducted in 2008.

20 Finance director, national newspaper group, interview conducted in 2008.

21 Trainee at a national newspaper, interview conducted in 2008.

22 Interview conducted in 2008.

23 This is contrary to Steensen who found that in feature journalism, audience participation 'challenges the traditional role of journalists as gatekeepers as it allows alternative flows of information to enter both the production and publication of journalism' (2009: 714).

24 Interview conducted in 2008.

25 Journalist working in the online community team at a national newspaper, interview conducted in 2008.

26 Online news executive, national newspaper, interview conducted in 2008.

27 Ibid.

8 Transparency and the ethics of new journalism

Angela Phillips

In a modern democracy, journalism derives authority from its claim to provide an essential contribution to democratic functioning. That authority in turn rests upon an expectation that journalists will behave according to a certain set of ethical standards, in relation to truth telling, fairness and the duty to inform citizens of events that matter (Hallin and Mancini, 2004: 37). Put simply, citizens in a democracy rely on access to information they believe to be reliable. This chapter asks whether it is possible for journalists always to behave ethically and provide material that is reliable, when commercial considerations, in an ever more competitive market, are pressing in on one side, and the free-wheeling and apparently ethic-free blogosphere is pressing in from another. It goes on to consider whether, in a context in which the need for speed is eroding standards of fact checking (Phillips, 2010) and web-only organisations are prepared to publish material without any checks (Pew Research Center for the People and the Press, 2008), it may be necessary to evolve new methods and procedures for ensuring that information is reliable, or new ways of presenting material which is not so dependent on speed.

In most democracies, there has been an assumption that the circulation of reliable information is best provided by a free press, via the unfettered working of the market. Where journalism is partisan, liberal press theory assumes that alternative voices will rise to counter the bias. In some instances, government subsidies, and publicly owned media, exist explicitly to provide such 'balance' (for example in Holland and Sweden, see Chapter 1). But markets function to maximise profit, not to maximise democratic debate, and therein lies the dilemma at the heart of any discussion about journalism and ethics.

We have written in earlier chapters about the tendency of media markets to move towards monopoly (Bourdieu, 2005) and of the ways in which the internet, via the use of algorithms, exacerbates that tendency (Hindman, 2009). As Bourdieu (2005) observes, this move towards monopoly is also a move towards the centre, as each media organisation seeks to establish the biggest possible presence by occupying the centre ground. The occupation of the centre ground, and the necessity to build ever larger audiences, funded online by advertising (see Chapter 1), has a tendency to tilt news organisations further towards the commercial pole. 'As television news has become commercialised, the need to make it entertaining has become a crucial priority for broadcasters' (Thussu, 2009). Not, of course, only for broadcasters. As news moves online it finds itself competing with, rather than being subsidised by, entertainment (see Chapter 1). A glance at the online version of the UK newspaper the *Daily Mail* reveals what this means. The online version has become a celebrity magazine – quite unlike its printed parent.

It is in this context of competition for the centre ground that we need to consider the question of journalistic standards and ethics, as specific collective practices,[1] rather than simply as individual attributes. Journalists, whatever their personal beliefs, work in the context of institutions which set ground rules. In most instances those ground rules are very clearly defined. The collective practices of news journalism vary both nationally and according to institutional culture but, as news media move outside their institutional 'comfort zones' and into a global arena, a need arises for an ethical practice which can traverse cultural boundaries. In order to establish an ethical practice for the future it is useful to consider the ethical practices of the present.

Neutrality, accuracy and sincerity

Neutrality

Neutrality is one 'virtue' that is often proposed as a universal journalistic ethic. It is certainly a very useful concept for news agencies (see Chapter 4), which need to ensure that their information can be used across the opinion spectrum by a very wide variety of outlets. It has also been useful as a regulatory requirement for network television. Television news regulation was devised in a period of 'spectrum scarcity' when a few major TV channels controlled all the information being piped into individual homes. The insistence on 'balance', 'fairness' and professional 'neutrality' was an attempt to offset that power. In countries where there is public provision of television, neutrality is normally a requirement for television journalists, on the grounds that, if the people are paying for it, or subsidising it, they should feel represented by it. However, while it is reasonable to expect that a public broadcaster should be fair, avoid extremism and give space to a variety of viewpoints, that is not the same as neutrality which assumes no opinion at all.

Neutrality is in fact almost impossible to achieve because the very act of selecting a fact requires a judgement to be made. Why is this fact more important than that one? Why is this person's version of events given priority over that one's? In general, 'neutral' tends to mean 'consensual' which is not the same at all (Golding and Elliott, 1979; Entman, 2003). I would argue that, far from being an ethical touchstone, the idea that news should always be neutral grew up as a way of making monopoly news providers more palatable in a democracy.

Neutrality is particularly prized as an ethical benchmark in the United States, where most newspapers are regional or local, and there has been very little competition for readers over the last half century (Hallin and Mancini, 2004: 27), journalism has developed an ideology of professionalism in which there is a presumption of neutrality. In European countries, where newspapers compete for audiences and take clearly observable political positions – Hallin and Mancini refer to this as 'political parallelism' (2004: 27) – neutrality is not a key ethical benchmark.

Accuracy

If neutrality cannot be an agreed standard for journalism, accuracy is generally considered to be the ethical bedrock upon which the 'profession' is founded. This does not mean an adherence to some non-negotiable essential version of events; it does mean that journalists, in telling their version of events, should be able to say with sincerity that they believe their version of events to be correct. 'Accuracy is the disposition to take the necessary care to ensure so far as possible that what one says is not false, sincerity the disposition to make sure that what one says is what one actually believes' (Phillips *et al.*, 2010: 53). While there is rarely one verifiable truth in any complex and changing situation, journalists – particularly those who adhere to the liberal or democratic corporatist traditions described by Hallin and Mancini – agree that they should at least make the effort to find and tell the truth by checking and verifying information (Fenton and Witschge, 2010).

Indeed, US media scholar Michael Schudson suggests that journalists, along with the judiciary and academics, have a duty to search for the truth:

> We cannot escape making sense of our world. But we are forbidden from trying to do so without making a conscientious appeal to the facts. As imperfectly as we are able to know them. As mute as they sometimes are. It is the least bad system of knowing that we have.
>
> (Schudson, 2009a: 113)

Sincerity and autonomy

The philosopher Bernard Williams (2002: 44) suggests that the two basic 'virtues of truth' or truthfulness are accuracy and sincerity. This allows for the possibility that a person may be wrong – as long as he or she sincerely believes that what they were saying was right at the time. It is a useful definition of 'truth telling', because it describes a process of discovery rather than a verifiable position. It makes more sense to judge the ethics of a journalist by their sincerity in looking for the truth than by the fact of having arrived at a truth. However, the ability to act with sincerity depends on a degree of autonomy. A person who always does what they are told, whether or not they agree with what they are told, is not acting ethically.

This is a particular problem for journalists because, although autonomy is prized as a journalistic norm within the profession, journalists do not always have the economic freedom to act autonomously (Bourdieu, 2005: 41). This is especially so in a news culture which does not encourage reflexivity. In the highly competitive

British market, some newspapers are run on industrial lines, in tightly controlled pyramid structures in which the editor has complete control. Others delegate decision making to subject specialists in collaboration with editors. Other national contexts may feature a greater reflexivity and debate about ethical standards. Cross-national research into the coverage of the Danish Muhammad cartoons affair, for example, found that there was more debate in newsrooms in Norway and Sweden than in the UK or USA (Eide, Kunelius and Phillips, 2008).

Without individual autonomy, ethical actions must be reduced to the status of a set of 'rules', which can be subsumed within journalistic practice, and against which employers can be held to account for the actions of their staff. While the detail of the rules may be obeyed meticulously, the spirit is often missing entirely. This desk editor on a mid-market tabloid explained just how the rules may be implemented in practice.

> It isn't [that it's] untrue. It is giving prominence to a minor feature. There has to be some kernel of truth. It may be twisted or biased but there must be some truth. [The paper] works on the presumption that negative news sells – always go for the negative line even if it isn't typical. There is nothing untrue but it isn't a balanced representation. It's been twisted to conform to an idea. If you leave ethics out, it's good professional journalism and it sells papers.
>
> (News editor, national newspaper, interview conducted in 2008)

This comment was made by a news editor, in a highly centralised, very commercial newsroom in which the attitude of editors tends to be: 'Do what we say or leave.' Clearly this journalist was not 'sincere' in believing that the newspaper provides an accurate portrayal of events. Truth is being held onto as a 'talisman' rather than as a virtue. In this particular newsroom debate is not welcome, and journalists learn that 'professionalism' is about ignoring personal ethical concerns in favour of producing the kind of material required by the editor. Journalists are theoretically allowed to decline to write a story they don't agree with, but there is a clear sense that they wouldn't last long in the job if they took that position (Phillips *et al.*, 2010: 55).

The newspaper mentioned above stands at the most commercial edge of the British journalistic field and is not typical of all newsrooms. However, even at the more autonomous end there is in fact very little space made for ethical debate (Phillips, 2003) and there is no legal protection offered to journalists who take a stand on ethical grounds (Phillips *et al.*, 2010: 51). In some Northern European newsrooms, a more reflexive approach is expected. However, international studies of journalism demonstrate that, although national attitudes differ in relation to ethical practices, globalisation works to homogenise practice as commercial considerations take centre stage (Hallin and Mancini, 2004: 277). This may be particularly pertinent in the English-language press, where competition for audience share is now international. For journalists to maintain ethical standards they need to have the freedom to act autonomously. However, in the fevered atmosphere of speed and commercialism that has infected so many newsrooms as a response to competitive pressures (see Chapters 1 and 4), journalists are too often forced to take short cuts with accuracy:

> Well, when all this, when this pressure started happening, I just had daily fights with them. I'd stand at the news desk and go 'but why do you want me to run it, it's not true'. And they, I mean you could actually see the veins in their neck kind of wobbling and they were going purple. But now, I just say 'yeah, fine, 600 words by 2 o'clock'. They don't care whether it's true or not. They literally do not.
>
> (Specialist reporter, national newspaper, interview conducted in 2008)

Ethical behaviour relies on the individual feeling able to act well of their own accord. In this atmosphere there is little room for acting autonomously.

Differentiate or die

Part of the pressure on journalists to leave their scruples at home comes from the pressure to find a celebrity angle to every story. Celebrity gossip comes high up amongst the most read topics on internet sites and some newspapers have massively increased their coverage of this material. According to the Pew Center research which looked at stories on Yahoo news for one week, 'the Most Viewed stories were often breaking news, more sensational in nature, with a heavy dose of crime and celebrity' (Pew Project for Excellence in Journalism, 2007). Publishing such stories has become part of a public relations 'game' in which 'truth' plays only a passing role. The stories get read and keep Google ratings high. Indeed their main purpose on news sites and in newspapers is to induce people to click or buy and, in doing so, to pull in the advertising pounds that news organisations depend on to pay their journalists. As businesses seek an audience, a certain proportion will simply give in to the gravitational pull of pure entertainment and seek to provide a bigger, flashier and faster way of offering it.

In an increasingly pressured and homogenised market, there is a temptation to slough off any pretension to provide a contribution to democratic debate and go entirely for high audience numbers, by jumping on the celebrity bandwagon and replacing truth with innuendo and facts with gossip. Bourdieu (2005), discussing field theory in relation both to individual journalists and also to news organisations, describes the paradox at the centre of the journalism field but at the same time points towards one possible solution for news organisations in an increasingly homogenised market:

> To exist in a field … is to differentiate oneself. It can be said of an intellectual that he or she functions like a phoneme in a language: he or she exists by virtue of difference from other intellectuals. Falling into undifferentiatedness … means losing existence.
>
> (Bourdieu, 2005: 39–40)

In the news industry, as Bourdieu (2005: 44) suggests, the fierce competition for differentiation is 'usually judged by access to news, the "scoop", exclusive information and also distinctive rarity, "big names" and so on'. However, he explains, commercial competition functions, paradoxically, to undermine the very differentiation it seeks, as competitive pressures force organisations to copy one another in order to monopolise the greatest number of readers. The results can readily be seen: as new technologies lower the cost of entry into news production, far from an increase in the number of different news outlets, competition has led to greater consolidation (Bourdieu, 1998; Herman and McChesney, 1997; House of Lords, 2008). There may be more outlets but they tend to be servicing the same people and largely with the same information (Redden and Witschge, 2010).

This trend is exacerbated by the practice of taking material from other news outlets without follow-up or attribution. Before convergence, newspapers were inhibited from simply taking copy from another paper by the necessities of the technology. They would have to wait for the early editions of rival newspapers before they were able to take any material, and then they would be limited by the sheer inconvenience of replacing large swathes at the last minute. A big newspaper scoop would give that publication a day to pick up new readers who were unable to get the same news elsewhere. Today news can be immediately 'scraped' off the site of a rival and re-organised a little. The intensity of competition on the internet, coupled with the lack of technical or temporal barriers to making use of information lifted from elsewhere, means that it is difficult for any news organisation to retain exclusivity for more than a few minutes. In this atmosphere it is hard indeed to ensure accuracy because that requires the journalist to take time and fact check. In one interview, a journalist remarked:

> I'd imagine people are really pissed off with me because I'm quite often told to take things. I put my by-line on there and it just looks as though I'm just stealing stuff all the time.
>
> (Junior reporter, national newspaper, interview conducted in 2008)

In the qualitative research undertaken to investigate changing relationships between journalists and their sources, journalists were interviewed in detail about the original and follow-up sources for recent stories. The practices at the *Telegraph*, the only national newspaper with a 'web first' approach at that time (early 2008), were different from those at other national newspapers. A third of the *Daily Telegraph* stories discussed had been lifted directly from another news organisation. None was attributed. *Telegraph* reporters also made fewer follow-up calls when covering a story. One explained:

> They go: 'Can you do 400 words on this', and it's something from the *Daily Mail* or something. I'd read it through, find out who the people are, try and move it forward a bit. So I was doing that one day ... , and the news editor came over and goes, 'You haven't filed that thing ... ', and I was like 'I'm

just speaking to the mother now to get some quotes', and he was like, 'don't bother with that, it's been in the *Daily Mail* just rewrite it'.

(Junior reporter, *Telegraph* newspaper, interview conducted in 2008)

On another story, the journalist states:

I got that [indicates story selected by interviewer] this morning when I came in. It's Page 5 in the *Sun* I think. That bit wasn't in it ... I added that in yeah, but all the quotes are from the *Sun*.

(ibid)

Clearly a reporter who copies the work of others without checking that it is accurate is not 'sincerely' seeking the truth. But there is an additional problem. The journalist who did the original work no longer gets the credit; the newspaper can no longer count on the added value of a scoop; and the incentive for original reporting starts to disappear. If all news is available freely online and all news organisations provide the same material, what reason is there to go out and spend money on one particular version of the news? In these circumstances, the most likely outcome will be further consolidation and a greater tendency to monopoly as weaker publications go to the wall (Häckner and Nyberg, 2008: 94).

The issue here is not simply one of ethics; it is also about commercial survival. The more each new organisation pulls into the centre to try and attract a mass audience, the harder it is to stand out as a unique and special place and to create audience loyalty (with the higher paying, premium advertising that goes with it). As the news industry reforms itself, news organisations will be forced to differentiate or simply be subsumed into one or two huge news providers (ibid). Differentiation will be the key to survival, and news organisations will need to reformulate old assumptions about ethical practice as they struggle to find themselves a place within a newly constituted journalism field.

The need for differentiation has not gone entirely unanswered, but the major form of differentiation so far has been via political polarisation. In the USA, Fox News sprang up to satisfy an audience that had long demonstrated its disaffection with what it perceived to be the 'liberal bias' of the TV news networks. In a 2010 poll (Public Policy Polling quoted by Pilkington, 2010), the Fox credibility rating was considerably higher than that of its more mainstream rivals. This form of differentiation may be a useful short-term business strategy for Fox but, according to Mike Hoyt, editor of the *Columbia Journalism Review*, 'Fox News is not really a news network, it's a commentary network. Its news output is a small island in a vast sea of very conservative commentary' (quoted in Pilkington, 2010).

In this it has much in common with the other new entrants to the news journalism market: the aggregators such as the *Huffington Post* and *The Daily Beast*. They also take their news from other sources and make their money by contextualising it. This has certainly been a cheap and useful strategy for a new internet business but it depends on an old and very expensive business model: the collection and dissemination of news by reporters. It does nothing to support that model financially. Like mistletoe clinging to a tree, it looks very attractive, it gathers audiences, but it may well kill off the host that supports it (see also Chapters 1 and 5). Differentiation will not be enough if news organisations are robbed of the value they invest in news-gathering. What is required is a re-evaluation of news as a product. News organisations need to find ways of making it much clearer that they are providing a product that is unique and valuable – and that means ensuring that the product they sell really is unique and valuable. In a market dominated by celebrity scandal (Pew Project for Excellence in Journalism, 2007), the adoption of clear and accountable ethical standards could be a means of differentiation as well as a contribution to democracy.

Evaporating trust

News is ephemeral and its existence as a viable product lies only in the value that audiences place in it. Trust is central to that value. Audiences may enjoy silly video clips on YouTube, and get a laugh from reading Pop Bitch, but they don't expect the information contained there to be accurate and truthful. Increasingly people are sceptical also of the news services, particularly online where people can easily move between completely unbelievable 'tall' stories and the day's news without very much difference in the form of presentation. 'Online news outlets are viewed with more scepticism than their print, broadcast and cable counterparts. Of seven organisations evaluated, none is viewed as highly credible by even a quarter of online users able to rate them' (Pew Research Center for the People and the Press, 2008).

A UK survey for the *British Journalism Review* demonstrated a sharp decline in trust for all journalists between 2003 and 2008 (Barnett, 2008). This research, however, also suggests that, though people are less trusting, they have not lost the ability to differentiate between more and less trustworthy sources. Audiences recognise that journalists working for the BBC, Channel 4 and 'up-market' and local newspapers are more trustworthy than those working on the mid-market and 'red-top' popular newspapers. Even those who habitually read 'red-top' popular newspapers see reporters on the 'up-market' newspapers and BBC journalists as more trustworthy. Similarly, in the USA the Pew Center found that those who are aware of the existence of the *Wall Street Journal* are more likely to trust that than to trust the newspaper they regularly read (Pew Research Center for the People and the Press, 2008).

These findings are important, not just because they underline a growing wariness, but because they make it clear that responsible journalism is worth preserving, not just for those who regularly consume it, but also as a benchmark and reference point for those who know that their regular paper is not a source of trustworthy information. This matters for the health of democracy because, even though a growing number of people do not regularly consume news from authoritative sources, and although they treat journalists and journalism with scepticism, they clearly have a sense of where they expect to find authoritative news should they need it. What they might not realise is how imperilled those authoritative sources actually are. The loss of respect is not something that occurs overnight. Audiences are loyal and take a while to notice that they can no longer trust the organisation they have always bought their news from. But once trust has gone, the collapse may be precipitous and the audience unreclaimable.

The following questions arise: what is responsible journalism? Where can it be found? And how should it be protected so that it is indeed still there when those who have spent their days reading celebrity blogs find that they have need of it? The answers do not lie in the futile exercise of trying to sort out the difference between bloggers, 'citizen' journalists and 'real' journalists. We must define what we mean by authority, and examine whether those who appear to have authority are actually acting sincerely. Anyone who diligently, and regularly, works to supply properly checked and sourced information, which they sincerely believe to be a correct representation of the facts, will eventually build up respect, trust and, through that, authority. Anyone who simply repackages other people's work, without checking that it is correct, should gradually lose both respect and authority. The test is not who they work for (although independence from sources will always matter), nor whether they are paid (although that is usually a pretty good indicator that they have the time to concentrate on the job); it is the effort they make to verify their facts. As news journalism roles out across the internet as a taken-for-granted stream of fact-bits, democracy (and journalists) requires a means by which people can learn which news organisations they can trust to do the digging on their behalf.

Is transparency the new fact checking?

Rigourous fact checking, following up sources and verifying information are the core skills that professional journalists believe set them apart from those whom they consider to be 'amateurs' (Fenton and Witschge, 2010). However, in practice the differences are sometimes paper-thin. As we discussed earlier (see also Phillips, 2010), if journalists are using material without either checking it or attributing its source, it is hard for them to claim greater rigour than amateurs. If audiences are in no position to know who wrote the original story, where the information originated or how it could be checked, then they are not in a position to use the comment facilities offered by the web, to correct mistakes or to check their own assumptions.

Online, where speed is considered to be more important than painstaking fact checking, accuracy and sincerity reside in transparency (Blood, 2002; Singer, 2007). The internet makes transparency possible through linking and attribution, so that audiences can (if they wish) follow up and check the facts. Traditional news organisations rarely make use of this potential. Bloggers on the other hand seem to view truth as a work in progress. They tend to publish rumours with links to their sources and wait for readers to react to them, allowing for the interactivity of the web to provide its own corrective. That is the reason why attribution on the web is one of the ethical norms agreed by bloggers: 'What truth is to journalists, transparency is to bloggers' (Singer, 2007: 86). If the 'public' is to act as a corrective, it needs to be aware of where the information originated.

That is the theory. As traditional news organisations are very quick to point out, however, in reality the essential facts may not emerge before real damage has been done to individuals and organisations, when rumours fly at warp-speed around the world (Solove, 2008). As the *New Yorker* reported of the *Huffington Post*:

> During the Hurricane Katrina crisis, the activist Randall Robinson referred, in a post, to reports from New Orleans that some people there were 'eating corpses to survive.' Arianna Huffington checked and found that the information couldn't be substantiated. It was taken down but by that time it was everywhere.
>
> (Alterman, 2008)

Similar, unsubstantiated rumours of rapes and murders in the New Orleans Superdome were being referred to as fact on news sites as far away as India and South Africa (Younge, 2008).

However, it is not enough for traditional news organisations to point out the mistakes made by bloggers. As news production speeds up, the ethic of transparency has much to recommend it. Not as a substitute for fact checking but as an addition to it. Transparency is a means of demonstrating sincerity. A professional journalist should feel able to say: 'I have checked this information, I stand by it, and I am not afraid to have you check it too.' The belt and braces of fact checking, plus attribution, should give professional journalists a clear edge in the battle to restore audience trust; and it has the additional benefit of allowing audiences to check for accuracy, which also helps to build trust (O'Neill, 2002). Sadly, even though the technology makes it increasingly easy to provide the necessary information, there is little evidence that professional news organisations are becoming any more transparent.

Attribution of sources is standard practice in academic circles and to re-use someone's work without attributing it would be considered an act of plagiarism. Yet a casual attitude towards attribution goes largely unquestioned in UK news-rooms. A specialist reporter on the *Guardian* remarked that her exclusive stories were routinely picked up by the *Daily Telegraph* within minutes of appearing on-line. They were slightly reorganised but never attributed. The attitude seems to be that taking copy from other news organisations is normal and accepted behaviour, part and parcel of the rough and tumble of journalism as it is practised. Janine Gibson, digital editor of the *Guardian*, was sanguine about this practice:

> When other newspapers take our stories and use them without attribution we have drawn it to their attention. We went through a period of sending notes but it's not worth it. There isn't much more you can do. If you start a war – it's pointless. In the end the user sees through it and will look for better places for news.
>
> (Interview conducted in 2010)

The *Guardian* newspaper's own policy has always been to attribute material. Its guidance to staff says:

Plagiarism: staff must not reproduce other people's material without attribution. The source of published material obtained from another organisation should be acknowledged including quotes taken from other newspaper articles. Bylines should be carried only on material that is substantially the work of the bylined journalist. If an article contains a significant amount of agency copy then the agency should be credited.

(Guardian, internal policy document, 2009)

Policy is not, however, always the same as practice. According to cross-national research comparing major newspapers with a significant online presence, it would appear that old media, as they have moved online, have not taken on the obligation of transparency. Indeed it seems to be moving in the opposite direction. As a study by Cardiff University (Lewis *et al.*, 2008) underlines, the use of agency copy is commonplace and, as our study indicates, use of copy from other news organisations is also common. Even so, Quandt (2008: 729) found that (with exception of *Le Monde*, in France, and *USA Today*) the standard approach, internationally, was to credit only one author for news items even when they are taken from several sources. This lack of concern for the copyright of others knows no bounds. Goldsmiths journalism students, working on the East London Lines news website, find that their copy is quite regularly lifted – without attribution or linking – by mainstream news organisations.

Research by Redden and Witschge (2010) found that mainstream British news websites rarely linked to other outside sources either. Where there are links in news items they are almost always to other parts of their own website or previous stories they have generated themselves. (The BBC and the *Independent* were cited as exceptions to this rule. The BBC consistently provided links to outside source material. The *Independent* provided links to Wikipedia.) Quandt (2008: 732) found a similar reluctance to link to outside organisations in all but two of the news organisations examined. One exception was the BBC; the other was Russian site Lenta.ru.

American news organisations seem to take the question of plagiarism a great deal more seriously than British newspapers. A journalist on the *Daily Telegraph* explained that, while it was common practice to lift material from other British news sites, similar rules do not obtain when handling journalism from the USA: 'You have to attribute American newspapers because they get annoyed', he explained.[2] The coverage of the Maureen Dowd plagiarism affair in May 2009 goes someway to show the difference in approach between the UK and the USA in relation to attribution, but more pertinently between newspapers and 'web native' publications.

Maureen Dowd, a respected columnist with the *New York Times*, was found to have lifted a paragraph from a blog (*TalkingPointsMemo*). The line was of no particular importance and, as plagiarism goes, it was of minimal significance, but it was clear that she had used someone else's formulation and bloggers were very quick to point it out: 'Now, I'm all for cutting and pasting. As a blogger I do it all the time, but I always give credit.'[3] Another blogger on the site where the material had been lifted commented:

If I was e-mailed a 40-plus-word block of text for this blog, and I used it, I'd include some sort of attribution – whether 'a reader writes in,' 'media insider points out' or whatever the case may be.

(Michael Calderone, 12:22, 18 May 2009, *TalkingPointsMemo*)

Maureen Dowd promptly published a correction (Dowd, 2009).

British newspapers were quick to jump on the discussion. The *Daily Telegraph* US editor, Toby Harnden, even entered the fray (2009). None of course pointed out that this sort of behaviour is commonplace on their own pages and rarely, if ever, is a correction or apology offered, even when they are caught in the act. For example, Brian Attwood, editor of *The Stage*, wrote to the UK *Press Gazette* complaining that the *Daily Telegraph* had lifted material without attribution and had not responded to a complaint (Attwood, 2008).

Investing in trust

British newspapers may prefer not to get into a fight about copyright, but there are other interests at stake here. When journalists are expected to steal the work of others and are given no time to check their facts, it is not enough to shelter behind arguments about 'commercial' necessity or 'popularity', or even cultural differences ('naughty', 'saucy', British journalism). This ethical deficit needs to be addressed, not at the level of the individual but structurally, so that normal practice becomes ethical practice again. One way would be to use the internet as a means of improving, rather than obscuring, transparency as indicated above. This is particularly important in the networked world of online journalism.

As things stand, with the merging of platforms, the flow of news has speeded up so radically that it is impossible for any casual observer to know where a story originated, or how to verify the information. Attribution is not only a means of allowing people to trace a story back and check it. It is also a means of giving credit to the originators of information. If professional journalism was to fully embrace the blogger's code and attribute story sources routinely, it would help to produce a different form of competition for cultural capital and differentiation. This should not be difficult for mainstream news organisations to do. The Media Standards Trust has produced software that enables newspapers to properly tag their stories.[4] The data are not intrusive; they are visible only to those who want to access them. The Associated Press has shown an interest (Smith, 2009) – for commercial reasons as it will allow them to keep tabs on their own material – but, at the time of writing (2010), no other significant news organisation had signed up.

Clearly there must be some limits to attribution (Allen, 2008). The obligation not to reveal a confidential source should still trump the obligation to be transparent, if journalists are to be able to investigate behind the scenes. However, protection of confidentiality is not an issue with the vast majority of material routinely handled by journalists. And there is absolutely no reason (beyond a distorted concern for commercial and brand protection) why journalists should not credit fellow professionals from other news organisations when the occasion demands that a real scoop should be recognised. Practice is slowly evolving to meet this policy. *Guardian* digital editor Janine Gibson said: 'It's a new way of doing things – crediting and linking conflicts with old journalistic practice. When we were working on newspapers, we came in and pretended that no other news organisation existed. You cannot do that now.'[5]

Routine use of attribution and linking would also make it rather more difficult for journalists to quote selectively, and in so doing completely distort the facts. But there would be other benefits too. If journalists could no longer pretend that the material they have lifted from another source is written by them, they would be able to use their time more fruitfully following up angles and investigating original stories.

This is a point that has not been lost on the *Guardian,* where, according to Janine Gibson, they have started publishing straightforward PA stories, unedited, under a Press Association byline. She said: 'We have stopped re-writing PA copy unless we are adding value to it.'[6] This doesn't sound very radical, but if all news organisations worked in this way, they would have more time to produce original stories and that would result in an expansion of the news pool. The value of original investigation would start to rise again and, with it, the cultural capital of journalists who produce it. If every time an original story is produced, it is properly credited and points traffic back to the source, then it will also, albeit at the margins, help to stimulate greater differentiation of content

Audiences demonstrate by their actions that they value sources they consider trustworthy. The BBC's Robert Peston, who helped British audiences understand the credit crunch of 2008, gets one million hits on his personal blog. He has earned that respect by doing serious research into his subject and explaining what he has learned. Emily Bell now of Columbia University said:

> They [the BBC] pay Peston to spend time understanding complex stories and cultivating sources ... This is basic stuff but oh so important, and there can be no better use of a news organisation's resource than allowing its journalists that space and time.
>
> (Bell, 2009a)

Space and time, accuracy and sincerity – these are the things that will reconnect journalism with its audience and rebuild the trust that has been lost. Accuracy and sincerity are as likely to be provided by amateurs as by paid journalists, but space and time have to be paid for and expertise must be nurtured. By embracing the transparency allowed by the internet, by using all the benefits the internet provides in terms of easy access to verifiable information, trust in journalism can be rebuilt. But this is not the same kind of trust that used to be invested in those lofty establishment figures that dictated the news from on high. The internet provides a new way of building trust by results. Journalists will be trusted only if they are prepared to give insight into the research process that lies behind stories, to listen to their audiences, and to retract and apologise when they are wrong.

News online has opened up the possibility of a more democratic way of doing journalism. Journalists still need jobs that provide them with the time they need to do the research, but they must also enter into a dialogue with the people they write for.

Notes

1 Philosopher Alasdair MacIntyre (1984: 175) describes a 'practice' as a form of collective human activity which has an impact on society as a whole. If performed well, a collective practice will enhance the experience of living for everyone in society. Journalism, according to Couldry (2006), can be seen as a practice in this sense as, for example, can the work of an academic producing research.
2 Interview conducted in 2008.
3 http://tpmcafe.talkingpointsmemo.com/talk/blogs/thejoshuablog/2009/05/ny-times-maureen-dowd-plagiari.php (accessed December 2010).
4 http://valueaddednews.org/ (accessed December 2010).
5 Interview conducted in 2010.
6 Ibid.

Conclusion

Changing the future of the news

Our research, starting in 2007 and concluding in 2010, has covered three of the most turbulent years in journalism history. As we go to press, our subjects – journalists – find themselves at the centre of a 'perfect storm', under pressure from all sides. There is acute competition in the job market and, at the same time, editors are under pressure to keep circulations as high as possible and to cut costs. Journalists are by far the highest cost in the production of news. In a culture in which it is considered acceptable for news organisations to take content from other sites without paying for it, and where the audience has the assumption that news is free, those organisations that pay for news-gathering are being undercut by those that do not. The pressure to square this economic circle is being applied firmly to the journalists. They are expected to work longer hours, for lower remuneration, and to master a whole range of unfamiliar technologies at the same time. This book has considered the context and implications of those pressures on the production and value of news journalism.

In a time of constant turmoil – that seems to characterise the current field of journalism – it has been tempting just to try and capture the moment as it occurs, but we recognise that what is most needed is for us to stand back and consider the changes in their context. In so doing, we have turned to the work of Bourdieu and field theory, which allows us to consider both the broader structures in which the field of journalism operates and the constraints it produces for individual journalists' actions. In taking this reflexive and theoretical perspective, we have tried to do justice to the complexity that characterises the field, where journalists are not just agents of the system but also, and maybe more so, workers within the system. Thus we have analysed journalistic practices in context and examined the way in which changes in structures – economic (Chapter 1), regulatory (Chapter 3) and technological (Chapters 2, 4 and 6) – have altered the relationships between journalists and their employers (Chapters 2, 4 and 5), the audience (Chapter 7), their information sources (Chapter 5) and with other journalists.

Looming in the background of our research was the economic crash of 2008, a once-in-a-generation event which accelerated a number of trends that were already underway. The audience for news – and the journalism field itself – shifts regularly, mutating as news organisations struggle to adapt to social, technological and economic change (see Chapter 5). The digital 'revolution' has not only transformed the journalists' means of production and distribution; it has also given their audiences those tools. The conventions of authoritative editorial agenda setting are challenged by alternative voices and a plethora of information sources. The audience has been recast as a 'stakeholder' with something to contribute, through interactive participation and the production of 'user-generated content' (UGC) (see Chapter 7). Coming from the egalitarian, laterally associative matrix of the net, these new sources are expected to act as a collective challenge to the authoritarian, linear traditions of conventional news.

This corrective has largely failed to materialise (see Chapters 1 and 7). While niche news groups in specialist areas (in particular technology) have emerged, the conventional news media are still the dominant source of general news. Even so, the field is rapidly shifting due to the entrance of a number of very large and unconventional new media players: in particular Google and Facebook. At the start of our research, Google was considered only peripheral in relation to its effect on the way in which news was selected and written. Facebook was mainly considered in the context of journalistic research, ethics and privacy (Phillips, 2010). Research by Redden and Witschge (2010) looked at the role of Facebook and YouTube in disseminating and responding to news but, at that stage (the research was conducted in 2008), neither of these hugely successful applications had themselves found a secure funding model, let alone one that could have threatened mainstream media, and neither of them played any serious role in news delivery, other than in spreading existing messages from mainstream media. Now, news aggregation sites and social media pose a considerable challenge to the traditional news media's model, most notably on the business models of news (Chapter 1), but also on the production and agenda setting of news (Chapter 6), and in terms of the homogenisation of news (Chapter 5).

One early effect of any economic downturn tends to be a reduction in advertising budgets, so the accelerated loss of advertising revenue in 2008 was not unexpected (Chapter 1). News organisations are used to slimming down their workforces and waiting out an advertising downturn. What was unanticipated was that the advertisers would use the recession as an opportunity to redouble their efforts to look for cheaper ways of getting their messages across, using social marketing and search advertising. It soon became clear that Google's presence and business methods were changing the whole business framework for news and that, as YouTube and Facebook found ways to monetise their massive audiences, they too would become major media players, with the power to transform the economic landscape (Auletta, 2009).

By 2010, Google mopped up around two thirds of all online advertising – and most of this was related to search. Facebook came late into the advertising market, but its massive audience and ability to target very precisely means that it was becoming increasingly attractive to advertisers. YouTube, now owned by Google, is also moving fast into the field. This significantly impacts on news journalism, as advertising has historically paid for most – if not all – of the cost of news, and when news organisations went online, the early assumptions were that it would pay here too. However, as we point out in Chapter 1, there is a serious concern that advertising will not return to traditional news media in anything like the quantity required to maintain the status quo, let alone to develop new outlets.

As advertising revenue drains away, it is the small to medium sized outlets that are most likely to collapse. The biggest organisations (News International, for example) are part of multinational, diversified corporations that can afford to cross-subsidise loss-making activities while they find a new model. BSkyB has concentrated its efforts on bundling television, telephony and broadband packages that have massively increased their market penetration and multi-media communications leverage. In this corporate world, news is less a key business proposition, more a loss leader. In the Sky Annual Review 2010, Sky News is only mentioned (briefly) by the chairman and chief executive in relation to Sky having launched the first HD news channel.[1] In March 2011, News Corporation offered to hive off Sky News as an independent company (which it would still bankroll for ten years and retain its 39 per cent interest in) to help ease its 100 per cent buyout of the remainder of BSkyB. In UK broadcasting, only the publicly funded public service broadcaster, notably the BBC, can still claim to put journalism at the heart of its operation.

Small, and in particular local, news organisations are disadvantaged by having little opportunity for diversification. Many have been forced into closure already (see Chapter 2) and, as we point out in Chapter 1, those that have attempted internet-based alternatives are also struggling. Furthermore, audiences – faced with the apparently unfathomable plenty which is the World Wide Web – are increasingly reverting to the walled gardens of safety, where familiarity and ease of use are becoming more important than the time-consuming effort of trawling the un-navigated web. So it is that organising software and websites – Facebook, news aggregators, iPad and TweetDeck – are increasingly attracting large audiences; and big business is poised to move in to take advantage of this trend (Anderson and Wolff, 2010).

At this time, it is impossible to say how the major media companies will respond to the emergence of these new oligopolies in the converged media world. One thing we can say unequivocally is that the much-heralded era in which the internet would allow 'a thousand flowers to bloom' – and transform democratic involvement in public debate – has not come to pass and is unlikely to do so, as we explain in Chapter 5. The internet provides access to more data but most people are still informed of that data by a shrinking number of conventional news organisations. Greater choice has lead, paradoxically, to greater homogenisation (see Chapter 5).

Online this tendency has been exacerbated by the effect of search engines which sort and list websites according to mathematical formulae (algorithms). Hindman (2009) describes the way in which search engines promote 'popularity' over 'authority'. Online businesses very quickly started to make use of the way in which web search can be manipulated, using search engine optimisation (SEO) to increase the chances of appearing at the top of an internet search page. Those at the top of the search list tend to attract the majority of 'hits', thereby confirming their popularity and increasing the chances of attracting more visitors. This tends to produce a 'winner takes all' situation, in which the biggest organisations dominate and even the middle-sized ones – which in a smaller market would get ample attention – get squeezed out. With audiences declining, advertising – which tends always to cling to the biggest players in any market – moves away. When the dust settles, we may find that some of the names have changed but global business will – unless regulatory action is taken – be in control of a slimmed-down number of news sources, each fighting to dominate the mass market in the 'centre ground'.

As news moves inexorably onto the single platform of the internet (considered in Chapter 4), new forms of regulation will be needed, but equally will be resisted by commercial interests. In the short term, such arrangements will be vital to counteract the tendencies toward market concentration by the big media companies (see Chapter 3 for an overview of regulatory frameworks). As we discuss in Chapter 5, the tendency towards cannibalisation of material, and the narrowing of the news pool (as more of the big players stop paying for news-gathering), pose significant challenges for citizens looking for information. Attempts to water down regulation in order to stimulate competition online are probably the worst possible means of countering the move to media concentration and ensuring that citizens are informed by a plurality of media.

None of this is good news for democracy, which depends on consistent, ethical news-gathering and a diverse news media for its public debate, and thus its legitimacy. Indeed the very fabric of democratic accountability must now be called into question, as indeed must the market system for news which, in a liberal democracy, should allow a pluralist media to survive. As we discuss in Chapter 1, the future of diverse news media is now a matter of widespread concern. In the UK, for example, the government is attempting to shore up local news by establishing local media consortia – creating local monopolies paid for by local advertising – though most commentators suggest that even these artificially constructed monopolies will fail to find a viable funding base.

Advertising became the key form of news subsidy in democratic societies because news provided the best way to get product information in front of the public. That model is now under threat, but it has never been the only, or even the best, option available for ensuring diversity. Curran and Seaton (2009: 29) point out that it was the rise of advertising in the mid-nineteenth century that killed off the radical press of that period. Advertising, says Curran, became a de facto form of 'licensing'; businesses did not care to advertise their wares in publications intended for 'readers [who] are not purchasers' (ibid: 30). Publications that did not deliver purchasers to advertisers were not economically 'licensed' to exist.

News journalism will, in some form, emerge from this paradigm shift in its means of distribution; but there may well be a need for new sources of funding to ensure that those organisations which emerge strongest from the current financial cataclysm are sufficiently varied to provide true diversity in news supply that a democracy requires. There are existing models for providing market-neutral funding support to a diverse local media (considered in Chapter 1). In European countries, there is a history of subsidy via forms of levy, or taxation. While this form of subsidy has also tended to support mainstream opinion rather than minority opinion, it has not, as critics in the United States argue (see Benson, 2010), led to a stifling of diversity or fettering of new businesses. On the contrary, in Sweden, where the second newspaper in every town is subsidised, newspaper circulations ducked the Anglo-American trend and actually rose between 2000 and 2006 (ibid: 189). When governments come to consider that the alternative to subsidy could well be the complete collapse of a diverse and relatively unfettered news media, some form of subsidy (considered in more detail in Chapter 1) may well start to seem the most obvious solution.

During a period of such massive change, it is hard to make predictions for the future. It is possible that the market will operate as its supporters intend that it should and new applications, coming on stream as we write, will restore a means by which audiences can (and will) pay directly for the news they access, with advertising losing its power to license what we can read. There are signs, however, that the online giants – Google and Apple – will move into the market with novel forms of news delivery that depend, even more than the existing ones, on vast international networks for their financial viability. Organisations with this kind of financial muscle are quite capable of moving into, and dominating, local markets and driving out competition. As many of those online giants do not actually produce news, but only disseminate it (and rely heavily on the traditional news producers currently under pressure), there is a real threat to the sustainability of the news cycle.

If the market in news seems likely to fail, then governments across the world should step in. Whether they will do so remains to be seen. The combined, globe-spanning, might of Google, Apple and Facebook may seem too much for mere governments to manage. However, to surrender something as precious to democracy as news to the monopolistic tendencies of massive global companies would be more than unwise.

Amidst all this uncertainty, we can say that journalism is indeed changing. It could well be entering an era of greater accountability, more access to data, exciting possibilities for two-way interaction with audiences and experimentation with modes of delivery. There is certainly no shortage of young journalists, ready and willing to explore new avenues and experiment with new technologies. The concern is that, without international intervention to regulate the news marketplace, and to provide properly constituted and accountable public support, the energy and excitement will be diverted away from democratic engagement. This is a critical moment for the future of journalism, and it will require the efforts of many people who are not journalists, as well as those who are, to ensure that genuinely accountable, free and diverse news media emerge from this 'perfect storm'.

Note

1 http://annualreview2010.sky.com/ (accessed November 2010).

Bibliography

Aaronovitch, D. (2006) *Twenty years after Wapping*, ESRC Society Today. www.esrc.ac.uk/
ESRCInfoCentre/about/CI/CP/Our_Society_Today/Spotlights_2006/wapping.aspx
(accessed December 2010).

Abramson, B. D. (2001) Media policy after regulation? *International Journal of Cultural Studies*,
4(3), 301–26.

Ackroyd, P. (2000) *London: The Biography*, London: Chatto & Windus.

Allen, D. S. (2008) The trouble with transparency: The challenge of doing journalism
ethics in a surveillance society. *Journalism Studies*, 9(3), 323–40.

Allen, K. (2007, 28 March) Online advertising share overtakes newspapers, *Guardian*.
www.guardian.co.uk/business/2007/mar/28/advertising.newmedia (accessed January
2011).

Allen, S. R. (2006, 9–15 March) Speaking truth to power: An interview with Laura Berg,
Alibi, 15. http://alibi.com/index.php?story=14352 (accessed November 2010).

Alterman, E. (2008, 31 March) Out of print, *New Yorker*. www.newyorker.com/reporting/
2008/03/31/080331fa_fact_alterman?currentPage=all (accessed December 2010).

Anderson, C. (2006) *The long tail: Why the future of business is selling less of more*, New York:
Hyperion.

Anderson, C., and Wolff, M. (2010) The web is dead. Long live the internet, *Wired Magazine*, September. www.wired.com/magazine/2010/08/ff_webrip/all/1 (accessed January
2011).

Andrejevic, M. (2008) Power, knowledge and governance: Foucault's relevance to journalism studies. *Journalism Studies*, 9(4), 605–14.

Andrews, R. (2010, 26 July) Why Hunt's local TV news idea is a non-starter, *PaidContent.
org*. http://paidcontent.org/article/419-why-hunts-local-tv-news-idea-is-a-non-starter/
(accessed January 2011).

Associated Press (2006, 2 August) VA nurse's letter to newspaper prompts sedition probe.
www.firstamendmentcenter.org/news.aspx?id=16438 (accessed November 2010).

Atton, C. (2004) *An alternative internet*, Edinburgh: Edinburgh University Press.

Attwood, B. (2008) Letter. *UK Press Gazette*, 14 August.

Auletta, K. (2009) *Googled: The end of the world as we know it*, New York: Penguin.

Avilés, J. A. G., and Carvajal, M. (2008) Integrated and cross-media newsroom convergence. *Convergence: The International Journal of Research into New Media Technologies*, 14(2),
221–39.

Bagdikian, B. H. (1992) *The media monopoly* (4th edn), Boston: Beacon Press.

Baker, C. E. (1994) *Advertising and a democratic press*, Princeton, NJ: Princeton University
Press.

Bakker, G. (2007) *Trading facts: Arrow's fundamental paradox and the emergence of global news networks, 1750–1900*, London: LSE. http://www2.lse.ac.uk/economicHistory/pdf/FACTSPDF/FACTs17GB.pdf (accessed December 2010).

Bakker, P. (2010) Free dailies 2010: The age of the happy monopolist. *InPublishing*, January/February, 19–20.

Bardoel, J. (2008) Dutch television, in D. Ward (ed.), *Television and public policy* (pp. 199–222), Abingdon: Lawrence Erlbaum Associates.

Barnett, S. (2008) On the road to self-destruction. *British Journalism Review*, 19(2), 5–13. www.bjr.org.uk/data/2008/no2_barnett (accessed December 2010).

Bauman, Z. (2007) *Liquid times: Living in an age of uncertainty*, Cambridge: Polity Press.

BBC News Website. (2005, 7 September) Yahoo 'helped jail China writer', BBC News website. http://news.bbc.co.uk/1/hi/world/asia-pacific/4221538.stm (accessed November 2010).

——(2007, 26 January) Pair jailed over royal phone taps, BBC News Website. http://news.bbc.co.uk/1/hi/uk/6301243.stm (accessed December 2010).

——(2010a, 9 July) Google says China licence renewed by government, BBC News Website. www.bbc.co.uk/news/10566318 (accessed November 2010).

——(2010b, 17 July) 'Nazi' jibe radio host loses legal bid, BBC News Website. www.bbc.co.uk/news/10611110 (accessed November 2010).

BBC Website (2009, 24 June) BBC Trust responds to Taste and Standards report, BBC Website. www.bbc.co.uk/bbctrust/news/press_releases/2009/june/taste_standards.shtml (accessed November 2010).

Beck, U., and Beck-Gernsheim, E. (2002) *Individualization: Institutionalized individualism and its social and political consequences*, London: Sage.

Beckett, C. (2008) *SuperMedia: Saving journalism so it can save the world*, Malden, MA: Wiley.

Bell, E. (2009a, 8 May) Lecture to Falmouth, Emily Bell(whether). https://emilybellwether.wordpress.com/2009/05/08/lecture-to-falmouth/ (accessed December 2010).

——(2009b) Response to Greenslade column on subbing, *Guardian*. www.guardian.co.uk/media/greenslade/2009/feb/13/national-newspapers-local-newspapers (accessed August 2010).

——(2009c, 9 March) The biggest mistake of the past 10 years? Too much stuff, *Guardian*. www.guardian.co.uk/media/2009/mar/09/emily-bell-media (accessed December 2010).

Benady, D. (1998, 5 March) M&S defeats Granada in TV libel case, *Marketing Week*. www.marketingweek.co.uk/home/ms-defeats-granada-in-tv-libel-case/2022305.article (accessed November 2010).

Benson, R. (2010) Futures of the news: International considerations and further reflections, in N. Fenton (ed.), *New media, old news: Journalism and democracy in the digital age* (pp. 187–200), London: Sage.

Benson, R., and Neveu, E. (2005) Introduction: Field theory as work in progress, in R. Benson and E. Neveu (eds), *Bourdieu and the journalistic field* (pp. 1–28), Oxford: Polity.

Bird, S. E. (2009) The future of journalism in the digital environment. *Journalism*, 10(3), 293–95.

Blood, R. (2002) *The weblog handbook: Practical advice on creating and maintaining your blog*, Cambrigde, MA: Perseus.

Bourdieu, P. (1977) *Outline of a theory of practice* (R. Nice, Trans.), Cambridge: Cambridge University Press.

——(1998) *On television and journalism*, London: Pluto Press.

——(2005) The political field, the social science field and the journalistic field, in R. D. Benson and E. Neveu (eds), *Bourdieu and the journalistic field* (pp. 29–47), Oxford: Polity.

Briggs, A. (1995) *The history of broadcasting in the United Kingdom* (new edn), Oxford: Oxford University Press.

Calcutt, D. (1993) *Review of press self-regulation*. www.official-documents.gov.uk/document/cm21/2135/2135.pdf (accessed January 2011).

Carey, J. W. (1992) *Communication as culture: Essays on media and society*, London: Routledge.

Carlson, M. (2007) Order versus access: News search engines and the challenge to traditional journalistic roles. *Media, Culture and Society*, 29(6), 1014–30.

Carpentier, N. (2009) Participation is not enough: The conditions of possibility of mediated participatory practices. *European Journal of Communication*, 24(4), 407–20.

Castells, M. (1996) *The rise of the network society*, Oxford: Blackwell Publishers.

Chittum, R. (2009, 19 August) Newspaper industry ad revenue at 1965 levels, *Columbia Journalism Review*. www.cjr.org/the_audit/newspaper_industry_ad_revenue.php (accessed August 2010).

Christoffersen, J. (2009, 2 March) Decline in newspapers renews idea of nonprofits, *Associated Press*.

Collins, R. (2008) Hierarchy to homeostasis? Hierarchy, markets and networks in UK media and communications governance. *Media, Culture and Society*, 30(3), 295–317.

ComScore (2008, 14 July) Americans view 12 billion videos online in May 2008, *ComScore*. www.comscore.com/Press_Events/Press_Releases/2008/07/US_Online_Videos (accessed January 2011).

Conboy, M. (2004) *Journalism: A critical history*, London: Sage.

Conboy, M., and Steel, J. (2008) The future of newspapers: Historical perspectives. *Journalism Studies*, 9(5), 650–61.

Cottle, S. (2003) *Media organization and production*, London: Sage.

Couldry, N. (2006) *Listening beyond the echoes: Media ethics and agency in an uncertain world*, Boulder, CO: Paradigm Books.

——(2010) New online sources and writer-gatherers, in N. Fenton (ed.), *New media, old news: Journalism and democracy in the digital age* (pp. 138–52), London: Sage.

Cranberg, G., Bezanson, R. P. and Soloski, J. (2001) *Taking stock: Journalism and the publicly traded newspaper company* (1st edn), Ames, IA: Iowa State University Press.

Croteau, D., and Hoynes, W. (2006) *The business of media: Corporate media and the public interest* (2nd edn), London: Pine Forge Press.

Currah, A. (2009) *What's happening to our news: An investigation into the likely impact of the digital revolution on the economics of news publishing in the UK*, University of Oxford: Reuters Institute for the Study of Journalism.

Curran, J. (2002) *Media and power*, London: Routledge.

——(2010) Technology foretold, in N. Fenton (ed.), *New media, old news: Journalism and democracy in the digital age* (pp. 19–34), London: Sage.

Curran, J., and Seaton, J. (2009) *Power without responsibility* (7th edn), Abingdon: Routledge.

Dacre, P. (2008). *Society of Editors: Speech*. (9 November). www.pressgazette.co.uk/story.asp?storycode=42394 (accessed November 2010).

Davies, N. (2008) *Flat earth news*, London: Chatto & Windus.

Davies, N., and Leigh, D. (2010, 25 July) Afghanistan war logs: Massive leak of secret files exposes truth of occupation, *Guardian*. www.guardian.co.uk/world/2010/jul/25/afghanistan-war-logs-military-leaks (accessed December 2010).

Davis, A. (2003) Public relations and news sources, in S. Cottle (ed.), *News, public relations and power* (pp. 27–42), London: Sage.

De Bens, E. (2007) The European newspaper market: Challenges and opportunities, in H. Bohrmann, E. Klaus, and M. Machill (eds), *Media industry, journalism culture and communication policies in Europe* (pp. 247–81), Köln: Herbert von Halem.

De Botton, A. (2009) *The pleasures and sorrows of work*, London: Hamish Hamilton.

Deuze, M. (2007) *Media work*, Cambridge: Polity.

——(2009a) Technology and the individual journalist: Agency beyond initiation and change, in B. Zelizer (ed.), *The changing faces of journalism: Tabloidization, technology and truthiness* (pp. 82–92), London: Routledge.

——(2009b) The people formerly known as the employers. *Journalism*, 10(3), 315–18.

Digital Britain. (2009) *Final report*, Department for Business, Innovation and Skills (BIS) and the Department for Culture, Media and Sport (DCMS). www.dcms.gov.uk/what_we_do/broadcasting/6216.aspx (accessed January 2011).

Domingo, D., Quandt, T., Heinonen, A., Paulussen, S., Singer, J. B., and Vujnovic, M. (2008) Participatory journalism practices in the media and beyond: An international comparative study of initiatives in online newspapers. *Journalism Practice*, 2(3), 326–42.

Doogan, K. (2009) *New capitalism? The transformation of work*, Cambridge: Polity.

Dowd, M. (2009, May 16) Cheney, master of pain, *New York Times*. www.nytimes.com/2009/05/17/opinion/17dowd.html?_r=2 (accessed December 2010).

Dusty (2009) Response to Greenslade column on subbing, guardian.co.uk. www.guardian.co.uk/media/greenslade/2009/feb/13/national-newspapers-local-newspapers (accessed August 2010).

The Economist (2009, 14 May) The news business: Tossed by a gale, *The Economist*. www.economist.com/displaystory.cfm?story_id=13642689 (accessed November 2010).

——(2010, 2 September) The web's new walls: How the threats to the internet's openness can be averted, *The Economist*. www.economist.com/node/16943579?story_id=16943579 (accessed November 2010).

Edgerton, G. (1996) Quelling the 'oxygen of publicity': British broadcasting and 'the Troubles' during the Thatcher years. *Journal of Popular Culture*, 30(1), 115–32.

Ehrenfeld, R. (2003) *Funding evil, updated: How terrorism is financed and how to stop it*, Los Angeles, CA: Bonus Books.

Eide, E., Kunelius, R., and Phillips, A. (2008) *Transnational media events: The Mohammed cartoons and the imagined clash of civilizations*, Gothenburg: Nordicom.

Engel, M. (1996) *Tickle the public: One hundred years of the popular press*, London: Gollancz.

Entman, R. M. (2003) *Projections of power: Framing news, public opinion, and U.S. foreign policy*, Chicago, IL: University of Chicago Press.

Erjavec, K., and Kovačič, M. P. (2009) A discursive approach to genre: Mobi news. *European Journal of Communication*, 24(2), 147–64.

Esfandiary, N. (2001, 16 August) YouTube should let Iranians speak, *Index on Censorship*. www.indexoncensorship.org/2010/08/youtube-should-let-iranians-speak/ (accessed November 2010).

Ettema, J., and Whitney, C. (1994) *Audiencemaking: How the media create the audience*, London: Sage.

Fenton, N. (2010) NGOs, new media and the mainstream news: News from everywhere, in N. Fenton (ed.), *New media, old news: Journalism and democracy in the digital age* (pp. 153–68), London: Sage.

Fenton, N., Metykova, M., Schlosberg, J., and Freedman, D. (2010) *Meeting the news needs of local communities*, London: Media Trust. www.mediatrust.org/uploads/128255497549240/original.pdf (accessed November 2010).

Fenton, N., and Witschge, T. (2010) Comment is free, facts are sacred: Journalistic ethics in a changing mediascape, in G. Meikle and G. Redden (eds), *News online: Transformation and continuity*, Basingstoke: Palgrave Macmillan.

Field, F., and Rees, D. (2009) Auntie's dying: Long live public service broadcasting [Electronic Version]. Retrieved November 2010 from www.frankfield.co.uk/~ff-resources/auntiesdying.pdf.

Financial Times (2010, 26 September) Cable should call Murdoch to heel, *Financial Times*. www.ft.com/cms/s/0/132051fa-c40d-11df-b827-00144feab49a.html (accessed November 2010).

Fiske, J. (1992) Popularity and the politics of information, in P. Dahlgren and C. Sparks (eds), *Journalism and popular culture* (pp. 45–64), London: Sage.

Fitzwalter, R. (2008) *The dream that died: The rise and fall of ITV*, London: Matador.

Fletcher, K., and Peters, L. (1997) Trust and direct marketing environments: A consumer perspective. *Journal of Marketing Management*, 13, 523–39.

Folkenflik, D. (2008, 8 April) Recording shows Tribune owner Zell's fiery side, National Public Radio. www.npr.org/templates/story/story.php?storyId=89446846 (accessed August 2010).

Foucault, M. (1977) *Discipline and punish: The birth of the prison* (A. Sheridan, Trans.), New York: Pantheon Books.

Franklin, B. (1997) *Newszak and news media*, London: Arnold.

——(2008a) Introduction newspapers: Trends and developments, in B. Franklin (ed.), *Pulling newspapers apart: Analysing print journalism* (pp. 1–35), London: Routledge.

——(2008b) The future of newspapers. *Journalism Studies*, 9(5), 630–41.

——(2009) *The future of newspapers: A comparative assessment (Evidence gathering on the current state of the Welsh newspaper industry)* (No. BSC(3)-03-09). www.assemblywales.org/bsc_3_-03-09 – paper_2a – prof_bob_franklin – cardiff_university.pdf (accessed January 2011).

Fredin, E. S. (1997) Rethinking the news story for the Internet: Hyperstory prototypes and a model of the user. *Journalism and Mass Communication Monographs*, September (163), 1–47.

Freedman, D. (2005) *How level is the playing field? An analysis of the UK media policy-making process*, London: ESRC.

——(2008) *The politics of media policy*, Cambridge: Polity Press.

——(2010) The political economy of the 'new' news environment, in N. Fenton (ed.), *New media, old news: Journalism and democracy in the digital age* (pp. 35–50), London: Sage.

Frost, C. (2010) The development of privacy adjudications by the UK Press Complaints Commission and their effects on the future of journalism. *Journalism Practice*, 4(3), 383–93.

Galtung, J., and Ruge, M. H. (1965) The structure of foreign news. *Journal of Research*, 2(1), 64–91.

Gans, H. J. (1979) *Deciding what's news: A study of CBS evening news, NBC nightly news, Newsweek, and Time* (1st edn), New York: Pantheon Books.

Gardam, T. (2009) Foreword, in A. Currah (ed.), *What's happening to our news: An investigation into the likely impact of the digital revolution on the economics of news publishing in the UK*, University of Oxford: Reuters Institute for the Study of Journalism.

Gillmor, D. (2004) *We the media: Grassroots journalism by the people, for the people*, Beijing; Farnham: O'Reilly.

Giugliano, F. (2010, 22 May) From mirror to looking glass, *Axess Programme on Journalism and Democracy*. www.axessjournalism.com/Blog/2010/5/22/from-mirror-to-looking-glass (accessed January 2011).

Golding, P., and Elliott, P. (1979) *Making the news*, London: Longman.

Greenslade, R. (2009, 13 February) Subeditors: Another attempt to explain why they are becoming redundant, *Guardian*. www.guardian.co.uk/media/greenslade/2009/feb/13/national-newspapers-local-newspapers (accessed August 2010).

——(2010, 22 September) Let Murdoch buy Sky – This is not a Berlusconi moment, *Evening Standard*. www.thisislondon.co.uk/markets/article-23880873-let-rupert-murdoch-buy-sky-this-is-not-a-berlusconi-moment.do (accessed November 2010).

Habermas, J. (1989) The public sphere, in J. Habermas and S. Seidman (eds), *Jürgen Habermas on society and politics: A reader*, Boston: Beacon Press.

——(1989) *The structural transformation of the public sphere: An inquiry into a category of bourgeois society*, Cambridge: Polity Press.

Häckner, J., and Nyberg, S. (2008) Advertising and media market concentration. *Journal of Media Economics*, 21(2), 79–96.

Hallin, D. C., and Mancini, P. (2004) *Comparing media systems: Three models of media and politics*, Cambridge: Cambridge University Press.

Harcup, T., and Neill, D. O. (2001) What is news? Galtung and Ruge revisited. *Journalism Studies*, 2(2), 261–80.

Harnden, T. (2009, 18 May) New media vs dead tree: Maureen Dowd and the plagiarism row, *Telegraph*. http://blogs.telegraph.co.uk/news/tobyharnden/9832768/New_Media_vs_Dead_Tree_Maureen_Dowd_and_the_plagiarism_row_/ (accessed December 2010).

Hemmingway, E. (2008) *Into the newsroom: Exploring the digital production of regional television news*, London: Routledge.

Hendy, D. (2007) *Life on air: A history of Radio Four*, Oxford: Oxford University Press.

Herman, E. S., and Chomsky, N. (1994) *Manufacturing consent: The political economy of the mass media*, New York: Vintage.

Herman, E. S., and McChesney, R. W. (1997) *The global media: The new missionaries of corporate capitalism*, London: Cassell.

Hermida, A. (2009) The blogging BBC: Journalism blogs at 'the world's most trusted news organisation'. *Journalism Practice*, 3(3), 1–17.

Hermida, A., and Thurman, N. (2008) A clash of cultures: The integration of user-generated content within professional journalistic frameworks at British newspaper websites. *Journalism Practice*, 2(3), 343–56.

Hibberd, M. (2008) Media policy in Italy, in D. Ward (ed.), *Television and public policy* (pp. 183–98), Abingdon: Lawrence Erlbaum Associates.

Hind, D. (2010) The return of the public, London: Verso.

Hindman, M. S. (2009) *The myth of digital democracy*, Princeton: Princeton University Press.

Holton, K. (2008, 17 June) UK online ad spending to overtake TV this year. www.reuters.com/article/internetNews/idUSL1748087420080617 (accessed 13 February 2009).

House of Lords. (2008) *The ownership of the news. Vol I: Report*, Norwich: Select Committee on Communications: Stationery Office Limited. www.publications.parliament.uk/pa/ld200708/ldselect/ldcomuni/122/122i.pdf (accessed January 2011).

Hutton, L. (2004) *Report of the Inquiry into the circumstances surrounding the death of Dr David Kelly*, House of Commons. www.the-hutton-inquiry.org.uk/content/report/index.htm (accessed December 2010).

Institute for Public Policy Research. (2009) *Mind the funding gap: The potential of industry levies for continued funding of public service broadcasting*. www.ippr.org.uk/members/download.asp?f=%2Fecomm%2Ffiles%2Fmind%5Fthe%5Ffunding%5Fgap%2Epdf (accessed August 2010).

iProspect. (2008) *iProspect blended search results study*. www.iprospect.com/about/researchstudy_2008_blendedsearchresults.htm (accessed August 2010).

Jansen, B., and Spink, A. (2005) An analysis of web searching by European AlltheWeb.com users. *Information Processing and Management*, 41(2), 361–81.

——(2006) How are we searching the World Wide Web? A comparison of nine search engine transaction logs. *Information Processing and Management*, 42(1), 248–63.

Jarvis, J. (2008) Whither the AP, *BuzzMachine*. www.buzzmachine.com/2008/06/18/whither-the-ap/ (accessed August 2010).

——(2009) *What would Google do?*, New York: Harper Business.

Kampfner, J. (2009) *Freedom for sale: How we made money and lost our liberty*, London: Simon & Schuster.

Koopmans, R. (2004) Movements and media: Selection processes and evolutionary dynamics in the public sphere. *Theory and Society*, 33(3), 367–91.

Kunelius, R. (2009) Journalism as robust secular drama. *Journalism*, 10(3), 343–46.

Lambourne, H. (2010, 29 September) Four-a-year limit planned under council paper curb, *HoldtheFrontPage*. www.holdthefrontpage.co.uk/news/100929consultation.shtml (accessed January 2011).

Lee-Wright, P. (2010a) Culture shock: New media and organizational change at the BBC, in N. Fenton (ed.), *New media, old news: Journalism and democracy in the digital age* (pp. 71–87), London: Sage.

——(2010b) *The documentary handbook*, Abingdon: Routledge.

Leslie, A. (2008) *Killing my own snakes: A memoir*, London: Macmillan.

Lessig, L. (2005) *Free culture: The nature and future of creativity*, London: Penguin.

——(2008) *Remix: Making art and commerce thrive in the hybrid economy*, London: Bloomsbury Academic.

Lewis, J., and Cushion, S. (2009) The thirst to be first. *Journalism Practice*, 3(3), 304–18.

Lewis, J., Williams, A., Franklin, B., Thomas, J., and Mosdell, N. (2008) *The quality and independence of British journalism*, Cardiff, UK: Cardiff University.

Lewis, S. C., Kaufhold, K., and Lasorsa, D. L. (2010) Thinking about citizen journalism: The philosophical and practical challenges of user-generated content for community newspapers. *Journalism Practice*, 4(2), 163–79.

Lindley, R. (2003) *Panorama: Fifty years of pride and paranoia* (updated edn), London: Politico's.

Livingstone, S., and Lunt, P. (2007) Representing citizens and consumers in media and communications regulation. *The Politics of Consumption/ The Consumption of Politics, The Annals of the American Academy of Political and Social Science*, 611(1), 51–65.

Lloyd, J., and Seaton, J. (2006) *What can be done? Making the media and politics better*, Malden, MA: Oxford: Blackwell Publishing.

Machill, M., and Beiler, M. (2009) The importance of the internet for journalistic research: A multi-method study of the research performed by journalists working for daily newspapers, radio, television and online. *Journalism Studies*, 10(2), 178–203.

Machill, M., Beiler, M., and Zenker, M. (2008) Search-engine research: A European-American overview and systematization of an interdisciplinary and international research field. *Media, Culture and Society*, 30(5), 591–608.

MacIntyre, A. C. (1984) *After virtue: A study in moral theory* (2nd edn), Notre Dame, IN: University of Notre Dame Press.

Madden, M. (2007) *Online video*, Pew Research Center. www.pewinternet.org/Reports/2007/Online-Video.aspx (accessed August 2010).

Marvin, C. (1990) *When old technologies were new: Thinking about electric communication in the late nineteenth century*, Oxford: Oxford University Press.

McNair, B. (1995) *An introduction to political communication* (4th edn), London: Routledge.

——(2000) *Journalism and democracy*, London: Routledge.

——(2009) Journalism in the 21st century – Evolution not extinction. *Journalism*, 10(3), 347–49.

McQuail, D. (1994) *Mass communication theory: An introduction* (3rd edn), London: Sage.

——(2001) *The consequences of European media policies and organisational structures for cultural diversity*, Strasbourg: Council of Europe. www.coe.int/t/dg4/cultureheritage/culture/completed/diversity/EN_Diversity_Bennett.pdf (accessed November 2010).

——(2009) Editorial: EJC symposium special issue. *European Journal of Communication*, 24(4), 387–89.

Media Standards Trust. (2009) *A more accountable press: Part 1, The need for reform*, London: Media Standards Trust. http://mediastandardstrust.org/publications/a-more-accountable-press/ (accessed November 2010).

——(2010) *Media Standards Trust proposes major reform of Press Complaints Commission to meet public expectations*, London: Media Standards Trust. http://mediastandardstrust.org/projects/press-self-regulation/recommendations-for-reform/press-release/ (accessed November 2010).

Meech, P. (2008) Advertising, in B. Franklin (ed.), *Pulling newspapers apart: Analysing print journalism* (pp. 235–43), London: Routledge.

Melvern, L. (1986) *The end of the street*, London: Metheun.

Mill, J. S. (1869) *On liberty* (republished 2008) Charleston, SC: Forgotten Books.

Mitchelstein, E., and Boczkowski, P. J. (2009) Between tradition and change: A review of recent research on online news production. *Journalism*, 10(5), 562.

Morozov, E. (2009, 18 November) How dictators watch us on the web, *Prospect Magazine*. www.prospectmagazine.co.uk/2009/11/how-dictators-watch-us-on-the-web/ (accessed November 2010).

Mosco, V. (2009) The future of journalism. *Journalism*, 10(3), 350–52.

Murdock, G. (1974) Mass communications and the construction of meaning, in N. Armistead (ed.), *Rethinking social psychology* (pp. 205–20), London: Penguin.

Muthukumaraswamy, K. (2010) When the media meet crowds of wisdom: How journalists are tapping into audience expertise and manpower for the processes of newsgathering. *Journalism Practice*, 4(1), 48–65.

Myles, P. (2008). *Public presentation*. Paper presented at Goldsmiths, University of London (October).

Naish, J. (2010, 9 July) Here come the super-taskers, *New Statesman*. www.newstatesman.com/scitech/2010/07/generation-university-media (accessed December 2010).

National Union of Journalists (2009) *Disappearing freelance work*, NUJ Freelance Industrial Council. www.nuj.org.uk/getfile.php?id=689 (accessed December 2010).

Newspaper Association of America (2009) *Total paid circulation*. www.naa.org/TrendsandNumbers/Total-Paid-Circulation.aspx (accessed December 2010).

Nossek, H. (2009) On the future of journalism as a professional practice and the case of journalism in Israel. *Journalism*, 10(3), 358–61.

O'Dell, J. (2010, 23 July) How the Internet is affecting traditional journalism, Mashable. http://mashable.com/2010/07/23/internet-journalism-survey/ (accessed August 2010).

O'Neill, O. (2002) *A question of trust*, Cambridge: Cambridge University Press.

——(2006, 13 February) A right to offend? *Guardian*. www.guardian.co.uk/media/2006/feb/13/mondaymediasection7 (accessed December 2010).

O'Sullivan, J., and Heinonen, A. (2008) Old values, new media: Journalism role perceptions in a changing world. *Journalism Practice*, 2(3), 357–71.

Ofcom. (2007) *New news, future news: The challenges for television news after Digital Switch-over*. www.ofcom.org.uk/research/tv/reports/newnews/newnews.pdf (accessed March 2009).

——(2009) *Annual report 2008–2009*, London: Office of Communications. www.ofcom.org.uk/about/annual-reports-and-plans/annual-reports/ofcom-annual-report-2008-09/ (accessed January 2011).

——(2010, July 13) High Court backs Ofcom's judgment in Jon Gaunt case, *Ofcom website*. http://media.ofcom.org.uk/2010/07/13/high-court-backs-ofcoms-judgment-in-jon-gaunt-case/ (accessed November 2010).

Oliver, L. (2008, 29 October) 'Post-moderated system' could reduce need for sub-editors, says Telegraph assistant editor, *journalism.co.uk*. www.journalism.co.uk/news/-post-moderated-system-could-reduce-need-for-sub-editors-says-telegraph-assistant-editor/s2/a532669/ (accessed December 2010).

——(2009) Mirror is standing out against the rush to SEO, *journalism.co.uk*. www.journalism.co.uk/2/articles/536769.php (accessed December 2010).

——(2010a, 9 January) Citizen journalism news site Oh My News to stop paying contributors, *journalism.co.uk*. www.journalism.co.uk/2/articles/533183.php (accessed August 2010).

——(2010b, 3 August) Demotix partners with Publish2 for new photo-sharing network, *journalism.co.uk*. www.journalism.co.uk/2/articles/539932.php (accessed August 2010).

——(2010c, 4 August) OhmyNews closes international citizen journalism site, *journalism.co.uk*. www.journalism.co.uk/2/articles/539939.php (accessed August 2010).

——(2010d, 11 May) Time running out for OhmyNews' members' club, *journalism.co.uk*. www.journalism.co.uk/2/articles/536382.php (accessed August 2010).

OpenNet Initiative. (2005) *Internet filtering in China in 2004–2005: A country study*, The Berkman Center for Internet and Society, Harvard University. http://cyber.law.harvard.edu/publications/2005/Internet_Filtering_in_China_in_2004_2005 (accessed November 2010).

Örnebring, H. (2008) The consumer as producer of what? User-generated tabloid content in The Sun (UK) and Aftonbladet (Sweden). *Journalism studies*, 9(5), 771–85.

——(2010) Technology and journalism-as-labour: Historical perspectives. *Journalism*, 11(57), 57–74.

Owers, J., Carveth, R. and Alexander, A. (2004) An introduction to media economics theory and practice, in A. Alexander, J. Owers, R. Carveth, C. A. Hollifield, and A. N. Greco (eds), *Media economics: Theory and practice* (3rd edn, pp. 3–47), Mahwah, NJ; London: Lawrence Erlbaum.

Parry, R. (2009) *Creating viable local multi-media companies in the UK*: Conservative Party Consultation Document. www.conservatives.com/~/media/Files/Downloadable%20Files/Creating%20Viable%20LMC%20Report.ashx?dl=true (accessed August 2010).

Paul, N. (2002, 30 June) Integrating old and new media newsrooms, *Poynter online*. www.poynter.org/content/content_view.asp?id=5678 (accessed August 2010).

Pérez-Peña, R. (2009, 6 April) A.P. seeks to rein in sites using its content, *New York Times*. www.nytimes.com/2009/04/07/business/media/07paper.html (accessed January 2011).

Peters, J. W. (2010, 5 September) Some newspapers, tracking readers online, shift coverage, *New York Times*. www.nytimes.com/2010/09/06/business/media/06track.html?_r=2 (accessed September 2010).

Pew Project for Excellence in Journalism. (2007) *The latest news headlines – Your vote counts*. www.journalism.org/node/7493 (accessed December 2010).

——(2010a) Community journalism, *The State of the News Media*. www.stateofthemedia.org/2010/specialreports_community_journalism.php (accessed August 2010).

——(2010b) *How news happens: A study of the news ecosystem of one American city*. www.journalism.org/analysis_report/how_news_happens (accessed August 2010).

——(2010c) *New media, old media: How blogs and social media agendas relate and differ from traditional press*. http://pewresearch.org/pubs/1602/new-media-review-differences-from-traditional-press (accessed August 2010).

——(2010d) *News leaders and the future*. www.journalism.org/analysis_report/news_ leaders_ and_future (accessed December 2010).

Pew Research Center for the People and the Press. (2008) *Key news audiences now blend online and traditional sources: Audience segments in a changing news environment*. http://people-press.org/report/444/news-media (accessed December 2010).

Phillips, A. (2003). Changing the frame: Can individual journalists change news discourse? Unpublished Research Paper.

——(2007) Press and publishing, in K. Coyer, T. Dowmunt and A. Fountain (eds), *The alternative media handbook*, London: Routledge.

——(2008) Advice columnists, in B. Franklin (ed.), *Pulling newspapers apart: Analysing print journalism*, London: Routledge.

——(2010) Old sources, new bottles, in N. Fenton (ed.), *New media, old news: Journalism and democracy in the digital age* (pp. 87–101), London: Sage.

Phillips, A., Couldry, N., and Freedman, D. (2010) An ethical deficit? Accountability, norms and the material conditions of contemporary journalism, in N. Fenton (ed.), *New media, old news: Journalism and democracy in the digital age* (pp. 51–68), London: Sage.

Picard, R. G. (2002) *The economics and financing of media companies*, New York: Fordham University Press.

——(2004) The economics of the daily newspaper industry, in A. Alexander, J. Owers, R. Carveth, C. A. Hollifield and A. N. Greco (eds), *Media economics: Theory and practice* (3rd edn, pp. 109–25), Mahwah, NJ: London: Lawrence Erlbaum.

——(2005) Money, media and the public interest, in G. Overholser and K. Hall Jamieson (eds), *The Press* (pp. 337–50), Oxford: Oxford University Press.

——(2006) *Journalism, value creation and the future of news organizations*, Harvard University: Joan Shorenstein Center on the Press, Politics and Public Policy. www.robertpicard.net/PDFFiles/ValueCreationandNewsOrgs.pdf (accessed February 2009).

——(2007) Subsidies for newspapers: Can the Nordic model remain viable? in H. Bohrmann, E. Klaus, and M. Machill (eds), *Media industry, journalism culture and communication policies in Europe* (pp. 236–46), Cologne: Herbert von Halem.

——(2008) The challenges of public functions and commercialized media, in D. A. Graber, D. McQuail, and P. Norris (eds), *The politics of news, the news of politics* (pp. 211–29), Washington: CQ Press.

Picard, R. G., and van Weezel, A. (2008) Capital and control: Consequences of different forms of newspaper ownership. *International Journal on Media Management*, 10, 22–31.

Pilkington, E. (2010, 27 January) Fox most trusted news channel in US, poll shows, *Guardian*. www.guardian.co.uk/world/2010/jan/27/fox-news-most-popular (accessed December 2010).

Pompeo, J., and Jedrzejczak, A. (2010, 9 July) A quick primer on the US newspaper collapse, *Business Insider*. http://read.bi/c1NqoC (accessed December 2010).

Pöttker, H., and Starck, K. (2003) Criss-crossing perspectives: Contrasting models of press self-regulation in Germany and the United States. *Journalism Studies*, 4(1), 47–64.

Powell, W. W., and DiMaggio, P. J. (1991) *The new institutionalism in organizational analysis*, Chicago: University of Chicago Press.

Press, A. L., and Williams, B. A. (2010) *The new media environment: An introduction*, Oxford: Wiley-Blackwell.

Quandt, T. (2008) (No) news on the World Wide Web? *Journalism Studies*, 9(5), 717–38.

Rantanen, T. (2009) *When news was new*, Oxford: Wiley-Blackwell.

Rebillar, F., and Touboul, A. (2010) Promises unfulfilled? 'Journalism 2.0', user participation and editorial policy on newspaper websites. *Media, Culture and Society*, 32(2), 323–34.

Redden, J., and Witschge, T. (2010) A new news order? Online news content examined, in N. Fenton (ed.), *New media, old news: Journalism and democracy in the digital age* (pp. 171–87), London: Sage.

Reinemann, C. (2004). *'Everyone in journalism steals from everyone else'. Routine reliance on other media in different stages of news production*. Paper presented at the International Communication

Association, New Orleans, LA (27 May). www.allacademic.com//meta/p_mla_ apa_ research_citation/1/1/2/6/3/pages112639/p112639–1.php (accessed December 2010).

Reporters without Borders. (2007) *China: Journey to the heart of Internet censorship*, Paris: Reporters without borders. www.rsf.org/IMG/pdf/Voyage_au_coeur_de_la_censure_GB. pdf (accessed November 2010).

Rheingold, H. (1994) *The virtual community: Finding connection in a computerized world*, London: Secker & Warburg.

Rice, R. E. (2008) Central concepts in media ownership research and regulation, in R. E. Rice (ed.), *Media ownership: research and regulation* (pp. 3–28), Cresskill, NJ: Hampton Press.

Robertson, G. (2010) Media inquiry ducked key reforms, *Guardian*. www.guardian.co.uk/ media/2010/feb/24/mps-media-legal-geoffrey-robertson (accessed January 2011).

Robinson, J. (2009, 13 October) How super-injunctions are used to gag investigative reporting, *Guardian*. www.guardian.co.uk/uk/2009/oct/13/super-injunctions-guardian-carter-ruck (accessed November 2010).

Romero, C. (2009, 2 November) European journalists: Comrades in arms? *European Journalism Centre*. www.ejc.net/magazine/article/European_journalists_Comrades_in_Arms/ (accessed December 2010).

Rosenblum, M. (2008, 24 February) A camera as the pencil, *Rosenblumtv*. http://rosenblumtv. wordpress.com/2008/02/24/a-camera-as-the-pencil/ (accessed August 2010).

Rusbridger, A. (2009) I've seen the future and it's mutual. *British Journalism Review*, 20(3), 19–26.

Russell, A. (2009) News bust; News boom. *Journalism* 10(3), 365–67.

Russial, J. (1998) Goodbye copy desks, hello trouble? *Newspaper Research Journal*, 19(2), 2–17.

——(2008). *Copy editors and the online revolution: In the trenches or missing in action?* Paper presented at the Association for Education in Journalism and Mass Communication, Chicago.

Schecter, D. (2010). *Keynote speech*. Paper presented at the Global Media and the 'War on Terror' conference, University of Westminster, London (14 September).

Schirrmacher, F. (2009) In the age of informavores, algorithms will replace journalists, *Guardian*. www.guardian.co.uk/media/pda/2009/dec/10/digital-media-newspapers-algorithm-journalism-informavores-schirrmacher (accessed December 2010).

Schlesinger, P. (1978) *Putting 'reality' together: BBC news*, London: Constable.

Schudson, M. (1978) *Discovering the news: A social history of American newspapers*, New York: Basic Books.

——(2009a) Factual knowledge in the age of truthiness, in B. Zelizer (ed.), *The changing faces of journalism: Tabloidization, technology and truthiness*, London: Routledge.

——(2009b) Ten years backwards and forwards. *Journalism*, 10(3), 368–70.

Seldon, A. (2010) *Trust: How we lost it and how to get it back* (2nd edn), London: Biteback.

Sennett, R. (2008) *The craftsman*, London: Allen Lane.

Shirky, C. (2008a) *Here comes everybody: The power of organizing without organizations*, London: Allen Lane.

——(2008b). *The Futureview address*. Paper presented at the Edinburgh International Television Festival (23 Augustus). www.mgeitf.co.uk/189/view.aspx (accessed November 2010).

Silberstein-Loeb, J. (2009) The structure of the news market in Britain, 1870–1914. *Business History Review*, 83(4), 759–88.

Singer, J. B. (2007) Contested autonomy: Professional and popular claims on journalistic norms. *Journalism Studies*, 8(1), 79–95.

——(2009) Convergence and divergence. *Journalism*, 10(3), 375–77.

Skillset. (2009) *Final report on scoping project for convergence journalism*, Skillset. www.skillset.org/uploads/pdf/asset_13678.pdf?1 (accessed December 2010).

Slattery, J. (2009, 20 April) A degree of despair, *Guardian*. www.guardian.co.uk/media/2009/apr/20/journalism-students (accessed December 2010).

Smith, A. (1978) The long road to objectivity and back again: The kinds of truth we get in journalism, in D. G. Boyce, J. Curran, and P. Wingate (eds), *Newspaper history from the seventeenth century to the present day*, London: Constable.

Smith, P. (2009, 10 July) AP, Media Standards Trust propose news microformat, *Paid Content*. http://paidcontent.co.uk/article/419-ap-media-standards-trust-propose-news-microformat/ (accessed December 2010).

Solove, D. J. (2008) *The future of reputation: Gossip, rumor, and privacy on the internet*, London: Yale University Press.

Soun Chung, D. (2007) Profits and perils: Online news producers' perceptions of inter-activity and uses of interactive features. *Convergence: The International Journal of Research into New Media Technologies*, 13(43).

Stabe, M. (2008) Media Wales puts online hub at the heart of its nerve centre. *UK Press Gazette*, 24 (September).

Standage, T. (1998) *The Victorian internet: The remarkable story of the telegraph and the nineteenth century's online pioneers*, London: Weidenfeld & Nicolson.

State of the Media Report. (2004) *Newspapers: Ownership, Centre for Excellence in Journalism*. www.stateofthemedia.org/2004/narrative_newspapers_ownership.asp?cat=5&media=2 (accessed August 2010).

Steensen, S. (2009) The shaping of an online feature journalist. *Journalism*, 10(5), 702–18.

Stephens, M. (1988) *A history of news*, New York: Penguin.

——(2010) The case for wisdom journalism – and for journalists surrendering the pursuit of news. *Daedalus*, 139(2), 76–90.

Tambini, D. (2010, 18 October) Ofcom cuts are grave assault on freedom, *Guardian*. www.guardian.co.uk/media/2010/oct/18/ofcom-cuts-threaten-freedom (accessed November 2010).

Tartakoff, J. (2010, 2 March) Yahoo News brings news commenting back, *PaidContent.org*. http://paidcontent.org/article/419-yahoo-news-brings-news-commenting-back-/ (accessed May 2011).

Thalhimer, M. (1994) High-tech news or just 'shovelware'? *Media Studies Journal*, 1(8), 41–51.

Thompson, G. (2003) *Between hierarchies and markets: The logic and limits of network forms of organization*, Oxford: Oxford University Press.

Thussu, D. (2009) *News and entertainment: The rise of global infotainment*, London: Sage.

Toynbee, P. (2009, 24 March) This is an emergency. Act now, or local news will die, *Guardian*. www.guardian.co.uk/commentisfree/2009/mar/24/regional-newspapers-lay-offs (accessed March 2011).

Trends in Newsrooms. (2008) *News at the crossroads*, Paris: World Editors Forum.

Tressell, R. (1914) *The ragged trousered philanthropists* (1955 edn), London: Lawrence & Wishart.

Tridish, P. (2007) Radio controlled: A media activist's guide to the Federal Communications Commission, in S. P. Gangadharan, B. de Cleen, and N. Carpentier (eds), *Alternatives on media content, journalism & regulation*, Tartu: Tartu University Press.

Tunstall, J. (1971) *Journalists at work: Specialist correspondents: their news organizations, news sources, and competitor-colleagues*, California: Sage.

Turner, G. (2009) Millennial journalism. *Journalism*, 10(3), 390–92.

——(2010) *Ordinary people and the media: The demotic turn*, London: Sage.

Ulf-Møller, J. (2001) *Hollywood film wars with France*, Rochester, NY: University of Rochester Press.

Van Dijck, J. (2009) Users like you? Theorizing agency in user-generated content. *Media, Culture & Society*, 31(1), 41–58.

Venice Commission. (2005) *On the compatibility of the laws 'Gasparri' and 'Frattini' of Italy with the Council of Europe standards in the field of freedom of expression and pluralism of the media*, Strasbourg: Council of Europe.

Wallace, S. (2009) Watchdog or witness? The emerging forms and practices of video-journalism. *Journalism*, 10(5), 684–701.

Watson, J. M., and Strayer, D. L. (2010) Supertaskers: Profiles in extraordinary multi-tasking ability. *Psychonomic Bulletin & Review*, 17(4), 479–85. www.psych.utah.edu/lab/appliedcognition/publications/supertaskers.pdf (accessed August 2010).

Weaver, D. H. (2009) US journalism in the 21st century – What future? *Journalism*, 10(3), 396–97.

Wilby, P. (2006, 13 March) The media column: Peter Wilby bids farewell to Sarah Sands, *New Statesman*. www.newstatesman.com/200603130007 (accessed December 2010).

——(2009, 1 June) Return of the old fashioned scoop, *Guardian*. www.guardian.co.uk/media/2009/jun/01/daily-telegraph-mps-expenses (accessed December 2010).

Williams, A. (2010, 22 July) An open letter to Alan Edmunds, Publishing Director, Media Wales, *openDemocracy*. www.opendemocracy.net/ourkingdom/andy-williams/open-letter-to-alan-edmunds-publishing-director-media-wales (accessed August 2010).

Williams, B. A. O. (2002) *Truth and truthfulness: An essay in genealogy*, Princeton: Princeton University Press.

Williams, R. (1983) *Towards 2000*, London: Chatto & Windus.

Witschge, T. (2009, 27 March) Street journalists versus 'ailing journalists'? *openDemocracy*. www.opendemocracy.net/article/street-journalists-as-an-answer-to-ailing-journalism (accessed August 2010).

Witschge, T., Fenton, N. and Freedman, D. (2010) *Protecting the news: Civil society and the media*, London: Carnegie UK. www.carnegietrust.co.uk/publications/protecting_the_news – civil_society_and_the_media (accessed December 2010).

Witschge, T., and Nygren, G. (2009) Journalism: A profession under pressure? *Journal of Media Business Studies*, 6(1), 37–59.

World Editors Forum. (2008) *Newsroom Barometer 2008*, Editors weblog. www.editorsweblog.org/analysis/2008/05/1_newsroom_barometer_2008_main_results_t.php (accessed August 2010).

Younge, G. (2008, 6 September) Murder and rape – fact or fiction? *Guardian*. www.guardian.co.uk/world/2005/sep/06/hurricanekatrina.usa3 (accessed December 2010).

Zelizer, B. (2004) *Taking journalism seriously: News and the academy*, Thousand Oaks, CA: Sage.

Index

www.routledge.com/media

The Ideal Companion to *Changing Journalism*

Journalism After September 11

Second Edition

Barbie Zelizer, University of Pennsylvania, USA, and **Stuart Allan**

Journalism After September 11 examines how the traumatic attacks of that day continue to transform the nature of journalism, particularly in the United States and Britain. Familiar notions of what it means to be a journalist, how best to practice journalism, and what the public can reasonably expect of journalists in the name of democracy, were shaken to their foundations.

Ten years on, however, new questions arise regarding the lasting implications of that tragic day and its aftermath.

Bringing together an internationally respected collection of scholars and media commentators, *Journalism After September 11* addresses topics such as: journalism and public life at a time of crisis; broadsheet and tabloid newspaper coverage of the attacks; the role of sources in shaping the news; reporting by global news media such as CNN; Western representations of Islam; current affairs broadcasting; news photography and trauma; the emotional well-being of reporters; online journalism; as well as a host of pertinent issues around news, democracy and citizenship.

This second edition includes four new chapters – examining Arabic newspaper reporting of the attacks, the perceptions of television audiences, national magazine coverage of the ensuing crisis, and the media politics of 'othering' – as well as revised chapters from the first edition and an updated Introduction by the co-editors. A foreword is provided by Victor Navasky and an afterword by Phillip Knightley.

Hb: 978-0-415-46014-9
Pb: 978-0-415-46015-6
eBook: 978-0-203-81896-1

For more information and to order a copy visit
www.routledge.com/9780415460156

Available from all good bookshops